STR	10/01	ALC	
SHI		ALM	
SHM		SDL	
KTN		HEN	
WEL		SOU	
HRB		SOM	

Greenhill Books

A RAIN OF LEAD

'We can scarcely understand the perfect peace which has so suddenly fallen on us after three months' rain of lead.'

2/Lt James Dalrymple-Hay, 2/21st Royal Scots Fusiliers
at the end of the siege of Potchefstroom

A RAIN
OF LEAD

The Siege and Surrender of the
British at Potchefstroom
1880–1881

IAN BENNETT

Greenhill Books, London
Stackpole Books, Pennsylvania

A Rain of Lead
First published 2001
by Greenhill Books, Lionel Leventhal Limited, Park House, 1 Russell Gardens,
London NW11 9NN
www.greenhillbooks.com
and
Stackpole Books, 5067 Ritter Road, Mechanicsburg, PA 17055, USA

British Library Cataloguing in Publication Data
Bennett, Ian H. W.
A rain of lead : the siege and surrender of the British at Potchefstroom
1. Great Britain – History, Military – 19th century
2. Transvaal (South Africa) – History – War of 1880–1881
I. Title
968'.0484

ISBN 1-85367-437-0

Library of Congress Cataloging-in-Publication Data
Bennett, Ian H. W.
A rain of lead / the siege and surrender of the British at Potchefstroom / Ian Bennett.
p. cm.
Includes bibliographical references and index.
ISBN 1-85367-437-0
1. Potchefstroom (South Africa)–History–Siege, 1880-1881. I. Title
DT2359.P68 B46 2001
968.04'5–dc21

00-066200

Typeset by DP Photosetting, Aylesbury, Bucks
Printed and bound in Great Britain
by MPG Books Ltd, Bodmin, Cornwall

Contents

List of Illustrations, Drawings and Maps

Illustrations

Drawings

Maps

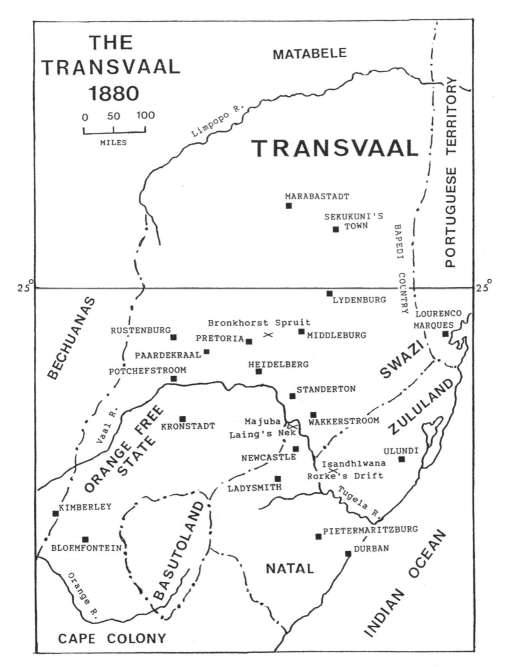

THE
TRANSVAAL
1880

0   50   100

MILES

MATABELE

Limpopo R.

TRANSVAAL

PORTUGUESE TERRITORY

MARABASTADT

SEKUKUNI'S
TOWN

BAPEDI COUNTRY

25°   25°

LYDENBURG

LOURENCO
MARQUES

BECHUANAS

RUSTENBURG

Bronkhorst Spruit

PRETORIA   MIDDLEBURG

PAARDEKRAAL

POTCHEFSTROOM

HEIDELBERG

SWAZI

Vaal R.

ORANGE FREE STATE

KRONSTADT

STANDERTON

WAKKERSTROOM

ZULULAND

Majuba
Laing's Nek

NEWCASTLE

ULUNDI

Isandhlwana
Rorke's Drift

KIMBERLEY

LADYSMITH

BASUTOLAND

Tugela R.

BLOEMFONTEIN

PIETERMARITZBURG

DURBAN

Orange R.

NATAL

INDIAN OCEAN

CAPE COLONY

Ian Bennett

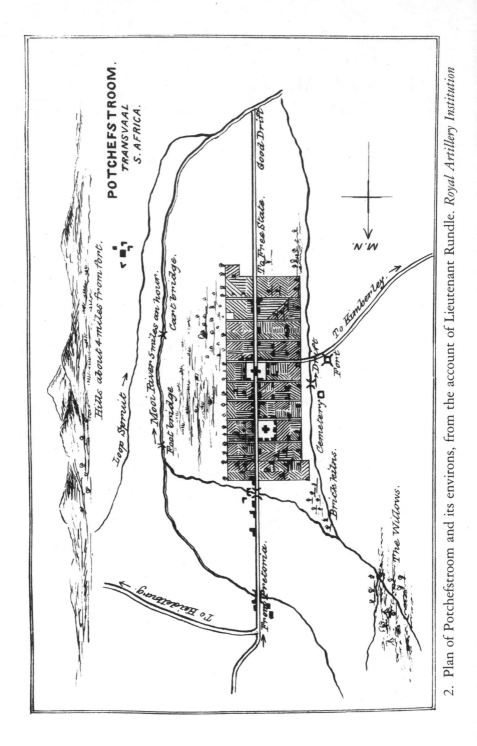

2. Plan of Potchefstroom and its environs, from the account of Lieutenant Rundle. *Royal Artillery Institution*

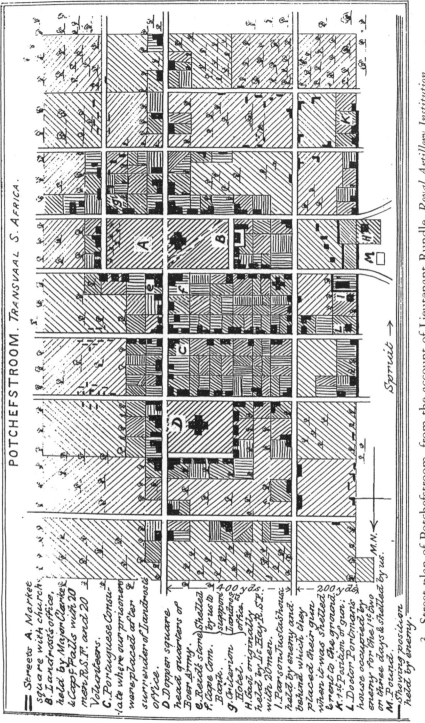

3. Street plan of Potchefstroom, from the account of Lieutenant Rundle. *Royal Artillery Institution*

4. Street plan of Potchefstroom, printed in the *Natal Mercury*.

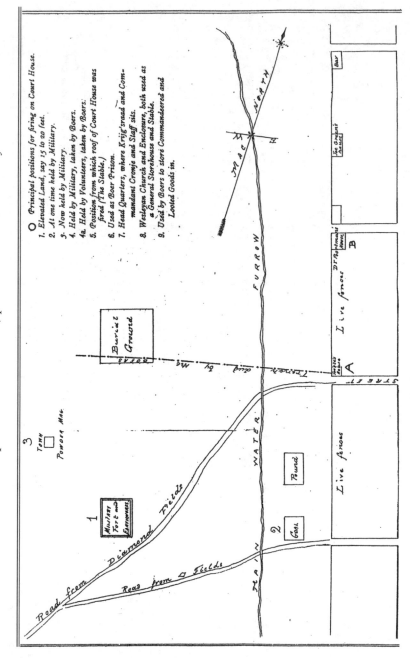

○ Principal positions for firing on Court House.
1. Elevated Land, say 15 to 20 feet.
2. At one time held by Military.
3. Now held by Military.
4. Held by Military, taken by Boers.
4a. Held by Volunteers, taken by Boers.
5. Position from which roof of Court House was fired (The Stable.)
6. Used as Boer Prison.
7. Head Quarters, where Krijgsraad and Commandant Cronje and Staff sits.
8. Wesleyan Church and Enclosure, both used as a General Storehouse and Stable.
9. Used by Boers to store Commandeered and Looted Goods in.

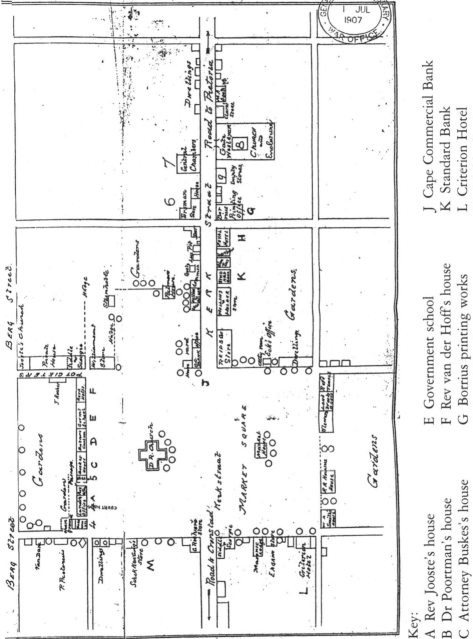

Key:

A Rev Jooste's house
B Dr Poortman's house
C Attorney Buskes's house
D Butner's canteen

E Government school
F Rev van der Hoff's house
G Borrius printing works
H Royal Hotel

J Cape Commercial Bank
K Standard Bank
L Criterion Hotel
M Schikkerling's store

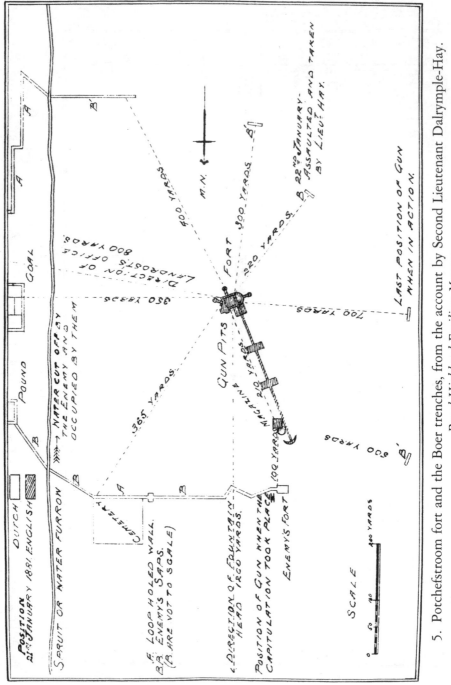

5. Potchefstroom fort and the Boer trenches, from the account by Second Lieutenant Dalrymple-Hay.
Royal Highland Fusiliers Museum

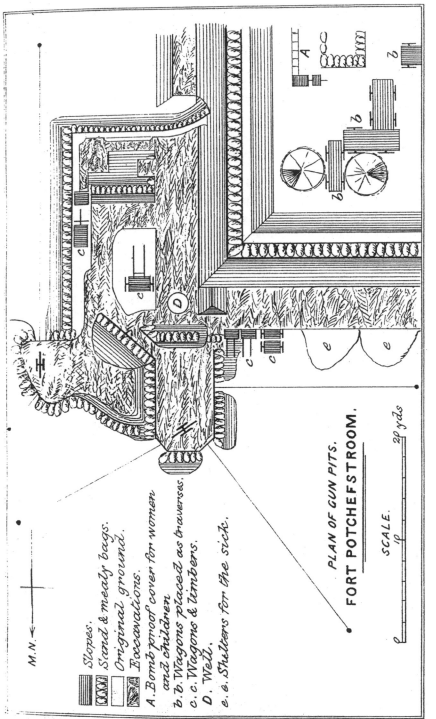

M.N.

Slopes.
Sand & mealy bags.
Original ground.
Excavations.
A. Bomb proof cover for women and children.
b.b. Wagons placed as traverses.
c.c. Wagons & timbers.
D. Well.
e.e. Shelters for the sick.

PLAN OF GUN PITS.

FORT POTCHEFSTROOM.

SCALE.

20 yds

6. Plan of the gun pits at Potchefstroom fort, from the account by Lieutenant Rundle. *Royal Artillery Institution*

Victoria Regina

July 3

A hot morning – Drove down to Frogmore with Beatrice & the 2 girls, & stopped just opposite the Gardener's Cottage, where the road from the Long Walk joins the others. Here was drawn up a Battery of Artillery, which had come into Windsor on Saturday & was billeted in the Town, on its way to Hay in S. Wales where it has its annual practice. Capt Bigge heard that there were in this Battery, 2 men, who had escaped from Isandlwhana, & who were at Rorke's Drift; – 5 who were with Lord Chelmsford on that day, as well as men who were at Ulundi, and in the Transvaal War with Sir George Colley. I annex a note by Capt Bigge about them. They marched past, then the men above mentioned, were brought up, & severally named, the Officers having been previously presented. They marched away. It was most interesting, & immensely gratified the poor men, who had been through so much. Leopold & Helen had followed us down, in a phaeton, & we all went on to Frogmore together & breakfasted under the trees. – Took a short walk afterwards, to the dear Mausoleum.

From
The Journal of Her Majesty Queen Victoria
For
3 July 1882

Acknowledgements

I should like to thank the many people who over the years have helped me to collect the material that has gone into the making of this book. In South Africa: Professor Gert van den Bergh, Potchefstroom University, who generously translated Weilbach and Du Plessis for me; Rita Van Wyk, Potchefstroom Museum; John Deare, the *Natal Witness*; Audrey Kemsley, a descendant of the Forssman family; the late Julian Orford and Ian Uys, who made their unpublished research papers available to me; Professor Joy Brain, Roman Catholic Archives, Natal; Fred Brownell, the State Herald of the Republic of South Africa; Dr Arthur Davey; Dr Gilbert Torlage and the staff of the Natal Archives, Pietermaritzburg. In Britain: Lady Sheila de Bellaigue and Frances Dimond, the Royal Archives, Windsor; Major Willie Shaw, Regimental Headquarters, The Royal Highland Fusiliers; Brigadier Ken Timbers and Bridget Timbers, Royal Artillery Institution; Captain Peter Starling, the Royal Army Medical Corps Museum; Yvonne Baker, South African High Commission, London. Illustrations 1 and 7 and the extract from the Journal of Queen Victoria (page 16) are reproduced by the gracious permission of Her Majesty Queen Elizabeth II.

Ian Bennett, 2001

Chronology

In 1652 Jan van Riebeck founded the settlement of Cape Town to victual Dutch ships trading with the East Indies. Over the next century Dutch, German and French Huguenot settlers merged to create the unique Afrikaner race, the Boers. During this era slaves were imported to the Colony from other parts of Africa and the East Indies. The Boers expanded their territory unhindered until 1702 when on the Eastern Cape border they clashed with the Bantu Xhosa people immigrating from the north, heralding the bloody and bitter struggles to come. During the Napoleonic Wars the British occupied the strategic Cape and in 1814 Holland ceded the Colony to Britain. The Boers resented British rule and events of the next sixty years would chart their determination to live beyond British jurisdiction.

1814   Cape Colony ceded by Holland to Britain.
1815   The Slagter's Nek Rebellion. The shooting of Cornelis Bezuidenhout by government troops led to a Boer revolt, which resulted in the inhumane hanging of five convicted rebels.
1820   British settlers established in Eastern Cape.
1833   The abolition of slavery, which resulted in severe pecuniary losses for the Boers.
1835   The Sixth Frontier War. Xhosa clans invade the Eastern Cape Colony, pillaging and devastating settlers' farms until driven out by British forces ably supported by Boer commandos.
1836   The Great Trek. The mass migration from the Cape Colony of Boer families no longer able to tolerate British rule or their policies towards the indigenous natives. By 1837 some 4,000 souls had crossed the Orange River, destined to create the Transvaal, the Orange Free State and Natalia.
1836   Cape of Good Hope Punishment enacted under which the British claimed legal jurisdiction over all citizens including Trek Boers as far north as the 25th Parallel.
1837   The Boers defeat the Matabele at Kapain and begin to occupy the Transvaal.
1838   Potchefstroom founded.
1838   The Boers defeat the Zulus under Dingaan at Blood River and found Natalia.

1842   British troops occupy Port Natal but are defeated by the Boers at Congella and are besieged in their camp.

1842   British reinforcements raise the siege of Port Natal and take control of Natalia.

1845   British forces defeat the Boers in a confrontation at Zwartkopjes in Transorangia.

1845   The British formally annex Natal.

1848   The British annex Transorangia and create the Orange River Sovereignty.

1852   The Sand River Convention by which the British recognise the independence of the Transvaal Boers.

1854   The Convention of Bloemfontein by which the British recognise an independent Orange Free State.

1857   The Constitution of the Transvaal Republic decrees that Potchefstroom shall be the capital and Pretoria the seat of government.

1865   Gold discovered in north-east Transvaal.

1867   First discovery of diamonds in South Africa, followed by major finds at Kimberley in 1869.

1872   Thomas Burgers elected president of the Transvaal Republic.

1875   Burgers travels to Europe to raise funds to finance the construction of a railway to the sea, which would make the Transvaal commercially independent of Britain.

1876   The Boer campaign led by Burgers against Sekukuni and his Bapedi people ends in ignominious failure.

1876 **(August)** Lord Carnarvon, British colonial secretary, holds London conference to plan the confederation of the South African states.

1876 **(October)** Sir Theophilus Shepstone appointed special commissioner to the Transvaal Republic.

1877   The Transvaal Republic bankrupt and in political turmoil as a consequence of Burgers's policies.

1877 **(April)** Shepstone annexes the Transvaal on behalf of Britain.

1877 **(April)** Sir Henry Bartle Frere arrives in Cape Town as high commissioner for all British South Africa, tasked to achieve confederation.

1877 **(May)** Paul Kruger leads a delegation to London requesting the restoration of Transvaal independence.

1877 **(October)** Ninth Frontier War. A tribal brawl escalates into a full-scale war between the British and Xhosa clans on the Eastern Cape border.

1878 **(January)** Sir Michael Hicks-Beach replaces Lord Carnarvon as colonial secretary.

1878 (April) Kruger leads a second delegation to London and warns that the Boers will fight if independence is not restored.

1878 (October) British forces under Colonel Rowlands fail in a campaign against Sekukuni.

1879   The Anglo-Zulu War. The Transvaal Boers refuse to participate. Battle of Isandhlwana (22 January), Rorke's Drift (22 January), Kambula (29 March). British ultimate victory at Ulundi (4 July).

1879 (March) Shepstone recalled to London and replaced as administrator of the Transvaal by Colonel Owen Lanyon.

1879 (April) Frere meets a mass assembly of armed Boers gathered threateningly outside Pretoria.

1879 (June) General Sir Garnet Wolseley arrives in Natal to replace Lord Chelmsford as military commander and becomes high commissioner for Natal, Zululand and Transvaal. Frere remained in office as governor of the Cape only.

1879 (September) Wolseley arrives at Pretoria.

1879 (December) Wolseley, having assembled a large force in the Transvaal, defeats and captures Sekukuni.

1880 (April) Wolseley departs from the Transvaal to be succeeded in July by Major-General Sir George Pomeroy-Colley.

1880 (April) Gladstone defeats Disraeli in the general election to become prime minister for the second time, increasing Boer expectancy of the restoration of their independence.

1880 (August) Frere recalled from the Cape.

1880 (11 November) The Bezuidenhout Affair. Boers at Potchefstroom prevent the government sale of a wagon belonging to Piet Bezuidenhout who was judged to be in default of taxes.

1880 (17 November) Commandant Raaff attempts to arrest Cronje and other leaders involved in the Bezuidenhout Affair.

1880 (18 November) British troops arrive at Potchefstroom in aid to the civil power.

1880 (29 November) Paul Kruger meets George Hudson, government secretary, and informs him that Boers will hold a mass meeting on 8 December.

1880 (30 November) Major Clarke assumes appointment of special commissioner at Potchefstroom.

1880 (8–13 December) Boers assembled at Paardekraal elect a governing Triumvirate, Kruger, Joubert and Pretorius, and declare the Transvaal independent.

1880 (15 December) A Boer commando led by Cronje enters Potchefstroom unopposed bringing the proclamation of independence for printing. British troops remain in the fort and government buildings where by evening they are joined by a number of civilians including women and children.

1880 (16 December) The approach of mounted Boers to the fort at Potchefstroom provokes an exchange of shots, so commencing the war.

1880 (16 December) Boers attack the British-held Landrost's office, fort and gaol.

1880 (18 December) Major Clarke surrenders Landrost's office and garrison. Later that night British evacuate gaol.

1880 (20 December) Bronkhorst Spruit disaster. A Boer commando successfully halts the 94th (Connaught Rangers) marching to Pretoria, inflicting heavy casualties.

1881 (1 January) Boers attempt a general attack on the Potchefstroom fort, opening fire with their cannon Ou Griet for the first time.

1881 (3 January) British occupy and fortify the Potchefstroom town powder magazine.

1881 (5 January) Boers commence digging trenches, which would eventually encircle the fort.

1881 (7 January) British attack and surprise Boers occupying the Potchefstroom town cemetery.

1881 (16–17 January) Boers attempt to lure the British out of the fort by a ruse.

1881 (22 January) British make a sortie against threatening Boer trenches.

1881 (28 January) Battle of Laing's Nek. Boers decisively repulse British attempt to break through into the Transvaal.

1881 (7 February) Fight at Ingogo. Boers successfully attack British troops under General Colley marching between Mount Prospect and Newcastle.

1881 (27 February) Battle of Majuba. The Boers drive British troops off Majuba Hill with heavy casualties, including General Colley killed in action.

1881 (6 March) Armistice agreement signed by General Evelyn Wood and Commandant General Piet Joubert half-way between Mount Prospect and Laing's Nek.

1881 (10 March) Boers under Cronje mount a general attack on the fort at Potchefstroom.

1881 (18 March) Lieutenant-Colonel Winsloe belatedly learns of the armistice.

1881 (19 March) Winsloe commences surrender negotiations with Cronje.

1881 (21 March) Capitulation agreement signed by Winsloe.

1881 (23 March) British garrison march out of Potchefstroom fort with
    honours of war and lay down their arms.

NOTE

The number of days under siege commencing on 15 December 1880 are
taken from the diary of Second Lieutenant J. R. M. Dalrymple-Hay. The
separate descriptions of events that occurred concurrently at the fort and in
the town lead to some overlap of dates in the text. Contemporary spellings
of place names are used throughout.

Biographies

Bezuidenhout, Pieter Lodewyk (1837–1905)
Bezuidenhout shared the Dutch forebears of Cornelis Bezuidenhout whose shooting led to the notorious Slagter's Nek hangings, but was not a direct descendant. In 1880 he had been a field cornet (a military office with the duties of a minor magistrate) for eighteen years and married for twenty with a large family. He was a staunch republican, ever ready to challenge British authority, and was a central figure in the 'Wagon Affair' at Potchefstroom, which set in train the events that led to war in 1880. He was a local character nicknamed 'Bontperde' after the dappled horses he bred. With a reputation as a dandy he habitually wore a top hat adorned with an ostrich feather. After the war he was elected to the Volksraad (1885–93) but never achieved prominence. When the British occupied Potchefstroom during the Boer War 1899–1902 he was placed under house arrest.

Browne, Lieutenant Peter William (b. 1857)
Browne was commissioned as sub-lieutenant in the 21st Royal Scots Fusiliers in 1876. He served with the 2/21st throughout the Zulu War, and with his men faced the most determined assault the Zulus made on the British square at Ulundi. He was mentioned in dispatches for service at Potchefstroom, where he commanded D Company, 2/21st and acted as adjutant to Winsloe. In 1881 he went with the 2/21st to India, being promoted captain in 1885. He served in the Burmese Expedition 1885–86, but curiously his name disappears from the Army list in 1887 and the regiment has no record of him after this date.

Buskes, G. H. (dates of birth and death unknown)
A doctor of law of the University of Utrecht, Buskes emigrated to the Transvaal and practised law in Potchefstroom. At one time he was clerk to the Landrost, resigning in 1878. At first he publicly supported Shepstone and annexation, but on the outbreak of war became more anti-British than most Boers. A leading Boer supporter during the siege of Potchefstroom, he was secretary to General Cronje and later a secretary to Kruger and the Triumvirate. He earned an unenviable reputation for devious behaviour and dishonesty.

Clarke, Major Marshall James (1841–1909)
(Later Lieutenant-Colonel Sir Marshall Clarke, KCMG)
Clarke was commissioned into the Royal Artillery from the Royal Military Academy, Woolwich, in 1863. From 1863 to 1865 he served in India where he lost the use of his left arm, having apparently fought a tiger when armed only with a carving knife. Following two years in Mauritius he was posted to South Africa where he was to spend the greater part of his career, employed more often in civil than in military appointments and frequently the centre of controversy. He attended the 'crowning' of Cetswayo as a member of Theophilus Shepstone's staff in 1873. Later in the same year he was engaged in the operations to suppress the Langalabilele revolt. In 1874 he was appointed resident magistrate at Pietermaritzburg only shortly after having been acquitted by a court-martial, lasting five days, of being implicated in the death of an African rebel prisoner. This was a *cause célèbre* at the time. He was ADC to Shepstone at the time of the annexation of the Transvaal in 1877. Sent to negotiate with Sekukuni in 1877, he was later appointed special commissioner for the Lydenberg area, which involved confrontation with the Bapedi until their defeat by Wolseley in 1879. The Transvaal Boers considered his conduct of affairs on the frontiers ill advised. As special commissioner at Potchefstroom in November 1880 he attempted to prevent any military confrontation with the Boers, but when fighting broke out he was forced to surrender the Landrost's office after a brief defence, and was held prisoner by the Boers until April 1881. After the war he became a resident magistrate in Basutoland in 1881, and commissioner of police in King Williams Town, Cape, in 1882. That same year he went to Egypt as colonel commanding the Turkish Regiment Egyptian Gendarmerie. There followed a series of prestigious civil appointments: resident commissioner, Basutoland, 1884–93; acting administrator, Zululand, 1893–98; resident commissioner in Southern Rhodesia, 1898–1905.

Cronje, General Pieter Arnoldus (1836–1911)
Cronje was a direct descendant of the Huguenot Pierre Cronier who arrived in the Cape in 1698. He received some education at Potchefstroom and with his brother Andries worked his father's farm, Goedevonden. He took part in a number of forays against natives and was made a field cornet serving under Kruger. Fiercely opposed to annexation, he entered public life in 1879 when made leader of the Boers in the Potchefstroom district. His conduct of the siege at Potchefstroom was criticised by Kruger, who reprimanded Cronje for putting local before national interests. His duplicity in obtaining the British surrender was a great embarrassment to the Boer Triumvirate. After the war he remained active in politics as a member of the Volksraad, supporting Kruger, and commandant of the Potchefstroom

district. He earned lasting military fame for his defeat of the Jamieson raid at Doornkop in 1896, receiving the plaudits of Russia, France and Germany. That same year he was appointed to the important government post of superintendent of natives. On the outbreak of the Anglo-Boer War in 1899 he was appointed assistant commandant-general and commander-in-chief of the republican forces on the western border. He laid siege to Mafeking and led the victory at Magersfontein, but shortly afterwards was defeated at Paardeburg and surrendered his forces to the British. Accompanied by his wife, Cronje was imprisoned on St Helena until the end of the war. Returning home he was ostracised by the Boers and in 1904 travelled to the USA to join a show giving dramatised representations of the Boer War. Disenchanted with his reception he returned home in 1905 to spend his remaining years at Palmietfontein, isolated, lonely and unhappy.

Dalrymple-Hay, Second Lieutenant James Reginald Maitland (1858–1923)

Commissioned in the Royal Ayr & Wigtown Militia in 1878, Dalrymple-Hay was granted a commission in the Regular Army in 1879, joining the 2/21st Royal Scots Fusiliers at Pretoria in April 1880. He defended the gaol at Potchefstroom with men of C Company, 2/21st for the first two days of fighting, and later led a bayonet charge against a Boer position. In 1886 he transferred to the West India Regiment, with which he saw campaign service in West Africa, 1897–98. He served in the Boer War 1899–1901 on the staff, was mentioned in dispatches and awarded the DSO in 1901. He commanded 2nd Battalion, West India Regiment in Sierra Leone in 1903, was promoted brevet colonel in 1907 and retired as honorary brigadier CB in 1917.

Dunne, Deputy Assistant Commissary-General Walter Alphonsus (1853–1908)

Dunne joined the Control Department (in what was to become the Commissariat and Transport Staff in 1880) as sub-assistant commissary (second lieutenant) in 1873. Posted to South Africa in 1877, he served in the Ninth Frontier War, 1877–78, and then in Rowland's Campaign against Sekukuni in 1878. Appointed senior Commissariat officer with No. 3 Column in Zululand, he played an active part in the defence of Rorke's Drift on 22 January 1879, and was recommended for the VC by Lord Chelmsford, although this was refused by the Duke of Cambridge. Immediately promoted DACG (captain) for gallantry, he served with Wood's Flying Column for the rest of the Zulu War, and was present at the battle of Ulundi. He then moved to the Transvaal and was at the storming of Sekukuni's Town and Fighting Kopje in November 1879. During the siege of Potchefstroom, in addition to his Commissariat duties, he took part in the defence of the gaol and led patrols. He went on to serve in the Egyptian Campaign, 1882, and in Sudan in 1885, being mentioned in dispatches on both occasions. He transferred in the rank of lieutenant-colonel to the Army Service Corps on its formation in 1888. He was appointed CB in 1896 and promoted colonel in 1897. Throughout the Boer War 1899–1902 he was at the War Office, responsible for the British Army Supply Services world-wide. Regulations that barred officers from the old Commissariat departments being promoted above colonel prevented his becoming the first ASC major-general in 1905. He retired in 1908.

Du Plessis, Charles Nicolaas Jacobus (1836–1928)
Little is known of his early life, but at the outbreak of war in 1880 Du Plessis was living in Potchefstroom where he kept a diary of events from 15 December 1880 until the end of hostilities. He took part in the siege as a corporal and also fought at Laing's Nek. After the war he supplemented his diary with other material and in conjunction with Commandant J. D. Weilbach published *Geschiedenis van den Emigranten-Boeren en van den Vrij-heids-Oorlog*, the first written Boer account of the war of 1880–81. Du Plessis seems to have been a restless individual, a romantic and a poet. A patriotic Boer, he fought against the Jamieson Raiders in 1896 and throughout the Boer War of 1899–1902.

Falls, Captain Alexander (1849–80)
Falls purchased his commission as ensign in the 21st Royal Scots Fusiliers in 1867. During the Zulu War he was left behind with his company at Fort Napier, Pietermaritzburg. He led his company in the Sekukuni Campaign of 1879, taking part in the storming of the Fighting Kopje. At Potchef-stroom he commanded C Company, 2/21st Royal Scots Fusiliers, and was killed defending the Landrost's office on 16 December 1880.

Forssman, Chevalier Oskar Wilhelm Alric (1822–89)
From an aristocratic Swedish family, Forssman was a qualified civil engineer who settled in Potchefstroom as a general trader in 1846. He became one of the biggest individual landowners in the Transvaal, owning more than one hundred farms and many properties in Potchefstroom, and was a justice of the peace. He held a concession for supplying the republican government with gunpowder, lead and stationery. He saw the great potential of the Transvaal and contributed much to the development of the country, encouraging mining of minerals and the advancement of agriculture. As a major exporter of goods to Portugal he was made consul-general by the Portuguese and a knight commander of the Order of Jesus Christ. He was a considerable personality and the friend of presidents, and much of the social life of Potchefstroom centred on his house. He accepted membership of the

British Legislative Assembly after annexation, arousing considerable animosity among the Boers. On the outbreak of war in 1880 he and his family sought protection in the British fort at Potchefstroom. After the war he returned to live in the Transvaal and although he never received compensation for his losses during the conflict he eventually rebuilt his fortunes to some extent.

Joubert, Petrus J. (Piet) (1831–1900)

Self-educated in the law, an astute businessman and law agent, Joubert first came to prominence as a politician rather than a soldier. He acted as president of the Transvaal in 1875 and 1876 during the absence of President Burgers in Europe. He was a member of the Triumvirate and elected commandant-general in 1880, an appointment he held until his death in 1900. He defeated the British at Laing's Nek and Majuba.

Kock, Johannes Hermanns Michiel (1835–99)

Kock fought against the British at Zwartkopjes aged 11 and at Boomplaats aged 13. His family then settled in the Potchefstroom district where Kock eventually became a government servant and a justice of the peace. He distinguished himself as a general under Cronje in the fighting at Potchefstroom in 1880–81, and after the war returned to government service achieving high appointments. On the outbreak of the Boer War in 1899 he had charge of a command in the invasion of Natal. After the battle of Talana he occupied Elandslaagte Station where he was decisively beaten by the British. Kock was seriously wounded during the battle and died a few days later, a prisoner of war, after much suffering.

Kruger, S. J. P. (Paul) (1825–1904)

Kruger accompanied his parents on the Great Trek when 10 years old. A field cornet at 17, he emerged as the principal Boer military leader during the formative years of the Republic. Elected vice-president immediately before the British annexation in 1877, he led the Triumvirate during the war of 1880–81. He was elected president of the Transvaal in 1883, 1888, 1893 and 1898. He fled to Switzerland in 1900 during the second Anglo-Boer War.

Lean, Second Lieutenant Kenneth (1859–1919)

A militia lieutenant in 6th West Yorks Militia, Lean transferred to the 2/ 21st Royal Scots Fusiliers for service in Zululand and took part in the Sekukuni Campaign, 1879. At Potchefstroom he was second officer with the Mounted Infantry Troop 2/21st. He was then commissioned in the Regular Army and went to India with the 2/21st, taking part in the Burmese Expedition of 1885–86. He held staff appointments in India during the 1890s. He served throughout the Boer War of 1899–1902, involved in many engagements in command of a Mounted Infantry battalion. He was mentioned in dispatches and promoted brevet lieutenant-colonel. He became a brevet colonel in 1908 and retired with the honorary rank of major-general in 1918.

Lemmer, Hermanus (1849–1900)
Lemmer was a commandant during the fighting at Potchefstroom 1880–81 and probably the officer who supervised the public execution of Hans van der Linden. After 1881 he took part in a number of native wars. He was elected to represent Potchefstroom in the Volksraad up to the outbreak of the Boer War in 1899. He then became a deputy to General de la Rey, fighting with great distinction until killed in action against the British on 9 December 1900. General Jan Smuts wrote of him that 'he combined the gentleness of a child with the courage of a lion'.

Lindsell, Lieutenant Charles Frederick (1852–1917)
Lindsell was commissioned in the 14th Hussars as second lieutenant, 1872, and transferred to the 21st Royal Scots Fusiliers in May 1878, serving with the 2/21st in the Zulu War. In addition to being involved in the first action of the war against the Boers on 16 December 1880 he played a leading part in the fighting throughout the siege, in command of the Mounted Infantry Troop, and was mentioned in dispatches. After Potchefstroom he went to India with the 2/21st and took part in the Burmese Expedition 1885–86. He was attached to the Egyptian Army 1886–87. Officially he retired from the 2/21st, and the Army list shows him as being employed by the Land Commission in Matabeleland and Mashonaland in the early 1890s. In 1896 he took part in the Jamieson Raid, as staff officer in charge of scouts at Doornkop where the Boers under General Piet Cronje defeated and captured the raiders. He saw service again in the Boer War from 1899–1901.

Martin, Trumpeter Nicholas Henry (1863–1912)
Martin enlisted as a boy soldier into the Royal Artillery at Falmouth on 23 July 1875, and proceeded to South Africa in February 1876 with N/5 Battery, serving in the Ninth Frontier War and the Zulu War. He escaped from Isandhlwana on 22 January 1879 when half of N/5 Battery was massacred. He rejoined N/5 Battery to serve in the Transvaal and at the age of eighteen was awarded the Distinguished Conduct Medal for rescuing a wounded man under fire on 22 January 1881 at Potchefstroom. He continued to serve with the Royal Artillery until 23 July 1896 when he was discharged in the rank of battery quartermaster sergeant.

Pretorius, Marthinus Wessels (1819–1901)
The son of Andries Pretorius, victor over the Zulus at Blood River in 1838, Marthinus Pretorius was elected commandant-general to succeed his father

in 1853. He desired the union of Boer republics and was elected president of the Transvaal in 1856 and also of the Orange Free State in 1859. He resigned the presidency of the Free State in 1862 and the presidency of the Transvaal in 1871, but returned to politics as a member of the Triumvirate in 1880.

Raaff, Commandant Pieter Edward, CMG (1849–93)

Raaff's father was of Dutch origin, an official employed by the British Government of the Orange River Sovereignty. Pieter Raaff was wounded in the Basuto war of 1865, aged sixteen, gaining a reputation for bravery. He unsuccessfully sought his fortune in the diamond fields, until, in 1876, he became one of the volunteers recruited by Burgers for his disastrous campaign against Sekukuni. He remained on the Bapedi border serving first the Boers and then the British, taking part in Colonel Rowlands's abortive campaign of 1878. At the outbreak of the Zulu War he was commanding 'Raaff's Corps'. After Isandhlwana he joined Wood's No. 4 Column at Kambula in command of the Transvaal Rangers, a mounted unit of mixed European and coloured troopers who fought with distinction. Raaff was appointed CMG for his services but the Zulu War medal was withheld for alleged financial irregularities in his unit. He attempted to settle down, married and opened a butcher's shop in Pretoria, and then in 1880 Sir Owen Lanyon appointed him court messenger and field cornet at Potchefstroom. He took a leading part in the defence of the Landrost's office, and after his capture he was court-martialled by the Boers and sentenced to death for high treason, but Kruger intervened ordering a retrial, which found him not guilty. In 1891 he joined the Bechuanaland police and became a resident magistrate. On the outbreak of the Matabele War in 1893, at the behest of Dr Jamieson, British South Africa Company, he raised a new force of rangers and led Raaff's Column in the pursuit of Lobengula. When their sister Salisbury Column was ambushed on the Shangani river with the loss of many officers and men the survivors insisted on Raaff taking command. He led the column safely back to Bulawayo, where he died on 28 March 1893. The circumstances of his death were suspicious and there were insinuations of murder, which were never proved.

Rundle, Lieutenant Henry Macleod Leslie (1856–1934)
(Later General Sir Leslie Rundle, KCMG)

Commissioned into the Royal Artillery from the Royal Military Academy, Woolwich, in 1876, Rundle was serving with 10/7 Battery RA in Mauritius when the unit was ordered to Zululand after Isandhlwana. The battery, arriving in Natal, was equipped with Gatling guns, one of the first RA units to handle this early type of machine gun. The battery took part in the battle of Ulundi where Rundle was in charge of a Gatling at a corner of the square, and was mentioned in dispatches. He was posted to N/5 Battery in the Transvaal in November 1879. For his invaluable part in the defence of the fort at Potchefstroom, where he was wounded, he was again mentioned in dispatches. He was to have a distinguished military career spanning many campaigns – Egypt 1882, the Nile 1884–85, Sudan 1885–87, Sudan 1889, Dongola 1896 – eventually becoming a lieutenant-general of the Egyptian Army. After the Khartoum Expedition of 1898 he was knighted KCB. There followed a number of senior appointments at home and abroad including command of the 8th Division during the Boer War of 1900–02 and the award of the KCMG. From 1909 to 1915 he was governor-general of Malta. He was colonel commandant, Royal Artillery, in 1907.

Sketchley, Dr Charles (dates of birth and death unknown)
There is no record of a Dr Charles Sketchley in the archives of the Royal College of Surgeons or the Royal College of Physicians in London, and consequently little is known of his background. He arrived in Potchefstroom as acting district surgeon some time in 1879, with a great reputation for his work during the Russo-Turkish War of 1877–78. Reports of the Stafford House Committee, which funded and organised medical support for the Turkish Army, contain many references to Assistant Surgeon or Dr Sketchley. He did sterling work at the siege of Plevna and during the retreat of the Turkish armies over 300 miles to Constantinople, and improvised a hospital to serve the military and civilians during an outbreak of typhus. Sketchley's presence in Potchefstroom is recorded by Judge John Koetze who attended the wedding of the doctor to Emily Forssman, one of the chevalier's daughters. On the outbreak of war in 1880 he took refuge with his wife in the fort and assisted Surgeon Wallis AMD throughout the siege. After the armistice of 1881 Dr Sketchley was seen in Newcastle, Natal, but no records of his subsequent history have come to light.

Thornhill, Major Charles (1838–86)
Thornhill was commissioned into the Royal Artillery from the Royal Military Academy, Woolwich, in 1857. Most unusually for an officer of this era, he had never seen campaign service before Potchefstroom in 1880. He had assumed command of N/5 Battery RA in May 1880 after the Zulu War, and was in command of British troops at Potchefstroom from 18 November to 12 December 1880 when he handed over to Lieutenant-Colonel Winsloe, 2/21st Royal Scots Fusiliers. Frequently ill during the siege, he did not play a leading role in the fighting, and was criticised after the war by General Wood for his lack of enterprise in handling his guns. Despite these shortcomings he was rewarded with brevet promotion to the rank of lieutenant-colonel. He was in command of the battery when seen by

Queen Victoria at Windsor on 3 July 1882. He retired from the Army in the rank of colonel on 1 April 1885.

Wallis, Surgeon Kenneth Sargeant (1852–1905)
A member of the Royal College of Surgeons, Wallis was appointed to the Army Medical Department in 1878. He was one of the surgeons sent to Natal as reinforcements after Isandhlwana and he saw service in Zululand. Later in 1879 he took part in the Sekukuni Campaign, was wounded during the storming of the Fighting Kopje while evacuating casualties, and was mentioned in dispatches. He was responsible for medical services during the siege of Potchefstroom. He continued to serve in the Army Medical Department until 1898, being promoted to the rank of lieutenant-colonel. He served in the Nile Expedition of 1884–85 in charge of a mobile field hospital.

Weilbach, Johan Daniel (1839–1906)
Weilbach was commandant of the Heidelberg Commando in the war of 1880–81, taking part in the siege of Potchefstroom, the battles of Laing's Nek, Ingogo and Majuba, and again in the Boer War of 1899–1902, leading the commando in the invasion of Natal and at Ladysmith. Later he was engaged in the fighting against Lord Roberts's advance on Johannesburg. He was soon seen to be too old and unequal to the demands of this war, and was relieved of his command. Weilbach's name appears as a co-author of the book on the war of 1880–81 with C. N. J. Du Plessis.

Winsloe, Lieutenant-Colonel Richard William Charles (1835–1917)
Winsloe purchased a commission in the 15th Foot in 1853, transferred to the 21st Regiment, Royal Scots Fusiliers, in 1854 in order to serve in the Crimean War, and was at Sebastopol and the amphibious operation to Kinburn that ended the war. He served with distinction in the Zulu War of 1879, being severely wounded at Ulundi, and was promoted brevet lieutenant-colonel. On his recovery he rejoined the 2/21st at Pretoria in December 1880 and was sent to Potchefstroom to command the British troops, relieving Major Thornhill. For his defence of Potchefstroom fort he was made ADC (1882–90) to Queen Victoria and promoted brevet colonel. After the war he was given command of the 2/21st and took the battalion to India, commanding it during the Burmese Expedition of 1886–87 and mentioned in dispatches.

Prologue

As the year of 1880 drew to a close some 200 British soldiers began the defence of a makeshift mud fort the size of a tennis court; with them were a number of civilian women and children. Although heavily outnumbered by encircling Boers they were to hold out under constant fire by day and night for ninety-five days, until starvation and numerous casualties, including women and children, forced them to surrender. Too late they discovered that they had been duped by a devious enemy. In recognition of their gallantry the emaciated garrison was permitted by the Boers to march out of the Fort with 'the honours of war', carrying their weapons, their home-made Union Jack flying and bugles playing. The place was Potchefstroom in the Transvaal and the conflict the First Anglo-Boer War of 1880–81.

Most of the garrison had fought in all or some of the campaigns undertaken by the British in South Africa during the immediately preceding years: the Ninth Frontier War, 1877–78; the Zulu War, 1879; the Sekukuni Campaign, 1879. Two had saved themselves from the massacre at Isandhlwana, others had survived the defence of Rorke's Drift, individuals had escaped from the near British defeat on Hlobane mountain and a significant proportion had participated in the final defeat of the Zulus at Ulundi. They had marched hundreds of miles in all weathers, often ill fed and clothed, seldom if ever with a roof over their heads. Yet with the exception of their commander and a few others, both officers and men were still in their early twenties.

The siege of the fort at Potchefstroom is unlikely now to enter the realms of military mythology along with Rorke's Drift and the Alamo, although Lady Florence Dixie, special correspondent of the *London Morning Post*, was inspired to write on 28 July 1881: 'Potchefstroom of all others held out the most gallantly, and under circumstances of privation and hardship which while the annals of glorious deeds and heroic actions last, must ever be remembered.'

Only by piecing together elements of all the eyewitness accounts is it possible to appreciate fully the appalling conditions endured inside the fort during endless days and nights under fire: heat of 30 degrees centigrade and more, but with incessant rain during the wettest summer season for thirty years; everywhere mud and stinking filth, and no shelter except for the women and the wounded, the latter lying on the wet floors of bullet-holed

35

leaking tents. Eighty-five were killed, wounded or succumbed to disease, over a third of the strength. One hundred and four gunshot wounds alone were treated; dressings and medical supplies were soon exhausted. The troops possessed no garments to change for their often rain-sodden clothing, while the women and children only had the clothes they stood up in. Rations barely adequate at the outset of the siege were steadily reduced to starvation level.

I first came upon the story of this siege when researching the life of Colonel Walter Alphonsus Dunne CB, who when one of the defenders of Rorke's Drift had been recommended for the Victoria Cross and less than two years later was in another tight corner at Potchefstroom. The tale appeared to have all the ingredients of the kind of patriotic military drama so beloved by the Victorians: the gallantry and fortitude of the soldiers and the womenfolk, colourful reports of Boer atrocities, spies publicly executed and British prisoners of war being forced to work in the enemy trenches under fire from their own unwitting comrades. I was curious to discover why the incident had never captured the contemporary interest one would have expected and also the parts played by the leading Boer personalities whose names were to figure in the history of South Africa over the next twenty-five years, particularly during the great Boer War of 1899–1902.

Regarded as of historical importance in South Africa as the First War of Independence, in Britain the Anglo-Boer War of 1880–81 has long since faded into obscurity and with it the story of events in a then remote corner of the Transvaal. Although completely overshadowed by the far greater war that began in 1899, it was this conflict beginning at Potchefstroom on 16 December 1880 which set in train the course of events that shaped the history of South Africa for over a century, indeed until the day in 1990 when Nelson Mandela was released from imprisonment. The war was a direct consequence of the policy instigated by Lord Carnarvon, colonial secretary in the Conservative government of Disraeli, to create a confederation of the diverse colonies and independent states in South Africa including the Boer republics. In pursuance of this goal the British annexed the Transvaal against the wishes of the people in April 1877. Gladstone seized upon this issue during the general election campaign of 1880 to vilify Conservative foreign and colonial policy. In a famous speech delivered in Midlothian on 30 March he accused Disraeli of 'mischievous, disquieting and disturbing schemes', continuing: 'That is the meaning of adding places like Cyprus and places like the country of the Boers in South Africa to the British Empire. And, moreover I would say this: that if those acquisitions were as valuable as they are valueless, I would repudiate them, because they are obtained by means dishonourable to the character of our country.'

Pamphlets spread these words widely across South Africa raising the expectations of the Transvaal Boers led by Paul Kruger, Piet Joubert and Marthinus Pretorius, soon to become the governing Triumvirate, that if elected a Liberal government would restore their independence. The Boers were to be swiftly disillusioned when immediately after taking office Gladstone told the Triumvirate: 'the Queen cannot be advised to relinquish her sovereignty over the Transvaal'. This decision was justified on the sanctimonious grounds of protecting the interests of the native population, particularly against slavery.

Peaceable attempts begun by the Boers immediately after the annexation to regain their independence, including sending two delegations to London led by Kruger, failed to change the attitude of successive British governments. At a mass meeting of Boers outside Pretoria in January 1879 that coincided with the British invasion of Zululand in which the Boers refused to participate, only the persuasive powers of Kruger and Joubert prevented open rebellion at this critical time. Once Gladstone had declared his hand the prospect of armed conflict rapidly grew, although such a likelihood was dismissed as improbable by the complacent British administrator at Pretoria, Colonel (later Sir) Owen Lanyon. In the fragile atmosphere of 1880 it took only a trivial incident at Potchefstroom involving the alleged non-payment of tax amounting to £27 5s to start the war.

A series of humiliating defeats, albeit only involving small forces, and the death of the high commissioner, Sir George Pomeroy Colley, killed in battle on Majuba Hill, pushed all other events into the background. Prime Minister Gladstone heading a divided and embarrassed ministry was eager to end the war almost at any price, hoping for the sake of his political reputation that the public would soon forget the whole sorry affair. However when it was learned that the Boer commander at Potchefstroom, General Piet Cronje, had engineered the British surrender by withholding the news that a general armistice had been signed, Gladstone's government made a great show of indignation. When a shamefaced Triumvirate offered to allow the British to reoccupy the fort, Gladstone accepted with alacrity. The objections of Major-General Sir Evelyn Wood VC, who had succeeded Colley, that such an adventure was militarily pointless were overridden by an insistent government grasping at an opportunity to salvage some national pride.

Wood's telegrams and reports were censored and their publication in parliamentary papers delayed until October 1882. The dearth of official information was compounded by the fact that there were none of the accredited special correspondents from the London press inside the Transvaal at the end of hostilities to telegraph home stories such as that of Potchefstroom. Reports that did appear in popular papers such as the *Penny Illustrated* of 8 April 1881 lacked accuracy and substance. This paper

contained a highly imaginative engraving depicting Colonel Winsloe and
his men marching out between mountainous walls, a few sentences out-
lining the conditions of their surrender and the comment that 'there was
much suffering among the garrison from dysentery'. Not surprisingly such
coverage aroused little interest from a public concerned about the health of
an ailing Disraeli and the prospect of a humiliating peace agreement to
conclude the war. This was the only war fought by the Army during the
reign of Queen Victoria for which no campaign medal was given, despite
pleas from General Evelyn Wood. Only about three dozen officers, NCOs
and privates who fought in all the Transvaal garrisons were eventually
rewarded, some with brevet promotions, others with honours and medals
for gallantry.

In the meantime the survivors of Potchefstroom were lost to the public
eye as they trudged 200 miles across the empty veldt of the neutral Orange
Free State with their sick and wounded. Not for thirty-eight days did they
reach Ladysmith in Natal where their arrival went virtually unremarked.

The day after crossing into the Free State, Lieutenant-Colonel Charles
Winsloe sat down under a tree beside the River Vaal and wrote his official
report, a concise factual summary of the main events, which apart from
appended reports by subordinates and correspondence with General Cronje
contained little detail. Even so, being one of the reports edited at the
direction of the Duke of Cambridge, commander-in-chief of the Army and
responsible for much of the censorship about Potchefstroom, it was not seen
by the public for many months.

By the time two of the special correspondents who had covered the war
published their books in 1882 – T. F. Carter, *A Narrative of the Boer War*,
and C. L. Norris-Newman, *With the Boers in the Transvaal* – any public
interest in Potchefstroom had waned. Both authors relied on hearsay and
their accounts of the siege were limited. That of Carter, the fuller of the two,
was largely based on newspaper interviews with Commandant Raaff,
commander of the British constabulary, who was captured on the second
day of the fighting and remained a prisoner of the Boers until the end of the
war, and the diary of G. F. Austen, a civilian resident in the town. Neither
author refers to the journal of events inside the fort accredited to an
anonymous 'Military Correspondent', which appeared in successive editions
of the *Times of Natal*, ending on 22 April 1881.

Much later an article by Winsloe appeared in *Macmillans Magazine* of
April 1883, and Lieutenant H. M. L. Rundle RA published his account in
the *Proceedings of the Royal Artillery Institution* in 1884. Often regarded as the
most authoritative account of the war inside the Transvaal, *The Transvaal
War 1881–82* by Lady Blanche Bellairs, 1885, but most likely to have been
written by her husband Colonel C. W. Bellairs, commander of the British

Forces in the Transvaal, is largely concerned with vindicating the lacklustre performance of the headquarters at Pretoria. The writer acknowledged that she based her account of Potchefstroom on the previous articles by Winsloe and Rundle. This limited contemporary view of events at Potchefstroom has misled most recent authors into trivialising the siege.

My research in Britain and South Africa over a period of nine years has uncovered forgotten or unpublished eyewitness accounts and much other relevant material from which emerges a very different picture of events and the people involved during those fateful days. From the nature of the content of the account in the *Times of Natal*, 22 April 1881, in particular the graphic details of casualties and medical matters, it is most likely that the anonymous 'Military Correspondent' was Surgeon K. S. Wallis, Army Medical Department, who was quoting from the daily journal routinely kept by Army doctors. The facts contained in the surgeon's account are corroborated with only rare differences by Second Lieutenant J. R. M. Dalrymple-Hay in his daily diary, extracts of which were published in the *Journal of the Royal Scots Fusiliers*, October 1929. Deputy Assistant Commissary-General W. A. Dunne wrote his story for the *Journal of the Army Service Corps* in 1891. Winsloe expanded his original article into a small illustrated book in 1896 but generally made light of events. A detailed picture of the fighting from the Boer perspective was left by two who were personally involved, J. D. Weilbach and C. N. J. Du Plessis, in their book, *Geschiedenis van den Emigranten-Boeren en van den Vrijheids-Oorlog*, 1882. Another aspect of the story which has been disregarded is that the fighting took place in and about a town with 3,000 residents of differing loyalties who attempted to continue their daily lives under what can only be described as military occupation.

The much-quoted diary of G. F. Austen provides a valuable chronological account of happenings in the town, but comparison with Weilbach and Du Plessis and reports in the contemporary press such as the *Natal Mercury* casts doubts on whether it was all compiled from the diarist's own immediate knowledge. However, together with papers from the Forssman family and archival material from the Potchefstroom Museum, these sources provide a vivid picture of life in a town under military occupation by the Boers as they laid siege to the British fort, their treatment of prisoners of war and public executions.

On a broader issue, none of the contemporary commentators recognised the significance of Potchefstroom in the overall conduct of the war. They concentrated on Pretoria, the seat of the detested British administration, which had become more and more Anglicised since the annexation. Potchefstroom on the other hand, which had been the old capital of the Transvaal until 1857, was steeped in the history of the people and was still regarded as their chief town by most Boers. Described as the gateway to the Transvaal it was a thriving commercial and agricultural centre standing in the heart of the most militant anti-British area of the country. For both sides, Potchefstroom and the 9-pounder guns kept there by the British were a key to the whole campaign.

While time has eroded the memory of their deeds, the places where the British and Boers fought at Potchefstroom in 1880–81 can still be seen today: the grass-covered outline of the fort and the adjacent little British burial place, the rebuilt magazine, the old town cemetery and the streets around the once market square on which stands the historic Hervormde Kerk. Some time after the war when the railway was being built to Klerksdorp and the engineers proposed cutting through the remains of the fort, President Kruger intervened ordering a diversion. In 1906 a party of Royal Engineers put the burial place in good order and erected a fine stone memorial. A *Government of South Africa Gazette* of 9 July 1937 proclaimed the old fort at Potchefstroom a national monument. The famous Boer gun 'Ou Griet' stands proudly in the Voortrekker Museum at Pretoria, while one of its lead cannon balls is displayed in the Potchefstroom Museum. In Britain a memorial to those who died in the Transvaal during the war of 1880 is housed in Saint Paul's Cathedral, and the home-made Union Jack fashioned during the siege is on display at the Royal Highland Fusiliers Museum, Glasgow.

The purpose of this work is simply to tell the forgotten story of the happenings at Potchefstroom, of the Boers who fought for their birthright, the British soldiers who fought for queen and empire, and the townsfolk who were caught in between.

CHAPTER 1

Prelude to War, 1880

The audacity of the Transvaal Boers who could muster no more than 7,000 fighting men in 1880 when they rose in rebellion against the might of the British Empire has been likened to David challenging Goliath. The truth was that British authority in the Transvaal barely extended beyond the main towns, and armed Boers roamed the country and were said to be intimidating waverers into supporting the independence movement.

The British in the Transvaal
Major-General Sir George Colley, who replaced Sir Garnet Wolseley as high commissioner in July 1880, was mainly concerned with the low morale of the British troops in the Transvaal, who were deserting in alarming numbers and no longer resembled the formidable deterrent that Wolseley had assembled the year before in response to Boer resistance to British rule. Their commander was Colonel William Bellairs, a soldier with considerable campaign experience in South Africa. He had been complaining since being appointed in May 1880 about the dangerous troop reductions and the faulty disposition of units that were the result of political decisions by the administrator, Sir Owen Lanyon, rather than military considerations. Battalions had been broken up and detachments were so widely dispersed as to be unable to render mutual support in an emergency. Economies had reduced transport to a level where it was impossible to effect a rapid concentration of units to create a mobile column at Pretoria, which had been the keystone of Wolseley's plan for controlling the Transvaal.

There was no longer a cavalry regiment in a country where every potential enemy was a horseman. The King's Dragoon Guards, the last Imperial cavalry regiment in all South Africa, was withdrawn in October 1880 for service in India. Their removal was mainly due to the excessive number of desertions, which was decimating the unit.

The troops, who generally hated the dreary monotonous life on the remote Transvaal veldt, had every reason to feel neglected. They had experienced nothing but hardship and discomfort for the last eighteen months. Since disembarking at Durban in April 1879 the infantry 2/21st and 94th had marched over a thousand miles in all weathers – burning sun, dust and rain – by the time they had participated in the Zulu War and defeated Sekukuni. In the haste to get the reinforcements to Natal many administrative matters had been overlooked; clothing normally due for issue in April and October 1879 did not reach the Transvaal until the beginning of 1880. On the long march from Zululand, boots had worn out – sometimes these were cobbled together with wire – and some men were left barefooted. Helmets used for pillows and carrying water were battered and shapeless. Civilian trousers of every hue were bought from wayside stores by the quartermasters. Colonel Anstruther commanding the 94th wrote home in January 1880:

> Nobody in England could believe what scarecrows they are. They have been through both campaigns in the suits they wear now and they are wonderful. They wear wideawake hats, black hats, fur caps, no caps – anything – and their coats and trousers are all colours – cords, blue serge, red ditto and any mufti they can lay their hands on patched all over with sacking, skin or anything.

The daily ration, basically a pound of meat and a pound of bread a day, was always indifferent to say the least, but tinned beef and biscuits were regularly substituted to use up surpluses left over from the Zulu War. Eggs, butter and milk usually bought by the men to supplement their rations were practically unobtainable and anyway cost more than they could afford. The mood of the men was captured by one deserter who left a note on his bed: 'Private —'s kit is complete. i am going to see if i can get a little better dinner somewhere else than i got here today – old Bully meat!'

Most lived in leaky tents and were charged threepence a month to cover any damages. When enough of the battalion was together the commanding officer would try to alleviate boredom with concerts by the regimental band, cricket matches, athletics and gymkhanas, but on detachment there was seldom anything other than a unit canteen or a local shanty housing a liquor bar. Brothels in the towns were the only possible contact with women. With a bottle of beer costing 10 shillings, ten days' full pay, drink – the Victorian soldier's panacea for boredom – had to be the fiery local gin and brandy, which caused widespread drunkenness. Between January and September 1880, almost 200 men of the 2/21st were fined for this offence. In units that had been brought up to strength only a few days before embarkation with volunteers of uncertain quality, harsh measures proved necessary to maintain discipline. Flogging was still a punishment on active service; twenty-one Fusiliers received the lash during the Zulu War and Sekukuni Campaign with a similar number of such punishments in the 58th and 94th. In an Army becoming increasingly literate, letters and newspapers from home became a lifeline for many and the means of making their complaints public.

The Boers steadily began to lose respect for the 'rooi batjes' ('red coats' – Boer slang for British soldiers). Bellairs referred to parties marching between military posts behaving towards the Boers as if they were in an enemy country. The Boers, whose shooting and fieldcraft were legendary, observed that the troops rarely practised live shooting but spent endless hours at drill, standing and kneeling in red-coated ranks firing mock volleys at an imaginary enemy. The British Army clung to the notion that teaching men to use cover in peacetime would only encourage cowardice in war.

So it was that the summer and autumn months of 1880 passed by with the British and their supporters believing that the Transvaalers had accepted the inevitability of their annexed status. Out across the veldt the Boers were biding their time until the next national meeting planned for January 1881 when the militants were determined to restore their republic by any means. Perhaps the last hope of peace was lost when the British prime minister, Gladstone, recalled Sir Bartle Frere (now governor of the Cape), who was one of the few to recognise the true state of affairs in the Transvaal, in August 1880. Back in London he bluntly warned the colonial secretary, Hicks Beach, that unless the Transvaal was given self-government there would be trouble.

The Wagon Affair

Had it not been for the tragic and far-reaching consequences, the incident that sparked off the First Anglo-Boer War of 1880–81 would have been farcical. Pieter Lodewyk Bezuidenhout, a diehard republican Boer, was sued by the British administration for outstanding taxes amounting to £27 5s, which according to Bezuidenhout was £13 5s more than he owed. At the time there were many similar cases where Treasury officials at Pretoria had made suspect claims against individual Boers. Over and over again people summoned for alleged tax arrears were able to provide receipts when they came to court proving they owed nothing. The number of suspect claims incensed the Boers who became convinced that an unscrupulous administration was prepared to squeeze money out of them even to the extent of acting illegally.

Bezuidenhout duly appeared before Mr Andries Goetze, Landrost (the government officer and magistrate) of the Potchefstroom district, and insisted that he only owed £14, which he was prepared to pay. Goetze referred the case to the authorities at Pretoria, who ordered the acceptance of £14 with 'costs' of £13 5s, raising the sum to the amount originally demanded. Bezuidenhout, not unnaturally, refused to pay this sham charge. The Landrost then ordered that a wagon belonging to Bezuidenhout be impounded and put up for sale at public auction the following month.

On the day of the sale, 11 November 1880, about a hundred armed

GEREGTSBODES VERKOOPING,
DISTRIKT POTCHEFSTROOM.

INGEVOLGE voorloopig vonnis van
het Hof van den Landdrost van Pot-
chefstroom, d.d. 25 September, 1880, en
lastbrief ter executie d.d. 6 October, 1880,
In zake
GOUVERNEMENT DER TRANSVAAL,
vs.
PIETER LODIWICUS BEZUIDENAOUT,
zal publiek verkocht worden, op DONDER-
DAG, den 11den November aanst., ten 11
ure in den voormiddag precies, voor het
Landdrost Kantoor alhier :—
EEN BOKWAGEN.
Zegt het Voort !
E. MOQUETTE, J. B.zn.,
Geregtsbode.
Potchefstroom, 19 Oct., 1880.   217 3

Public notice of the sale of the wagon belonging to Pieter Bezuidenhout.
(Potchefstroom Museum)

Boers who had gathered in Potchefstroom, led by republican Piet Cronje, succeeded in disrupting the proceedings and making off with the wagon. Sir Owen Lanyon authorised the Landrost to enrol special constables to restore order, and appointed Captain Pieter Raaff as court messenger and field cornet of Potchefstroom town and district. Colonel Bellairs was ordered to send troops to Potchefstroom, specifically to provide Raaff with escorts in the event of his being unable 'to procure sufficient competent men to act as assistant messengers [constables]'.

However, the tone of a dispatch that Lanyon sent to the colonial secretary in London on the same day, 14 November 1880, shows that he had no comprehension of the gravity of the situation: 'Whilst the occasion demanded that prompt measures should be taken in order to support the civil authority, and to show these misguided people that the law cannot be defied, I do not anticipate any serious trouble will arise out of the affair.'

Tensions Rise

The arrival of Commandant Pieter Raaff CMG at Potchefstroom on 16 November 1880 introduced a colourful character to the scene. Although given the rank of captain in official British correspondence he was usually known by the colonial title of commandant. He was a flamboyant little man, only 5 foot 4 inches tall, who over the years had not endeared himself to the Boers. Indeed his appointment to be field cornet at Potchefstroom was greeted with a vitriolic article in the Pretoria republican newspaper *De Volksstem* on 27 November 1880, which concluded this 'detective and informer' was 'a bad selection'. There is no apparent single reason for this antipathy other than the perception that he had abandoned his Afrikaner roots in favour of the British. Originally one of the mercenary officers recruited by Burgers for operations against Sekukuni, after annexation he transferred his allegiance to the British. He continued to serve on the Bapedi border until he took his roughneck volunteers to the Zulu War where he earned his CMG.

On arriving at Potchefstroom on 16 November 1880, Commandant Raaff reported to the Landrost and took the necessary oaths of office. Once installed he was issued with warrants for the arrest of the ringleaders of the 'wagon affair', Piet Cronje, Pieter Bezuidenhout, Johannes Basson and Cornelious Coetzee. All were living on their farms between nine and thirty miles from Potchefstroom.

After his attempts on 17 and 20 November to arrest first Coetzee and then Cronje on their farms were thwarted by groups of armed Boers, Raaff agreed to put forward a proposal by Cronje to the Pretoria authorities: that the Boers should be allowed to hold the mass meeting they had convened for 8 January 1881 without any interference from the British in the way of attempting to collect taxes or to arrest anyone concerned in the Bezuidenhout wagon affair. In return the Boers would remain quiet, but Cronje warned Raaff that any government officials who came into the district to collect taxes or make arrests would be shot. Raaff promised to return in eight days with the government reply.

Arrival of British Troops at Potchefstroom

Early in the afternoon of 18 November 1880 a British field force marched into Potchefstroom. Given only twenty-four hours to prepare and move the troops, it had covered 104 miles in ninety-six hours in appalling wet, cold weather. This speed was achieved by carrying the infantry on mule wagons enabling them to keep up with the Royal Artillery and the Mounted Infantry.

The force, which represented a considerable proportion of the Pretoria garrison, was under command of Major Charles Thornhill RA who as the officer commanding N/5 Battery RA was *de facto* the senior artillery officer in the Transvaal. The force comprised the Right Division of N/5 Battery, two 9-pounder guns with their limbers and wagons, twenty-five Mounted Infantry from the 2/21st Royal Scots Fusiliers and C Company of the same regiment, seventy-five men strong. These fighting troops were accompanied by a surgeon of the Army Medical Department with his medical staff and two ambulance wagons. There was also a Commissariat officer with soldiers of the Army Service Corps and sixty civilian drivers and leaders for the water carts and wagons carrying the infantry, provisions, ammunition and equipment.

As the column marched through the streets of the town to make camp on the western outskirts it must have presented quite an impressive spectacle to the inhabitants who were unaccustomed to any military presence. Two days after arriving, Thornhill was reinforced by D Company, 2/21st, numbering forty-nine men commanded by Lieutenant Peter Browne, who marched in from Rustenburg.

When Thornhill reported to Goetze, the Landrost, he was told of the initial failed attempt by Raaff to make arrests and learned that the whole situation was far more serious than the authorities at Pretoria appreciated. He now understood the full implications of the warning given to him by a friendly farmer on the march down that the Boers intended to fight. At the time he had not taken the man seriously, only passing the warning on to Pretoria with the remark: 'I think it right to mention these statements for what they may be considered worth.'

Thornhill became increasingly unhappy as constant contact with Goetze and Raaff kept him abreast of events in the deteriorating situation. He began to send written reports to Army headquarters at Pretoria at least once a day. He was particularly concerned at the prospect of being required to send his men to assist the civil authorities to make arrests at farms up to thirty miles away over the veldt. To achieve the speed and mobility required, the infantry would need to ride in mule wagons; such convoys would give the Boers ample warning of their approach and be extremely vulnerable to attack.

Thornhill began to receive information from Mr Grey, the justice of the peace at Ventersdorp, who despite fears for his safety and business interests reported that a significant number of armed Boers were concentrating in his area. This intelligence was confirmed by Raaff, who further warned Thornhill that if troops were moved out of Potchefstroom they would certainly be attacked. Grey also warned Thornhill that there were Boer spies everywhere, even in the Landrost's office at Potchefstroom. There were widespread rumours that the British were preparing to march on the Boers at Ventersdorp, who were more than ready for a fight. Raaff told Thornhill that many of the Boers living in and about Potchefstroom threatened to take action against local loyalist, that is pro-British, shopkeepers if the troops marched out. Faced with this dangerous, volatile situation, Thornhill and Raaff were convinced that no military operation should be mounted without the prior sanction of Sir Owen Lanyon himself as any British failure would have disastrous consequences.

Goetze as Landrost was ultimately responsible for the conduct of local affairs and he was later widely criticised for being indecisive at this critical time, but in reality there was little more he could have done in the circumstances. The policies initiated by Wolseley and subsequently implemented by the cheeseparing British government had left both inadequate and unsuitable military forces in the Transvaal.

The Boers Muster

The ensuing days saw mounting political activity on both sides. The Boers convened near Ventersdorp on 25 November and resolved to bring forward the meeting of the national convention at Paardekraal from 8 January 1881 to 8 December 1880. Sir Owen Lanyon sent George Hudson, the colonial secretary, to take charge of affairs and undertake any negotiations that might be needed after Raaff had met Cronje as planned on 27 November. Hudson's presence was a temporary measure to cover the gap until Major Marshall Clarke RA could take up his appointment as special commissioner at Potchefstroom on 30 November.

On 27 November Raaff returned to Ventersdorp and presented the government's reply to Cronje's proposal: the Boer representative was to meet Hudson at Potchefstroom. Eventually the Boer leader Paul Kruger persuaded Cronje to acquiesce, although Cronje insisted that the venue be changed to Kaalfontein, a farm twenty miles from Potchefstroom and well away from British troops. Raaff reported back to Hudson and expressed his opinion that the Boers were determined to fight.

At this point in time the impetus for a head-on collision with the British was coming from a hard core of ordinary Boers and not from their national council. If on his own admission Kruger himself was unaware of the current strength of Boer feeling and resentment it is not surprising that Lanyon and his staff were misguided and taken unawares.

The colonial secretary, George Hudson, left Potchefstroom early on the morning of 29 November for the crucial meeting accompanied only by a special constable, Ribas, who drove their cart. Hudson was given a very cool, sullen reception. Kruger appeared nervous and apprehensive as to the unpredictable behaviour of the Boer crowd, which Hudson numbered at about 400.

The meeting took place indoors between a solitary Hudson and Kruger supported by a committee of ten burghers. It proved an acrimonious affair, in essence Kruger demanding that the Boers be left unmolested by tax collectors, arrests and other legal actions until after their meeting on 8 December 1880, and Hudson insisting that the government could not be blackmailed in this fashion. When the argument came round to the Bezuidenhout affair it transpired astonishingly that Hudson claimed not to be familiar with the 'particulars' of the case, but patronisingly said he would look into it when he returned to Pretoria. It is little wonder that an exasperated Kruger retorted that government actions had run their course; now he would let the Boer people decide what must be done. They were being called to a meeting and he warned that if the government interfered he, Kruger, would wash his hands of all responsibility. Expressing his hope that the Boers would reach the right decision, Hudson left the meeting escorted away from the hostile gathering by three mounted burghers.

The preliminary skirmishing was at an end.

CHAPTER 2

The Garrison at Potchefstroom

The military, who had now been encamped on the western outskirts of Potchefstroom for nearly two weeks, had begun in a desultory way to construct a small earth fort. They showed little urgency or enthusiasm for the task, hoping to be withdrawn to Pretoria as soon as the present furore had subsided. From a personal letter that Thornhill wrote to Bellairs on 20 November 1880, it is clear that he had been ordered to commence building this redoubt immediately on arrival at Potchefstroom. However, as he explained to Bellairs, he had not yet been able to start but intended to do so shortly using convict labour from the civil gaol. His next routine report to Pretoria dated eight days later contained the sentence: 'A redoubt has been commenced and will be carried out according to orders.'

The embryo fort took shape beside the camp close to a fork in the main road from the Kimberley diamond fields to Potchefstroom. The two roads then crossed the Grootvoor to enter the town at either end of the western side of the market square. The southern fork ran past the gaol, joining the square adjacent to the Landrost's office giving a direct link between the camp and the government buildings.

Building the Fort

Guidelines for the construction of redoubts and the layout of camps in outlying stations had been laid down by General Sir Garnet Wolseley a year before on 31 December 1879 in anticipation of any trouble that might arise from a meeting of the Boers expected to take place in April 1880:

A good square redoubt is to be constructed (if this has not already been done). The parapets are only required to be proof against rifle bullets, but should be about 8 feet high, and the ditches should be wide and deep. The sides of the square should be about 25 yards long inside, and the entrances should be very narrow and easily closed, arrangements for closing it being prepared. The greatest care should be paid to the drainage of these redoubts; if the ground admits, the ditches should be drained, so as to prevent any accumulation of stagnant water. Each redoubt should be near water and when any disturbance is threatened, say for instance, before the next Boer meeting comes off, all possible arrangements should be made for storing water within the redoubt, barrels or old biscuit tins being used for this purpose. Preserved meat, biscuits and groceries for the permanent defensive garrison for thirty days must always be maintained within the redoubt, these supplies not to be drawn upon if possible, food being obtained as long as possible from the general reserve at each station, or by purchasing from the adjoining village. Forty boxes of small arms ammunition will be kept in each redoubt as a reserve, in addition to what the men have in their pouches.

Until actually threatened with an attack the garrison to be encamped outside the redoubt, in ordinary times about 100 yards from it. When the Boer meeting or any other exciting event takes place, the camp should be moved close to the ditch on the side where the entrance is; latrines and cooking places should be kept outside the fort as long as possible. If seriously threatened, all horses and mules might perhaps with advantage be picketed in the ditch, and the wagons, if there are any, be placed so as to form an obstacle, care being taken to remove one or two wheels from each wagon. No civilian to be allowed into or near these redoubts at any time. This is very important.

The events at Potchefstroom were to prove the wisdom of this instruction. Although there was no Royal Engineer officer to advise him, Major Thornhill as a graduate of the Royal Military Academy would have understood these requirements and appears to have followed the basic instructions fairly meticulously. Most of the infantry officers were likely to be familiar with *Notes on Military Engineering 1870*, the Army manual that contained detailed instructions for the actual construction of a 'temporary fortification'; for example it specified that the ditch should be 'not less than six feet deep and ten feet wide at the top'. The amount of earth to be dug and piled up to construct even a small fort was formidable. Traditionally British soldiers hated this dreary heavy manual work, hence Thornhill's intention to employ convict labour from the civil gaol. The general lack of urgency and enthusiasm was compounded by a shortage of tools, and seventeen days later when the siege began the walls were still only 4 foot 6 inches high.

The accommodation bell tents, probably numbering about thirty, were pitched in neat rows to the rear of the fort. When the latter began to take shape the Commissariat marquee was erected within the walls in accordance with the Wolseley instruction, together with five hospital bell tents. The men, who slept fourteen to a tent, had been wet through every night since leaving Pretoria, the tents being worn out and already condemned as unfit for use. Thornhill had complained to Army headquarters at Pretoria saying he was surprised that more men were not sick and insisting that new tents be supplied if the troops were to remain at Potchefstroom for any length of time. An as yet unfinished shelter trench had been dug to enclose a laager area between the fort and the town magazine. Inside the laager nearest to the fort were the two 9-pounder guns of N/5 Battery together with their limbers and wagons. In the centre were the animal lines where 76 horses and 114 mules were picketed. Beyond them a space was kept for the 128 oxen when they were brought in from grazing. On the far side nearest the magazine were parked the empty Commissariat wagons. Assistant Commissary-General Le Mesurier at Pretoria, remote from events, entertained the quaint idea that in an emergency the mules could be put into the town cemetery where although possibly under fire they could feed themselves thus doubling the fodder available for the horses.

The Officers and Men

Drawn as they were from the British units at Pretoria, the officers and men who were to garrison the fort at Potchefstroom represented a cross-section of the troops stationed in the Transvaal.

With the notable exception of their commander, Major Thornhill, most of the garrison at Potchefstroom had experienced their baptism of fire during all or some of the campaigns undertaken by the British in South Africa in recent years: the Ninth Frontier War, 1877–78, the Zulu War, 1879 and the Sekukuni Campaign, 1879. All had been hardened by marching hundreds of miles in all weathers under rigorous campaign conditions for months on end, ill fed and badly clothed. Lately they had endured the boredom of garrison duties in the Transvaal with few creature comforts, let alone luxuries. With relatively few exceptions the majority of both officers and men were still in their early twenties but they were hardly the unseasoned recruits criticised by the opponents of the short service system.

Major Charles Thornhill, aged forty-two, had assumed command of N/5 Battery RA at Standerton after the Zulu War, in May 1880. He was married and his wife was living at Pretoria. As the senior Royal Artillery officer in the Transvaal he was the artillery adviser to the commander of the district. In sending Thornhill to Potchefstroom, Colonel Bellairs deprived himself of a key member of his staff. Thornhill was rather naïve concerning what would be expected of him at Potchefstroom; he had brought his battery pay sergeant with him intending to catch up on arrears of routine work such as the battery pay lists.

In direct command of the two 9-pounder guns, which formed the Right Division of N/5 Battery and were manned by forty-three men of the Royal Artillery, was Lieutenant H. M. L. Rundle, aged twenty-four. He had joined N/5 Battery after serving at Ulundi with distinction. Most of the men in the battery were in their mid-twenties and on average had served for five years. Many had been with the battery during the Ninth Frontier War and the Zulu War, including the fateful day when half their number were killed and

two guns lost at Isandhlwana. Notable among these were Trumpeter
Nicholas Martin and Driver Elias Tucker, who had escaped with their lives
from the slaughter. Driver Thomas Lewis, previously a bombardier, and
Abraham Evans had taken part in the defence of Rorke's Drift.

The majority of the garrison was provided by the 2/21st Royal Scots
Fusiliers: a half troop of Mounted Infantry, twenty-four NCOs and men
commanded by Lieutenant C. F. Lindsell; C Company, seventy-five NCOs
and men commanded by Captain Falls; and D Company, forty-nine NCOs
and men who had fought at Ulundi, commanded by Lieutenant P. W.
Browne.

The Army Medical Department was represented by Surgeon Kenneth
Wallis, aged twenty-eight, and his medical staff of four NCOs and men of
the Army Hospital Corps.

In charge of supplies and transport for the garrison was 27-year-old
Deputy Assistant Commissary-General (DACG) Walter Dunne. His early
promotion to this rank, which equated to a captain, had been an immediate
award for his gallantry during the defence of Rorke's Drift. He had been
personally recommended for the Victoria Cross by Lord Chelmsford but the
award had been turned down by the Duke of Cambridge. He was regarded
by his superiors as 'a man of very excellent judgement'. The men of the
Army Service Corps commanded by Dunne numbered seven: two NCOs
and three men of the supply branch and two NCOs from the transport
branch. He also controlled a civilian conductor and sixty transport drivers
and leaders (voorloopers), all Africans or Cape Coloured, men of mixed
blood.

Although the advent of Major Clarke had relieved Thornhill of any direct
responsibility for political affairs, his military problems were becoming
increasingly complicated. His defence plan, which Clarke endorsed, envis-
aged holding what he called a 'citadel', an area reaching into the town from
the fort, embracing the magazine, the gaol and the Landrost's office. The
implementation of such a plan in an emergency was dependent on enough
loyalist volunteers joining the military to hold the extensive open flanks of
such a perimeter. Early enquiries worryingly indicated a marked reluctance
among the civilians to become involved in any confrontation. Perhaps it is
not surprising that Thornhill wrote plaintively to Bellairs: 'I am rapidly
getting into arrears of work still greater, no doubt all will end somewhere in
time – how I do not see.'

Rumours of War

Thornhill was not at first bothered by the rumours that sprang up as the
Boers began gathering for the mass meeting at Paardekraal, called for 8
December 1880 by Paul Kruger and the national committee.

The loyalists living in Potchefstroom became increasingly agitated as threats of raids on their stores and businesses and even threats of attacks on the Army camp began to circulate. The garrison at first appeared singularly indifferent to the developing events and the scare stories. No extra effort was put into the construction of the fort. Thornhill discounted the rumours until Major Clarke warned him on 4 December that the Boers had declared it their intention to prevent any supplies entering the town once their meeting began four days later on 8 December 1880. Clarke believed it would then become impossible for any small detachments of men or convoys of ammunition and stores to be sent down the road from Pretoria. Clarke advised Thornhill to make sure the garrison had sufficient reserves to meet all their needs for six weeks. He also urged Thornhill to find out what stocks of food and fodder were held by local contractors in the town as these might ultimately be the only source of supply.

Thornhill and his commissary, Dunne, now faced some serious problems. Although the Commissariat held sufficient rations for roughly a month this was not strictly a reserve; part of these stocks were consumed daily as part of the men's ration, being replenished from Pretoria as required. There was a serious shortage of animal forage, mainly mealies, and orders placed with contractors had not yet been delivered. This immediate shortfall had made it necessary to put the mules on half rations and turn them out to graze.

The holding of ammunition was not complete to war scale, a serious deficiency. This perilous situation had come about because the force sent to Potchefstroom had been regarded by Colonel Bellairs as a 'flying column' equipped to cope with a temporary difficulty and not intended to undertake any prolonged operations. Consequently they had marched from Pretoria with only fourteen days' rations and far less than the proper scale of ammunition. The infantry had only 180 rounds as opposed to 300 per man, the Mounted Infantry only 100 rounds per man instead of 200, and each artillery gun crew a total of 50 rounds of small arms ammunition between them as opposed to an entitlement of 200 rounds. The quantity of 9-pounder ammunition held by the division of N/5 Battery was more satisfactory although not complete: 201 rounds for each gun, carried 148 in the limbers and 53 in their mule wagon. The reserve of 150 rounds per gun had been left at Pretoria.

Alarmed by the reports of the deteriorating political situation being sent in by Thornhill, and alerted at last to the possibility of the troops at Potchefstroom being cut off a hundred miles from reserves at Pretoria, the headquarters there took steps to increase stocks up to the emergency level of thirty days as held at other outstations. On 26 November 1880 Captain Churchill, the deputy assistant adjutant-general, gave written orders to the commissary-general of ordnance instructing him to issue the additional ammunition required to complete the garrison at Potchefstroom to scale. This amounted to 120 rounds for each infantryman and 100 rounds for every mounted soldier. Churchill also stipulated that sixteen more rounds for each 9-pounder should be sent.

It took Markwick, the ordnance commissary, two days to obtain transport and arrange for the Pretoria garrison commander to provide an escort. Eventually Markwick dispatched fourteen boxes of Martini Henry rifle ammunition and four boxes of Martini Henry carbine cartridges for the Mounted Infantry but he sent no gun ammunition. When the consignment was checked on arrival at Potchefstroom it was realised that Markwick had not provided for D Company, who had come from Rustenburg, sending only enough for the troops who had left from Pretoria – an error that could have had dire consequences. Fortunately the ammunition arrived before the blockade expected by Major Clarke, but by the time news of the shortfall got back to Pretoria it was too late to risk another convoy.

The additional reserve rations also reached Potchefstroom by 4 December 1880. The Commissariat marquee inside the fort then contained crates of Australian tinned beef, boxes of hard tack biscuits, sacks of flour and a variety of groceries, which included tea, coffee, sugar, salt and rice. There were items to prevent scurvy, lime juice in wicker-covered demijohns, preserved vegetables in tins and a new innovation first tried in the Zulu War, erbswurst. This was a cheap long-lasting sausage made of peas and chopped smoked meat developed by the Germans as an iron ration for the Franco-Prussian War. Eaten cold or boiled up in water, it was said 'a small quantity would suffice a man for a day'. Intended by the British as an emergency substitute for tea or coffee, it found little favour with British troops. The Army Medical Department were unenthusiastic; experience during the Zulu War showed that unless the sausage was properly boiled it caused diarrhoea.

Importantly, beside these general items were special foods for hospital patients: tins of preserved milk, essence of beef in pots, canisters of sago and arrowroot. Not least there were 204 bottles of port wine and 203 bottles of French brandy. There was also a small quantity of ration rum. Among the miscellaneous items were hundreds of candles, which were routinely issued to the men. During the siege to come they were the only source of light for surgery during the night.

When Thornhill's column arrived at Potchefstroom the first task for Commissary Dunne had been to arrange contracts in accordance with normal peacetime procedures for the supply of slaughter cattle and bread, which with tea and coffee were the basic components of the Army daily ration. Contracts were also required for the supply of animal forage. These contracts had to be negotiated as troops had never been regularly stationed at Potchefstroom. There was an abundant available supply of beef cattle, but obtaining forage proved unexpectedly difficult. The local practice was for forage to be delivered from outside town direct to customers for their immediate use. As a result there were no storage depots actually in the town. The needs of the Army would have to be brought in from some distance. The numerous trading stores in town could provide all the foodstuffs required by the civil population and, according to the advertisements in local newspapers, luxuries ranging from a wide variety of fine teas to Yarmouth bloaters, English jams and sweets – good news for the officers but way beyond the purse of the rank and file.

When Dunne heard the warning from Major Clarke that the delivery of supplies might be cut off by the Boers, he had accumulated only sufficient mealies for eight days' animal forage. The stack of a hundred or so mealie sacks outside his marquee must have awakened memories of Rorke's Drift where under Zulu fire he had turned such a pile into the last defensive redoubt. Dunne hoped a further five days' forage promised for delivery by the contractor, Erasmus, before Monday 6 December would avoid the threatened Boer blockade. However he was less optimistic about the arrival of the next consignment amounting to fourteen days' stock of mealies and kaffir corn (millet) due at the end of that week. Having already placed his own mules on half rations, Thornhill now caused the Landrost to prohibit the export of grain from the town. In the end the scheduled deliveries were made and by 10 December 1880 sufficient mealies and millet to last the animals for twenty days were stacked in sacks at the camp. Erasmus the contractor assured Dunne that he had a further two weeks' supply stored outside the town.

Winsloe Arrives

Early in the afternoon of Sunday, 12 December 1880, Lieutenant-Colonel Richard Winsloe, 2/21st Royal Scots Fusiliers, accompanied by his soldier servant was driven into the camp at Potchefstroom in a buck wagon drawn by twelve mules. Announcing he had come to relieve Thornhill and take command, his arrival was completely unexpected by Clarke, the special commissioner, and Thornhill, neither having received any warning.

Three days previously when out for an evening ride in Pretoria, Winsloe had decided to make a social call on Sir Owen Lanyon who greeted him with the words, 'Have you seen Bellairs?' Winsloe hardly had time to reply in the negative before Bellairs himself came up and told him that he must go at once to Potchefstroom to release Thornhill, who was required at Pretoria urgently. Bellairs was planning to organise a mobile column by concentrating troops from outstation at Pretoria and he required Thornhill to arrange the artillery support.

Winsloe was elated at the prospect of an independent command. He had only recently rejoined the battalion from sick leave in Britain where he had been recovering from a serious wound in his chest near the heart, which he had received at the battle of Ulundi. His services in the Zulu War had been rewarded with a brevet promotion to lieutenant-colonel but it was likely in the normal course of events to be a long time before he was considered for command of his battalion.

Having received his orders from Bellairs, Winsloe obtained a wagon from the Commissariat and left for Potchefstroom the following morning. He covered the 104 miles in forty-eight hours despite bad roads and having to negotiate several rivers, camping on the veldt each night in the heart of the country being crossed by the Boers moving around outside Paardekraal. Miraculously he had not been intercepted by any of these hostile bands, although friendly travellers whom he met indicated that one Boer party must only just have missed him.

Much to the disappointment of Major Clarke and the other officers, Winsloe brought no official information from Pretoria and he admitted to knowing as little as they about the events unfolding in the Transvaal. After a look around the camp, followed by dinner, Winsloe was taken by the officers to meet Chevalier Forssman and his family at their elegant house in the town. Friends of the chevalier dropped in to meet Winsloe and lost no time in expressing their opinion that fighting would soon break out, a view that Winsloe politely dismissed as unlikely. In the relaxed social atmosphere of the Forssman ménage he was disposed to enjoy the company of the ladies, and General Redvers Buller, in his report after the siege, wrote that Winsloe 'had been so taken up with Mrs S [Sketchley] that he let all things slide'.

CHAPTER 3

Proclamation of War

3 December to Day 1 of the Siege, 15 December 1880

In early December, after Kruger had informed Hudson that the Boers would be meeting on 8 December at Paardekraal, Bellairs sent a Royal Engineer officer accompanied by the government surveyor-general, a civilian, to reconnoitre the area. They reported that the locality, a plateau situated among rocky hills with good all-round visibility overlooking the main Pretoria to Potchefstroom road, offered a very strong, natural defensive position that would be difficult to attack. The Boer occupation of such a base within a day's march would constitute a great threat to Pretoria. Bellairs thought this was justification enough immediately to plan the withdrawal of guns and troops from Potchefstroom. By adding these to the 94th, already ordered to march in from Lydenburg, and the Pretoria garrison, he could create a column, as proposed by Colley, capable of attacking the Boers if necessary. Senior military officers at Pretoria who had always regarded the deployment of troops to Potchefstroom as a mistake saw this as an opportunity to retrieve the situation. However, the plan was soon overtaken by events.

The Boer Perspective
The Boers began streaming into Paardekraal on 8 December 1880 but because of the distances many had to travel it was two or three more days before most were assembled and the full meeting began. The speed with which so many of this scattered nation were brought together – Kruger estimated there were more than 7,000 men under arms by 14 December – was probably an accident of fate. Traditionally at this time of year most Boer families were collecting at their homes to prepare for the great Christmas Nachtmaal (the quarterly gathering for communal religious worship) and the New Year celebrations. Consequently wagons, animals and equipment were assembled and in good order ready for the trek. Supplies of food and other stores needed for several days of celebration away from home had been gathered in, and much had been cooked and baked in readiness. In military parlance, the Boers were mobilised. There were many

57

women present and it has been said that they were among the most
vociferous militants who goaded their menfolk to stop talking and take
positive action against British rule.

Rumours filtering back to Potchefstroom increased the tension among
the already unsettled inhabitants. The loyalists with political leanings
towards the British and who supported the annexation were greatly outnumbered by those whose sympathy lay with the Boers. The bulk of the
commercial community were inclined toward the British but they were
currently collectively owed between £70,000 and £80,000 sterling by Boer
customers, a vast sum in 1880. The traders could not afford to alienate these
debtors. Their pragmatic attitude was made abundantly clear when an
attempt by Major Clarke and Thornhill to raise volunteers to assist the
military in an emergency met with total failure. Clearly it was imperative for
Clarke to obtain accurate and reliable information as to the Boer intentions.
His only regular source of intelligence was Raaff, who sent out pairs of his
mounted constables to scout in the direction of Paardekraal. With the
passing days the Boers became more confident and belligerent, soon
showing no hesitation to fire warning shots in the direction of any
approaching British vedette.

Whether he was attempting to boost loyalist morale or just behaving
with his customary arrogance, Raaff was alleged to have told an anxious
group gathered on the stoep (veranda) of a house in the town: 'Don't worry
about the Boers. If and when they come to the town, I shall be standing
under a tree by the bridge with a large pot in my hand. We shall fire one
cannon and I shall strike the pot with a single blow with a stick. All the
Boers will flee and that will be the end of the affair.'

True or not, the yarn quickly spread among the Boers even to the
assembly at Paardekraal. When the commando later rode into Potchefstroom, one of their number was to record: 'We galloped over the bridge.
One would think we should have been afraid. But no. After all Raaff was
absent with his tin dish and the cannon was silent.'

Raaff persuaded two men to attend the meeting at Paardekraal and send
reports back to himself and Major Clarke. Hans van der Linden was already
one of his volunteer constables. A native of the Transvaal, he was a married
man who lived in Potchefstroom. He joined the assembled Boers and was
appointed a sub-cornet (corporal) in a commando. The second of Raaff's
informants was a well-known local figure, 'Doctor' Woite, a tailor who had
acquired a knowledge of medicine and especially the treatment of the ill-
nesses common in South Africa. Being on friendly terms with many
prominent Boers including Cronje, his presence at the meeting was accepted
without question. In due course he was to send his son back to Potchefstroom with a letter for Major Clarke that gave details of the proceedings of

the meeting and Boer intentions. Once read, Clarke kept this letter in his pocket with fatal consequences for Woite.

The Proclamation

The climax came on 13 December with the election of the Triumvirate and passing of a draft proclamation that declared the re-establishment of the South African Republic independent of direct British government. The ruling Triumvirate was to comprise Paul Kruger as vice-president, the post to which he had been elected before the annexation (there was to be no president for the time being), Marthinus Pretorius, an elder statesman who had once been president, and Piet Joubert as commandant-general. The Hollanders Dr Edward Jorissen and Willem Bok became respectively state attorney and state secretary (Hollanders were natives of Holland who emigrated to the Transvaal, usually professional men such as lawyers and doctors). Members of the former Volksraad who were present resumed their sittings.

The proclamation was a substantial document containing thirty-eight clauses, which set out the Boer grievances. It covered the re-establishment of their own government, and future relations with the British, which did not preclude some form of confederation. The document ended with the declaration: 'And, finally, we declare and make known to all and everybody that from this day the country is declared to be in a state of siege and under the provisions of martial law.'

With religious solemnity, as had been done at Blood River forty-two years before, each burgher present put a stone on a cairn pledging himself to the cause of Boer freedom.

The following day Cronje with his commando set out for Potchefstroom to have the proclamation printed at the only press available to the Boers. Another commando was dispatched to intercept the 94th Regiment en route from Lydenburg to Pretoria. They carried a letter telling the unit to halt pending a decision from Lanyon at Pretoria as to whether the two sides were at war. It warned the British commander that if he failed to comply he would be responsible for the consequences. By 16 December 1880, Dingaan's Day, the largest proportion of the Boer forces together with the Triumvirate had moved to Heidelberg, which was to become the temporary capital. On that historic anniversary of Dingaan's Day, marking the Boers' victory over the Zulus in 1838 and the founding of the Republic of Natalia, with the hoisting of the Vierkleur the Republic was re-established.

Among their other activities the Boers had on 15 December cut the telegraph line between Pretoria and Natal, and then prevented two Royal Engineer linemen from making repairs. The last telegraphic communication to get through was on 14 December telling Colley of the election of the

Triumvirate but saying future Boer intentions were unknown. An attack on
Potchefstroom was regarded as doubtful but it was forecast that any conflict
might commence with an attack on the marching column of the 94th from
Lydenburg.

On 17 December before news of the outbreak of fighting at Potchefstroom had reached Heidelberg, the Triumvirate sent a 'diplomatic agent',
Hendrick Schoemann, to Pretoria with a copy of the proclamation and a
letter for Lanyon. Schoemann arrived at about 11 o'clock at night and had it
not been for the intervention of Hudson, the colonial secretary, who personally served him with a brandy and soda, he would have received rough
treatment as a rebel. The letter addressed to Lanyon protested the Boer
desire for a peaceful outcome to the present crisis but requested that the
British give up the keys to the public offices without bloodshed as the Boers
had done at the time of the annexation in 1877. Ominously the letter ended
with a thinly disguised ultimatum: 'We expect your answer within twice
twenty-four hours.'

Predictably the next day, 18 December 1880, Lanyon issued a proclamation declaring the province to be in a state of rebellion. Schoemann was
kept waiting until 19 December before he was given copies of the British
proclamation together with only a covering letter from the colonial secretary acknowledging the 'communications' he had brought from Heidelberg.

Lanyon had so little understanding of the situation and the determination
of the Boers that even after another month of open war he still wrote to Lord
Kimberley at the Colonial Office giving his opinion that the Boer proclamation of 13 December must be regarded as 'the result of a sudden
impulse'.

British Preparations
Winsloe, however, was becoming unhappy with the defensive arrangements
he had been shown at Potchefstroom by Thornhill and contrary to the
critical remarks later made by Wood and Buller he quickly took some
positive steps to improve the position.

Thornhill had sited his camp on the open gently rising ground that
looked on to the western edge of the town. The position was about half a
mile from the main government building known as the Landrost's office,
which housed Goetze's office and the magistrate's court together with the
post office. Half-way between the Landrost's office and the camp stood the
town gaol. About 200 yards to the north was the town magazine where
local trading firms secured their stocks of ammunition and gunpowder. Also
on this side of the town about 400 yards to the north-east was the large
town cemetery, which was enclosed by a substantial wall. The camp had
access to a plentiful supply of running water from the Grootvoor, the town's

main furrow which, fed by springs three-quarters of a mile to the north at a place known as the Willows, carried water along the western edge of the town feeding numerous smaller furrows which supplied houses and gardens. The Grootvoor entered the Mooi River to the south of the town. Thornhill was later to be heavily criticised for choosing this site, but it must be remembered that he only expected to be giving 'the moral support of their presence to the Landrost and other civil officers of the district'. Without the benefit of hindsight, Thornhill made a logical decision in positioning his camp adjacent to the centre of the civil administration and where the vital commodity water was available.

Winsloe considered the camp had been wrongly sited, being within easy rifle range of the cover offered by the houses, walls and gardens that extended along the edge of the town behind the gaol. The Grootvoor, the only source of water, running midway between the camp and the fringe of the town, would be completely under enemy observation and fire in the event of hostilities. The incomplete redoubt afforded little protection, being still hardly more than a shelter trench with an earth parapet; this was only about $4\frac{1}{2}$ feet high except at the corners, which had been built up slightly more. The long, roughly entrenched laager that encompassed the Royal Artillery guns and the animal lines stretching out to include the wagons parked near the town magazine was obviously too extended and indefensible. The magazine, which contained several thousand rounds of rifle ammunition as well as barrels and sacks of gunpowder belonging to civilian trading firms in the town, stood in isolation. The contents would be invaluable to the Boers in the event of a war.

Winsloe ordered that the 9-pounder guns with their limbers and ammunition wagons be brought into a more secure position just outside the north-east corner of the redoubt, from where they could be brought into action facing parts of the town. He also directed that the horses of the artillery and the mounted infantry together with the mules were to be picketed in the ditch surrounding the redoubt. He positioned wagons on the outside of each corner of the redoubt. If more than these few were brought any closer to the low parapets of the redoubt they would have masked the fire of the defenders, and consequently the remainder were left where they were. The redoubt was beginning to take on the semblance of the fort it was to become. The Commissariat oxen were rounded up and under guard of their drivers and voorloopers were to be kept within the protective range of the guns. Anxious about the vulnerability of the water supply, Winsloe ordered that a well be dug just outside the fort.

Winsloe also turned his attention to the emergency plan conceived by Thornhill in conjunction with Clarke to defend the key government buildings using mainly soldiers. He found that rations had already been positioned: ten days' for forty men in the Landrost's office and seven days' for twenty-one men in the gaol. Winsloe learned that some of Raaff's men would be used to supplement the soldiers in the Landrost's office while others, reinforced it was hoped by volunteers from the town, would hold various civilian properties around the market square, being positioned so as to give fire support to those in the Landrost's office. The viability of this plan depended entirely on sufficient volunteers coming forward to secure the road between the fort and the Landrost's office, which ran past the gaol, by occupying buildings and gardens on the flanks.

An attempt by Major Clarke to raise volunteers in the town having previously failed totally, he arranged for Winsloe accompanied by Thornhill to attend a meeting of townsmen on 13 December hoping to persuade loyalists to pledge their support in an emergency. In the event only four people offered their services: Chevalier Forssman, Dr Sketchley, now acting district surgeon, Mr Smart, manager of the Standard Bank, and Joe Green, the post cart contractor. Winsloe returned from the meeting disappointed but not unduly concerned because in his own words, he 'did not believe anything untoward would happen'.

For the remainder of that day and the next, Tuesday, 14 December 1880, despite being in constant touch with Clarke, Winsloe appears to have remained oblivious to the mounting tension in the town. They did discuss an unrealistic idea to locate twenty-five Fusiliers in the Forssman house, but this was probably prompted by some chivalrous notion to protect the ladies rather than any serious defensive measure. Winsloe and his troops busied themselves with their military routine. Men digging the well bored through 16 feet of solid rock, reaching a depth of 27 feet to produce only a dribble of water. The artillerymen dug shallow gun pits for their 9-pounders and measured ranges to the cemetery and points in and about the market square. The usual guards were mounted, equipment and weapons cleaned and inspected, and horses groomed, watered and fed. Water carts were filled and brought into the camp, meals cooked and the area cleaned. The multitude of mundane activities that filled the peacetime military day were carried out by a no doubt bored garrison.

Each evening Winsloe and his smartly uniformed officers left the camp, going down to the Forssman house to enjoy a typical Victorian soirée, the young with music, singing and dancing, charmingly broken by flirtatious walks with the ladies, while their elders, Forssman and his friends, played their usual whist and chatted.

At this time Thomas Leask, a prominent citizen and trader from the nearby township of Klerksdorp, arrived in Potchefstroom on business. He had recently returned from a holiday in Scotland and the rumours of war that met him on landing in Natal made him decide to leave his family in

Durban and travel post-haste to the Transvaal to take care of his commercial interests. He found Potchefstroom alive with rumours and the residents talking of leaving or sending their families away. Leask quickly concluded that he would be safer in Klerksdorp where he was well known and planned to leave as soon as possible next morning.

Without any certainty of official communications with Pretoria and conscious of the increasing disquiet among the civilian inhabitants of the town Clarke was becoming desperate for reliable information as to Boer movements and intentions. As he waited for news from Woite and van der Linden attending the meeting at Paardekraal and the return of the scouts sent out by Raaff on 13 December, he came to an arrangement with John Nelson, son of a justice of the peace who farmed fifteen miles north-east of Potchefstroom, who undertook to send in intelligence. On Tuesday, 14 December Raaff dispatched two more pairs of scouts in the direction of Paardekraal. Later that night Clarke was told that Bezuidenhout was in town warning his friends to leave for the Orange Free State as there was going to be fighting.

The first positive news came early on the morning of Wednesday, 15 December when Trooper Benson and his companion, the first of Raaff's patrols, rode in. They reported that they had been fired at on the previous evening by Boers laagered close to the road midway down from Paardekraal. Wondering if this meant the Boers were moving out from their meeting, Clarke waited anxiously for confirmation from the other two pairs of scouts. They never came, having been captured by the approaching Boers, but events began to gather momentum when, soon after Benson arrived, Wilhelm Woite rode in with a letter from his father. This letter, which Clarke fatefully thrust in a pocket to be found later by the Boers, gave details of the Paardekraal meeting, the declaration of a South African Republic and the election of Paul Kruger as vice-president to head a governing Triumvirate. Having delivered the note, young Woite gallantly rode back to rejoin his father. About 11.30 am two of Raaff's men who had gone out half an hour before galloped in to report that a large party of Boers were approaching and were only about five miles away.

Unaware of events, Leask was standing in the yard of the Criterion Hotel waiting for his horses to be harnessed into his cart for the journey home when he noticed a 'Cape boy', obviously tired, squatting beside a horse in a lather of sweat. Curious, Leask questioned the man who turned out to be one of Raaff's returning scouts, probably Carolus. He claimed he had come from the road to Pretoria and seen the Boer commando, which would be in Potchefstroom by that afternoon. Expressing disbelief, Leask stared the man straight in the eyes to be told, 'Master, it is the truth.' Although not wholly convinced, Leask wasted no time in mounting his cart and driving off.

Passing some friends he jocularly called out, 'The Boers will be here this afternoon.' Happy to be on his way home to Klerksdorp, he was unaware of what was happening at the other end of the town or that his facetious remark would later be taken by loyalists to indicate that somehow Boer friends had given him an early warning.

The Commando Enters Potchefstroom, 15 December 1880

On a very hot Transvaal summer morning General Piet Cronje, leading a commando over 500 strong, rode resolutely down the Pretoria road to Potchefstroom. His mission was to have the Boer proclamation of independence printed at the press owned by Mr Borrius, editor of the Dutch-language newspaper, the *Potchefstroomer*.

Under strict orders from the Triumvirate not to open fire unless attacked, Cronje carried with him a letter addressed to Major Clarke, as the special commissioner, which read:

> We have the honour to inform you that the Government of the South African Republic, hereby restored wants a certain document to be printed at once. We trust that from your side no measures will be ordered or taken to hinder us, as it is pressing, and of the most serious importance to both parties. The publishing of this document all over the world is very likely to prevent bloodshed – at least so is our intention. Therefore it must be done and shall be done. We take it that considering the seriousness of this matter you will not make this a casus belli. If so, we throw the responsibility for this step on your shoulders, and take the liberty to remind you that in a very same state of affairs three years ago when Sir Theophilus Shepstone wanted the Annexation Proclamation to be printed, the then Government of the Republic was generous enough to allow the Government printer to print the same. We are of the opinion that the representative of Her Majesty the Queen will, in generosity not be behind the President of a small Republic. At all events, we know that the civilised world, and the people of England, in this matter will be on our side.

Although their approach would be screened from the town by trees, the Boers anticipated that the British would be expecting their coming, having been alerted by the scouts they had fired on the previous evening. About half a mile before reaching the main road bridge into the town over the Mooi River, the commando extended into line, formed a half-circle facing the bridge and halted. The Boer manoeuvre was seen by locals living on the outskirts of the town and the news of their arrival quickly spread. Eight Boers cautiously rode forward before making a sudden swift dash over the bridge to dismount and take up firing positions to secure the bridgehead. To

Boer surprise there was no British reaction, no cannon fire. Raaff's arrogant threat, which had prompted their caution, had not materialised.

Reassured, the main commando confidently reformed into double file, galloped over the bridge and then continued on into the town. Their immediate objective was the house of ex-President Pretorius, now one of the Triumvirate, which stood about three-quarters of a mile ahead. On reaching the house the leading group of a dozen riders paused and then, detaching themselves from the main body, cantered on through the town to the Borrius printing works in Kerk Street. The commando halted on the open ground opposite the Pretorius house deploying into an extended line facing into the town centre. The Boers dismounted but remained standing by their horses. Men frequently broke ranks in the heat to drink from a nearby water furrow. The commando, poised for action, waited expectantly for some British reaction to the foray into the heart of the town. When all had remained quiet for an hour a large contingent remounted and rode on to reinforce the party already at the printing office. The remainder, numbering around a hundred, unsaddled and turned their horses loose to graze.

While the Boers knew that Borrius was a sympathiser they feared that under pressure from the British he might refuse to print the proclamation. In this event they were prepared to compel him and occupy his office and works. They need not have worried; Borrius willingly complied.

Shortly after one o'clock that afternoon the British authorities in the person of Major Clarke accompanied by Commandant Raaff put in their first appearance. Riding up to the printing office Clarke demanded to see Cronje or some other Boer leader. He was confronted by Andries Cronje (the brother of General Piet Cronje) who, speaking in Afrikaans translated by Raaff, warned Clarke, 'If you will take my advice you will go away at once.' Clarke repeated his request twice more, only to be told to go away. No attempt was made by the Boer leaders to deliver the letter to Clarke that they had brought from the Triumvirate.

Thwarted, Clarke with Raaff returned to the Landrost's office where he wrote a letter, which he sent down to Borrius warning him that he would be held responsible for any seditious matter that might be printed by him. Borrius showed the letter to Piet Cronje who promptly ordered a strong guard to be mounted on the works to prevent any British interference with the printing in progress.

By mid-afternoon the Boers effectively controlled the whole town except the market square. Initially Boer activity was confined to riding up and down the streets as far as the north edge of the square. As time passed they became more confident, blatantly posting armed pickets on each corner and street crossing. Some boldly infiltrated into the area between the Landrost's office and the British camp. At first the Boers did not interfere with anyone

moving about the town and some were even prepared to discuss their
reasons for being in Potchefstroom with passers-by.

The townspeople were in a turmoil of excitement, bewilderment and
apprehension as they watched the Boers exert their authority with no
challenge from the British Army sitting quiescent in their encampment.
Several of the men who had ridden in from Paardekraal themselves came
from the Potchefstroom area and on seeing friends and acquaintances called
on them to get their rifles and join the commando, which some did. Other
residents who were fearful of what was about to happen left their homes or
sent their families out of town. The more confident among the British
element had no inhibitions about telling the Boers that they would soon be
killed by the British.

As evening fell it started to rain, and armed Boer patrols began to stop
ordinary people walking on the streets. One in particular, Mr Smart,
manager of the Standard Bank, who was making his way home from a visit
to the Landrost's office, was seized by a large party of Boers sixty or seventy
strong. They took his revolver and forcibly detained him all night in a side
street with only the hedge to protect him from the pouring rain. At much
the same time that Smart was apprehended Major Clarke was returning to
the Landrost's office after visiting Colonel Winsloe at the camp. Suddenly
Clarke was rushed by half a dozen Boers, one grabbing the bridle of his
horse. Clarke drew his revolver and the Boers, who were under orders not to
provoke a confrontation with the British, hastily exhorted him not to shoot
and let him pass. Clarke was alarmed by this encounter but still hoped to
avoid any fighting. Nevertheless immediately on reaching his office he
issued a warning to people living near the square telling them to seek
protection in the school house or the church as they could be in danger if
firing began and they were still in their own houses. Although he knew that
there were between 600 and 800 Boers in the town, Clarke still optimis-
tically believed they would leave peaceably once their proclamation had
been printed.

Weakness in the British Position

The advent of Lieutenant-Colonel Winsloe to assume command of the
military created an anomalous situation that would later give rise to some
recrimination. Major Clarke as special commissioner held the ultimate
responsibility for any decision to deploy troops in aid of the civil power, but
he was still a serving Army officer junior in rank to Winsloe. Previously the
situation had been uncomplicated as Clarke and Thornhill were both majors
in the Royal Artillery and although Clarke was the junior he was by far the
most experienced campaign soldier. Thornhill had never been to war.
Clarke, in his determination to avoid armed confrontation if at all possible,

kept Winsloe informed of Boer activities but does not appear to have authorised him to make any preparations to intervene other than to implement the defence plan. Consequently Winsloe was completely wrong-footed by the next series of events.

Apparently oblivious to happenings on the far side of the town, shortly after 12 midday Major Charles Thornhill took leave of Winsloe and rode off towards the town intending to board the post cart at the Royal Hotel, which would take him to rejoin Army headquarters at Pretoria. Only minutes later the garrison was startled at the sight of Thornhill returning at full gallop. After his departure he had only got as far as the Landrost's office when he was stopped by Clarke who sent him back to tell Winsloe that the Boers had entered the town, all troops must be confined to camp and the emergency plan implemented.

As the strident notes of 'Assembly' were sounded by a bugler, the inertia and boredom of the past weeks immediately fell away. Orders were shouted, the tented camp struck, the parapet of the redoubt manned by the Fusiliers while the Gunners prepared the 9-pounders for action in their shallow pits. The horses and mules were brought into the ditch as planned and the Mounted Infantry saddled up ready to ride out if required. Troops were detailed off to occupy the government buildings. Captain Falls with two sergeants and twenty-two men marched briskly down to the Landrost's office carrying bags of extra ammunition. Another party of Fusiliers under Lieutenant Dalrymple-Hay moved off to occupy the gaol. Later Winsloe sent the experienced DACG Walter Dunne to support the young Dalrymple-Hay at the gaol.

If when he had assumed command Winsloe had 'considered the position of the Fort ill chosen', his misgivings as he saw his men being dispersed in isolated penny packets to meet Clarke's orders are captured in the words he was to write later:

Between the Fort and the Gaol, a distance of three hundred sixty yards, was open 'veldt', sloping from the former to the latter, crossed by a water furrow about one hundred and fifty yards from the Fort.

Between the Gaol and the Landrost's Office, a distance of about four hundred yards, the space was intersected by walls and hedgerows, and the latter was by no means a nice place to retreat from. We all knew it was not an advisable place to occupy, but I felt bound by the orders of a superior authority and there was no time for remonstrance.

When it transpired that Raaff could muster a group of about only twenty-five constables and civilian volunteers, most of the latter being government employees on the Landrost's staff, the inherent weakness of the British position was exposed. Plainly there were insufficient men to secure the long, open flanks of the British enclave.

The occupation of the Landrost's office was essential for British prestige, as it contained the government offices and records, the magistrate's court and the post office. The Union Jack flying from the flag-pole on the corner of the building was the visible symbol of British authority. However unless the flanks and rear of the building were secured the place was ultimately indefensible.

The long, thatched building filled quite a large section of the south-west corner of the market square. The façade, which was interspersed with three doors and several large tall windows, looked out over the open square, and was exposed to hostile fire from all sides of the square. The church, which might be occupied, was only 100 yards to the front. Next door, on the left, distanced only by a narrow gap containing a tree was the store belonging to the Algemenen Boerenwinkel, the farmers' co-operative. This building formed the street corner where the fork of the Kimberley road, which ran past the fort and the gaol, entered the market square. The other end, housing the post office, was separated from a brick stable by an open passage about 10 yards wide. This stable adjoined the house of Attorney Buskes, sometime clerk to the Landrost. The rest of the buildings on that side of the square – Butner's canteen, the government school, the residence of the Reverend van der Hoff, pastor of the Hervormde Church in the square – extended all cheek by jowl on to the corner of Potgieter Street where the second fork of the Kimberley road came into the square.

To the rear of the Landrost's office and the neighbouring buildings was the maze of hedges, outbuildings and walled gardens that worried Winsloe. These extended back across a lane known as Berg Street to within 100 yards of the gaol from which only the roof of the Landrost's office could be seen. This lack of visibility rendered the gaol virtually useless as an intermediate position to support the garrison in the Landrost's office.

The gaol, standing alone in comparatively open ground, was a single-storeyed whitewashed brick building about 30 feet square and 20 feet high, with a flat roof, and built round a quadrangle with the gaoler's quarters on the front and cells on two sides opening into the yard. A wall with a wooden gate completed the rectangle. In front of the gaoler's rooms a small garden surrounded by a 3-foot high mud wall faced on to the Kimberley road. The rooms and cells were roofed with corrugated iron surmounted by a parapet one brick thick and 18 inches high.

Each of the Fusilier detachments included a signaller who was intended to maintain communications between the detachment and Winsloe by means of semaphore flags.

With so few men at his disposal, Raaff could only reinforce the Fusiliers in the Landrost's office and occupy a few buildings around the square, which could give supporting fire to that position. He placed men in the Algemenen Boerenwinkel and a house across the street belonging to Impey, the Landrost's clerk. This was intended to secure the corner of the road leading down from the fort. Another party took over the Schikkerling house and store, now abandoned by the owners, from where they could cover the front of the Landrost's office. A third group remained in the Criterion Hotel, which was already in use as a billet for the constables and their horses. The Criterion, standing in the far south-east corner of the square, gave observation over the back of the church and the corner occupied by the Cape Commercial Bank from where Kerk Street led out to the Borrius printing works occupied by the Boers.

The afternoon was spent by the military improving their defences. Work continued on the ditch and parapet of the fort. Convicts were brought back from the gaol to supplement the Fusiliers. More ammunition was sent up to the Landrost's office where Captain Falls used sandbags, which had been pre-positioned, to block up the windows. At the gaol, Dalrymple-Hay ordered the windows of the gaoler's quarters to be barricaded and loop-holed. He received orders from Winsloe to release and arm the ten military prisoners if fighting broke out.

At seven o'clock in the evening Chevalier Forssman and his family including two married daughters, Mrs Palmer whose husband was away on business and Mrs Sketchley accompanied by her husband Dr Sketchley, arrived at the fort asking for protection. They were joined by several other ladies who lived around the market square, two of whom were teachers at the young ladies' seminary. This first group of refugees totalled sixteen and Winsloe willingly took them in, a decision he was to regret.

Dr Sketchley was one of the only four townspeople who had answered Clarke and Winsloe's appeal for volunteers. The chevalier, despite his status as Portuguese consul and his loyal, inestimable services to the Transvaal Republic before the annexation, believed it was his duty as a member of the British legislative assembly to support the special commissioner in the maintenance of law and order. However he was anathema to many Boers for having accepted a place on the British legislature. He could not risk leaving his wife, five teenage daughters and nine-year-old son at his house, which was literally just across the street from the Borrius premises, now the very centre of Boer activities in the town. The fort was seen by the other refugees as the only sanctuary when it became obvious that the government school and church proposed as safe havens by Clarke in his warning letter were vulnerable to shooting from all around the market square.

The refugees brought with them into the fort only the clothes they were wearing, but fortunately each was clad in a topcoat (ulster) against the rain.

Perhaps they feared the Boers would have prevented them leaving their homes had they been seen carrying baggage, but in any event they expected to return home the following morning. Everyone shared the optimistic British belief that the Boers would leave the town once their proclamation had been printed and was ready for distribution across the Transvaal.

As an eventful day drew to a close the Boers were effectively in control of the town except for the market square. Their numbers had swollen to about 800, outnumbering the British by four to one. Boer confidence had increased throughout the day as the British offered no challenge to their presence other than the appearance of the special commissioner, Major Clarke, with Commandant Raaff at the printing office early in the afternoon. By dark Boer patrols acting with impunity challenged and stopped anyone moving in the streets. Several groups like those who had boldly accosted Major Clarke and apprehended Smart, the bank manager, had freely infiltrated into the gardens and across the lane between the Landrost's office and the gaol. Frightened townspeople, in particular those who did not wish to become involved on either side in the event of a conflict, made plans to leave themselves or send their families away to safety. The Reverend Jooste, whose house was particularly exposed standing between the town and the fort, prepared to abandon his property.

All remained quiet, rain fell steadily and sentries, British and Boer alike, stared into the darkness uncertain of what might occur next.

Goetze the Landrost slept at his house on the opposite side of the square to his office. In the early hours of the morning with astonishing *savoir-faire* or defiant bravado, Major Clarke left Captain Falls and Raaff in command of the Landrost's office and returned to his rooms in the Royal Hotel only yards from the Boer headquarters.

CHAPTER 4

The Siege Begins in Earnest

16 December 1880: Day 2

Just about nine o'clock on the morning of Thursday, 16 December 1880, the date commemorated each year by the Boers as 'Dingaan's Day', the first shots were fired at Potchefstroom starting the war between the British and the Transvaal Boers.

Having spent the night under canvas, probably no more uncomfortably than they often experienced when travelling on the veldt, the Forssman family and the other refugees had breakfasted with their military hosts sitting on the grass outside the fort. The young ladies no doubt enjoyed the novel experience of being waited on by the officers and their soldier servants. No one dreamed there was any danger of a Boer attack as Colonel Winsloe with his officers, the ladies and children sat about in scattered groups chatting or strolled around the outside of the fort. A number of the soldiers looked on, taking their ease sitting on the parapet of the fort relaxing after a damp night in the open interrupted by spells of guard duty. All were passing the time until the departure of the Boer commando permitted them to return home or go about their normal affairs. The Mounted Infantry were saddling their horses ready for morning exercise.

Suddenly to everyone's surprise the tranquil scene was broken by the appearance of eight mounted Boers, rifles at the carry, butts on thigh, who rode slowly out from the edge of the town towards the fort. Passing quite close under the walls of the gaol the Boers provocatively jeered in Afrikaans at the 'rooi batjes', Dalrymple-Hay and Dunne, standing on the roof with their Fusiliers, rifles at the ready, crouching behind the low brick parapet. As they looked down impassively there came a taunt in English: 'Why don't you damned English fire, you cowards?'

Dunne then identified one of the party as Erasmus, a beef and forage contractor who had pretended to be loyal to the British and was well acquainted with the strength and composition of the garrison. The two young officers were close to being provoked. Dunne was to relate: 'Only a strong sense of grave responsibility prevented us from firing on them.'

The Boer horsemen arrogantly continued their progress at a leisurely walk until reaching a point about 150 yards from the fort they insolently

71

paused, almost halting. Then wheeling away to their left they rode off towards the Kimberley road on the far side of the gaol as though to re-enter the town. They were watched suspiciously by Dunne and Dalrymple-Hay, while the audience at the fort looked on somewhat bemused.

Opening Shots

However, this show of contempt was too much for Colonel Winsloe, who broke the rule of non-intervention imposed by the special commissioner. He ordered Lieutenant Lindsell to take half his troop of Mounted Infantry, thirteen men, and catch up with the Boers to enquire what they wanted and warn them not to approach the vicinity of the fort again. Given the order 'Mount – gallop march' and urged on by cheers from the fort, away they went in pursuit. The Boers promptly broke into a trot, and then accelerated to a gallop down the Kimberley road until they turned left at the crossing with Berg Street. According to Forssman, who watched from his refuge in the fort, Lindsell and his men followed round this corner and were fired at twice by Boers concealed behind a wall, who then leapt on their horses galloping off after their fleeing comrades. Lindsell ordered three men to dismount and return the fire. The volley appeared to wound two Boers and drove the remainder back into the town. Hearing the shots, Winsloe immediately ordered a bugler to sound the recall. The notes of the 21st Mounted Infantry ditty, 'Oh dear, what can the matter be', followed by the 'Retire' brought Lindsell and his men galloping back to the fort.

At the time these events were about to happen Major Clarke was still at the Royal Hotel. He had breakfasted and was about to return to the Landrost's office when he met and spoke with the Roman Catholic Bishop of Natal, Bishop Jolivet, who was entering the hotel. From the Landrost's office, Commandant Raaff could see armed Boers moving about in the area and was becoming increasingly anxious at their infiltrating between the Landrost's office and the gaol. In need of direction from his superior he rode off to find Clarke whom he met almost immediately in the market square. Significantly in the light of subsequent allegations made by the Triumvirate, Clarke appears to have walked out of the Royal Hotel in broad daylight and made his way to the market square unnoticed by any Boers in the vicinity. As Clarke and Raaff spoke, two shots rang out from the direction of the fort, followed by a volley. Raaff's experienced ear identified the first shots as being fired from Boer rifles. They spotted some men running back into the town from the area where Raaff knew the Boers had posted pickets during the previous night. Getting to the Landrost's office as fast as possible, Clarke signalled to Winsloe at the fort asking for an explanation as to what had occurred.

Extraordinarily the shots seem to have gone unremarked either by the crowd of Boers who were gathered around the printing office waiting for Borrius to deliver the completed proclamation or by customers, including the coach passengers, breakfasting in the Royal Hotel across the street.

Parties of Boers were still whiling away their time riding about the streets, but they no longer interfered with townspeople who were beginning to emerge apprehensively from their houses to go about essential business. Not surprisingly observers felt a pervading air of tension and suspense, no one, Boer or townsman, quite knowing what might happen next.

Earlier in the day, around 6 am, the Kimberley mail coach had clattered into the town from Pretoria. On its regular schedule, the coach had stopped at the Royal Hotel to set down the passengers, Bishop Jolivet and his aide Monsieur Beauve, before continuing on to the post office in the Landrost's building to deliver and pick up mail. The normal timetable allowed a couple of hours for the passengers to breakfast and stretch their legs while the coach returned to the hotel, changed horses and prepared for the onward journey to the diamond fields. Bishop Jolivet records how he saw armed Boers everywhere when he arrived, but although they stared at him, he was allowed to make his leisurely way into the Royal. Here he was welcomed by Young, the manager, who was an old friend, Major Clarke, Smart of the Standard Bank and Mr de la Hunt, postmaster-general of the Transvaal.

In a single moment at exactly 9.30 am, the situation erupted. A young burgher came charging up the street to where General Piet Cronje was sitting on the stoep of the Borrius office, like his men, waiting for the proclamation. Pulling his horse to a stop he shouted, 'Oom Piet, the Reds have shot at us!'

The startled onlookers heard Cronje ask, 'Where did this happen, and what has been done about it?'

Before the young man could reply a second rider galloped up, shouting at the top of his voice, 'The Reds have shot at us and Commandant Robertsee has lost an arm!'

The crowd round the printing office was electrified, but the usually volatile Cronje immediately took a firm grip of the situation calling together his 'commandants and field cornets'. Giving orders for the commando to saddle up, he directed one section to proceed to the Landrost's office to investigate the shooting and deployed three other sections to positions overlooking the market square and the British fort.

It must be remembered that apart from a sprinkling of immigrants who had undergone military service in Europe, none of the men setting off to confront the British regulars had any military training and the commando lacked any formal organisation as a combatant force.

When the burghers received their orders the tension brought on by waiting was replaced by euphoria. The long-awaited hour of liberation had come; God controlling their national destiny had ordained the events of this 16 December 1880, Dingaan's Day.

The controversy as to who fired the first shot at Potchefstroom was to continue *ad infinitum*, both sides holding the other responsible. The Triumvirate claimed that Clarke was acting on instructions, issued on 16 December, to prevent armed bodies of men approaching within one mile of any town in the province. However, Clarke did not reach the Landrost's office, where he would have received any mail delivered that morning, until after the shots were heard, and there is no evidence that instructions reached him any other way. Neither the behaviour of the British, casually breakfasting outside the fort, nor the impassive attitude of the detachment occupying the gaol, even after provocation, suggests that they were under orders actively to prevent any approach by armed Boers. The one fact about which there can be little doubt is that by the time the shots were fired open war was probably inevitable.

The section dispatched by Cronje to the Landrost's office numbering about a hundred rode calmly down Kerk Street in the direction of the market square headed by an advance guard of half a dozen burghers. Their instructions were to investigate the cause of the shooting and although some thought the time had come to fight there is no evidence to suggest any intention of an immediate attack on the British.

From the Landrost's office Major Clarke could see between the houses across the square and caught sight of the approaching Boers. He ordered Raaff to send a man to warn them that they would be fired on if they entered the market square. Lieutenant Wright, one of the small group of volunteers Raaff had enrolled to act as mounted constables on his arrival in Potchefstroom, met the Boer advance guard by the Cape Commercial Bank on the corner where Kerk Street joined the square. He delivered the message, whereupon the six horsemen turned about and rode back to the main body.

Within five minutes a first wave of twenty-five or thirty Boers galloped into the square ignoring warning shots fired over their heads. When more horsemen followed a number of men and horses were brought down by a volley from the Landrost's office, the survivors scattering to find cover behind the church and buildings bordering the square. The Fusiliers were laughing so much at the way the Boers appeared to have run away they even forgot to count the casualties they might have inflicted. Their derision was short-lived as the Boers now hidden from view retaliated with heavy, accurate fire sending plaster and brickwork flying off the buildings occupied by the British. Within half an hour their company commander, Captain Falls, was dead. He had been in the passage between the office and the court-room leaning against the front door talking to Raaff when a bullet penetrated the soft wood hitting him in the heart. According to Raaff he blurted out, 'Oh God', and dropped dead.

The clash in the market square finally unleashed the pent-up anti-British feelings among the Boers and the momentum for an attack on the fort was unstoppable.

The First Attack

At the fort, the garrison stood to, rifles cocked, their helmeted heads and shoulders exposed above the low, unfinished parapets, although on rising ground their view of the town was limited to the forty or so houses bounded by a low mud wall and screened by trees that formed the immediate fringe. From the gaol directly to their front, frantically waving semaphore flags sent back information as to what Dalrymple-Hay could see of the cause of the rising crescendo of rifle fire coming from the market square. Quite soon look-outs in the fort glimpsed large numbers of men, about 500 of them, moving in the area to the left of the gaol between two prominent houses, those of the Reverend Jooste and Dr Poortman, which stood on the corners of roads leading into the town and were separated by a couple of hundred yards of orchard and shrubs. At the same time more men were observed assembling among buildings on the edge of the town, way out on the far right of the gaol. Winsloe concluded that a general attack on the fort was developing from both flanks and he realised the vulnerability of the 9-pounders, which were standing in full view of the Boers with hardly any protection.

Isolated and left to his own devices in the gaol, Dalrymple-Hay released and armed the ten soldier prisoners, increasing his strength to thirty men. He detailed two men to fire from each of the three barricaded windows and placed most of the remaining Fusiliers behind the low parapet surrounding the roof. From the roof Dalrymple-Hay and Dunne could see only one corner of the square, the rest being obscured by trees. Dunne spotted 'a commotion of mounted men'. The intelligence was immediately semaphored back to the fort. Whenever a signaller emerged from the back of the Landrost's office he was driven back inside by Boer snipers who denied any communication between Major Clarke, the gaol and consequently Winsloe in the fort. Cut off from the control of the special commissioner, the military decisions at last rested with Winsloe, who lost no time in ordering the artillery to open fire, sending a salvo into the corner of the square indicated by the officers at the gaol. Whatever the effect on the Boers, the shells terrified women and children all over the town, immediately clearing the streets.

Almost simultaneously with the shelling, a group of twenty or thirty mounted Boers led by Cronje himself charged out from behind the

Poortman house and galloped across the 500 yards of open veldt to reach the town cemetery. Having survived British volleys from both the fort and the gaol, they dismounted and opened fire on both the British positions from behind the cemetery wall. They added their weight to the increasing volume of fire already hitting the British from marksmen concealed in the area of the Poortman house. Fire being returned from the roof of the gaol became increasingly erratic as the Fusiliers were forced to duck or fall flat between their shots by Boer bullets that smashed into the parapet scattering lumps of brick or ricocheted away over the prostrate soldiers. The 9-pounders quickly switched to the cemetery, landing shells among the Boers who appeared to take casualties to both men and horses. Alarmed, Cronje and his men mounted and galloped back into the shelter of the town. The guns now engaged a fresh target, firing on the centre of the Boer line where a large number of horsemen appeared to be concentrating. A salvo on the Poortman house destroyed the front of the building, also killing two horses belonging to Cronje that were being sheltered there. Another shell blew open Jooste's house exposing walls covered with pictures cut from the *Illustrated London News* and the *Graphic*, all scorched and burnt by the explosion.

This shelling deterred any advance by the Boers in the centre of their line but a daring attack was launched from the end of the town out to the right of the gaol. Racing over the open ground in loose formation, the horsemen got to within 400 yards of the fort before the first line of seven or eight men was hit by a British volley that emptied five saddles. The attack disintegrated and all along their line the Boers, numbering up to 800, went to ground. Taking advantage of the plentiful concealment they remained hidden while raking the British positions with fire at short range, precisely the situation Winsloe had feared when he first viewed the site of the fort.

The flight of the Boers gave Winsloe a chance to seize the initiative. He sent the Mounted Infantry dashing across to the cemetery to ensure it was clear of the enemy. Boer fire brought down the horse of one of the Fusiliers, who calmly removed his saddle, caught a loose horse left behind by Cronje and his men, mounted and rode back to the safety of the fort.

In the background to these dramatic and serious events, continuous shooting could be heard coming from the market square. The Landrost's office was also under siege. In a matter of minutes rather than hours a tense but essentially passive situation had escalated into a fierce little battle that began the war.

The impetuous Boer attack on the fort exposed the naïvety of Cronje and his subordinate commanders as they threw two uncoordinated mounted charges against the British fort. Their tactics even resembled the classic Zulu attack formation, the 'chest' or main body centred around the Jooste and

Poortman houses while the right and left 'horns' fanned out from either side of the town.

Had the British held their artillery fire a few minutes longer the Boer centre would probably have advanced into the open, coming into the killing zone of the close-range volley fire at which the British infantry were adept. These same Fusiliers had decimated the Zulus at Ulundi the previous year; the effect on the Boers might have been devastating. In his official report Winsloe admitted: 'At the time my guns were in the open and I kept up a hotter fire at the commencement than I might have done and this I am afraid prevented as decisive engagement as I should have liked.'

Had Cronje suffered heavy casualties in this initial attack and been forced to withdraw from Potchefstroom the course of the whole war might have been very different. Without the pressure he perceived to relieve the garrison of Potchefstroom, Colley would not have taken the precipitate steps that led to the disaster at Laing's Nek and the ultimate débâcle on Majuba Hill. A letter from Colley at Newcastle to Lord Wolseley, dated 17 January 1881, explains his forced decision to attack at Laing's Nek: 'Unless I can in some way relieve the pressure on Potchefstroom before the middle of next month, I am afraid that garrison and its guns must fall into Boer hands. This it is which has determined me to move without awaiting further re enforcements.'

In the event the British shells and some erratic long-range rifle fire drove the Boers into safe cover with few casualties other than horses.

Despite their contemptuous remarks about British marksmanship the Boers never again risked coming out into the open to attack the fort.

Seemingly unaffected by the excitement and activity being generated around the printing office as reports of the clash between the Mounted Infantry and the Boers were brought in to Cronje, the Kimberley mail coach stood outside the Royal Hotel across the street ready to depart.

Bishop Jolivet and his fellow passengers, refreshed after breakfast, came out to take their seats, shepherded by the coach agent, Mr Faure. They were unaware that General Cronje had just ordered that the coach be prevented from leaving and the mail impounded. To the consternation of the passengers, twenty armed men, some mounted, some on foot, suddenly surrounded the coach, ordering them to get down and telling the driver to unhitch the horses. The startled passengers grabbed what personal luggage they could, and then 'fleeing like mice' scuttled back into the hotel menaced by the Boer riflemen.

Before boarding the coach the bishop had entrusted Young, the hotel manager, with a letter to be posted to a friend at Pretoria describing events at Potchefstroom. Finding himself virtually a prisoner of war he decided it was prudent to retrieve and destroy the letter.

Faure the agent, who protested to the Boers, was hit in the mouth by one of the burghers, while Young, who had come out to assist the elderly bishop, was struck on the back of the neck with a rifle butt for his trouble. The Boers, clearly angered by the turn of events, adopted an equally threatening attitude towards the cluster of curious townspeople who were gathered around the area, attracted by the happenings beside the printing office and the mail coach.

Jacobus Scheepers, a local burgher who enjoyed a certain celebrity for having been imprisoned by the British for taking ammunition from a store without a licence, marched across to the onlookers. Self-importantly introducing himself as a commandant, he ordered the group to disperse within five minutes, also saying that those who were for the British should go to the fort and Boer supporters should cross to the printing office. When someone pointed out that to reach the fort they would have to pass through the heavy rifle fire that could now be clearly heard, Scheepers replied that was their look-out.

The onlookers wisely went on their way, a few into the Royal Hotel, most into surrounding houses and stores in Kerk Street. Subsequently the Boers discovered between twenty and thirty men who had barricaded themselves inside the Hollins and Holder store only a few buildings down Church Street, not a stone's throw from the Cape Commercial Bank from where Boer marksmen were firing on the Landrost's office.

From cynical stories that circulated among the Boers, it was believed that about this time the Reverend Jooste, who had tended Commandant Robertsee after he had been wounded by the Mounted Infantry, scrambled on to his horse and, leading a second, galloped out from the ruins of his house. Dashing past the fort he ran the gauntlet of British shots to escape to friends in the country. Jooste had made himself unpopular with many Boers as far back as 1877 when he had written a letter to the *Zuidafrikaan* newspaper that had also found its way into the British press in which he said only Kruger and a few irreconcilables were against the annexation. This was seen as another clash between the new free-thinkers in the Dutch Church and the Doppers (the puritanical sect of whom Kruger was a leading figure).

As the morning wore on, Boer fire on the fort and gaol slackened, petering out at about 11 o'clock. It was barely two hours since the initial exchange of shots between the Boers and the Mounted Infantry had begun the fighting. The British were hemmed in to their positions by the Boer riflemen hidden among the houses, gardens and trees along the edge of the town. Marksmen concealed within about 150 yards of the gaol had put shots through the barricaded windows and made life for the Fusiliers attempting to fire from the roof very dangerous indeed, although up to now they had suffered no casualties. Similarly by some miracle no one in the fort had yet been hit. However, the crack and thump of the Westly Richards bullets had left the defenders with no illusions as to their lack of protection, particularly that of the Gunners, who were in the open. The civilian women and children refugees, huddled in the bottom of their tents, the exposed tops of which were already becoming riddled with bullet holes, must have been very frightened.

The British Reaction

Taking advantage of the lull the garrison wasted no time in raiding the Commissariat stores to improve the defences. The heavy sacks of mealies stacked inside the redoubt were heaved out to build a wall to protect the guns and to heighten the lip of the ditch where the horses were sheltering. Precious crates of canned beef and boxes of biscuits were carried out from the Commissariat marquee and piled on top of the earth parapet to give added protection to the interior of the fort. There was no shortage of labour as Conductor Klien with his sixty drivers and voorloopers had abandoned their wagons parked by the magazine and taken shelter in the fort when the fighting began. The drivers afterwards could not be persuaded to leave the fort. In consequence the trek oxen and slaughter cattle they were supposed to guard gradually strayed further and further away from the fort seeking grazing and water.

With the increasing noonday heat and the thirsty, heavy work being done on the defences, the lack of water was acute. The thirsty animals cooped up in the ditch were becoming restive. The well commenced on the orders of Winsloe had struck rock 14 feet down, and a further 16 feet of hard labour had so far produced only 9 gallons of virtually liquid mud in a night. Winsloe was to refer over-optimistically to this as 'striking water' in his report of 16 December to Colonel Bellairs at Pretoria.

As the afternoon wore on and the Boers remained quiet, it was decided that the artillery should risk an attempt to water their parched horses at the Grootvoor between the fort and the gaol, the operation being covered by fire from both these positions. The Gunners were caught in the open by heavy fire from the left of the Boer line. Driver Moss was seriously wounded, a horse was killed and four others wounded before the artillerymen with their animals could get back to safety covered by shelling from the guns and rifle fire from the fort and gaol. Clearly the enemy could deny this source of water to the British, and providing this commodity vital to their survival became Winsloe's most pressing concern. The nearest water lay at the Willows, about 1,200 yards away across the open veldt beyond the town magazine. Any attempt to reach the Willows would have to wait until after dark.

From the gaol what little could be seen of the town gave the impression that it was deserted. The Fusiliers snatched a meal of bully beef and biscuits, but the civilian gaoler with his prisoners had to make do with food left over from the previous day. Dalrymple-Hay signalled back to the fort requesting additional rations and ammunition for the ten released soldier prisoners. Boer snipers still prevented any regular semaphore communication between the Landrost's office and the gaol.

In the fort, Winsloe prepared a report to be sent to Pretoria at nightfall. Carried by a faithful native who was to prove his loyalty by returning in mid-January, this last dispatch from Potchefstroom for ninety-five days was delivered to Colonel Bellairs on 21 December 1880. It read:

From Major and Brevet Lieut.-Colonel R. W. C. Winsloe, Royal Scots Fusiliers, commanding troops, Potchefstroom, to the Deputy-Assistant Adjutant-General, Pretoria

The Camp, Potchefstroom,
16th December 1880.

I have the honour to report that I have been menaced by the Boers since yesterday at 12 noon. This morning a party of Boers threatened the fort about 9 A.M., and fired on the Mounted Infantry. It was rumoured that a proclamation was to be read on the market-square at 9 A.M. today announcing a Republic. Major Clarke, R.A., is in Landrost's office with Captain Falls and about 20 volunteers under Captain Raaf. Lieut. Hay and D.-A. C.-Gl. Dunne are at jail. Major Thornhill is with me here. At about 9 A.M. a party of the Mounted Infantry was fired upon, and they returned the fire. Almost simultaneously we heard firing from the Landrost's office, which we occupy. The camp was shortly afterwards vigorously attacked on three sides, and this has continued more or less all day. The enemy have retreated repulsed on all sides, but stray shots have been fired all day into camp from the environs of the town, and firing has been going on continuously from the market-square and jail. It is impossible to hold more than the jail, Landrost's office, and the camp with the present force, owing to this being a very straggling town. Not a volunteer is forthcoming, and nearly the whole town are to all appearance on the side of the enemy. The enemy occupy the town, with exception of that portion covered by our fire. Communication with the Landrost's office is very difficult, the whole distance each side being under fire of houses occupied by the enemy. Chevalier Forssman and family, and many ladies and children, have taken refuge in my camp. Probability of water-supply being cut off. Horses can only be watered and water obtained for our use under the enemy's fire. I am sinking two wells (struck water in one of them), and so I don't anticipate much difficulty on that. I consider our position a very grave one, chiefly from the fact that the greater part of the population is undoubtedly hostile to us. Unless affairs take a better turn shortly, I may be forced to take the field, as I am using my ammunition very fast. I am embarrassed by the presence of ladies and children. The soldiers under my command are behaving admirably. Major Clarke has asked me to open communication with him, but I am unable yet to do so. Casualties as known to me up to the present are entered below.

When darkness fell a fresh flurry of activity overtook the fort. Mules loaded with three days' rations together with ammunition were sent forward to the gaol, returning without incident. The operation to fetch water from the Willows began with the departure of the water carts escorted by the Mounted Infantry, who left through the ditch at the rear of the fort. A party of thirty Fusiliers on foot also went out, taking up a covering position to prevent any Boer interference with the water convoy. The remainder of the garrison lined the parapet and manned the guns, anxiously listening to the clearly audible rumble of the water carts on their journeys to and from the springs. The noise must have been heard by the Boers but they did not react. Two return trips were needed to fill all the containers in the fort and also end with full carts. Only then was the third hazardous task of taking the horses and mules to drink completed.

Why the Boers had not seized the Willows remains a mystery, but the British had gained a breathing space and now had enough water to give everyone a ration of two or three pints for the next two days – little enough to cover all the needs for drinking, cooking and washing for men labouring in the heat, digging wells and building the defences.

Soon after dark, much to the consternation of Winsloe, more civilian refugees arrived at the fort asking for protection, which he could not refuse. He recorded: 'Twenty one women and children, three gentlemen from a neighbouring farm (the Nelson brothers), two loyal Dutchmen and one Kaffir.'

With the exception of some sporadic shooting from around the market square, the remainder of the night passed in relative quiet. At the Landrost's office, Captain Falls and another casualty, a volunteer named Woods, were buried without ceremony in the hen-house at the back of the building. Four other defenders lay wounded inside the offices.

The Boers had become more organised. Brigadier-General Jan Kock had assumed command of the right flank positions confronting the fort and the gaol, while Commandant Andries Ousthuizen, leader of a commando from the Gatsrand on the Vaal River, took charge of the left or south side of the market square.

So ended 'Dingaan's Day' 1880, a day which arguably changed the course of the history of South Africa.

CHAPTER 5

Major Clarke Surrenders the Landrost's Office

17 and 18 December 1880: Days 3 and 4

The garrison of the fort stood to at 4 am and watched the sun come up over Potchefstroom on the morning of Friday, 17 December 1880. As day broke, the Boers once again opened fire on all the British positions. Surgeon Wallis wrote in his journal:

> For how long this disagreeable state of affairs is to last it would be madness to attempt to guess. Not even a dog is to be seen abroad in the streets of the Town: every store is either robbed or closed, every house darkened or barricaded and the noise of the guns in the hands of the secreted rebels, the barking of dogs, and the crowing of cocks are the only symptoms of the existence of life, making a man say to himself when he thinks of some little town of his early haunts 'God save you from civil war.'

Apart from the sound of isolated shots fired around the market square, people in the town had passed the night in relative quiet. The Boers had posted pickets all over the town, believing the inhabitants in general to be hostile to their cause. Their attitude reflected the deep mistrust of town dwellers held by the majority of veldt Boers. In reality they could have little to fear at Potchefstroom where there were only eighty British families among a total population of over 3,000 souls.

During the night word circulated among the Boers that their casualties on the first day of fighting had been only one man killed and two wounded, one of whom was Commandant Robertsee, hit during the very first encounter with the Mounted Infantry. If accurate, these reported casualties were remarkably light considering the fact that there were numerous dead horses lying in the market square, around the cemetery and marking the scene of the failed attack on the fort mounted from the edge of the town south of the gaol. These bloated carcasses began to stink as the day grew hotter, attracting the macabre attention of vultures, which circled overhead before dropping down to gorge themselves.

At the Royal Hotel the passengers ejected from the mail coach, together with local customers who had taken refuge in the hostelry, mostly remained in the safety of their rooms. However, they were virtually prisoners of war. They were served by the hotel staff, who having fled during the initial panics of the previous day had returned to work. Quite soon Boer officers from Cronje's headquarters across the street came into the hotel ordering food and liquor for which they either declined to pay or offered 'commandeering orders'. Commandeering orders were in effect promissory notes to be honoured in due course by the new republican government. Much more was to be heard of this controversial practice.

Young's troubles were compounded when an agitated servant ran in to tell him some Boers were busily removing bundles of oats from the forage loft over his stables. Rushing out he remonstrated with the 'thieves' only to be told curtly that the men were acting on the orders of Cronje himself and if he valued his life he would disappear back into his hotel. Young could only look on while the Boers appropriated the stables for their own use, not only looting the forage but also removing all the horses they found including the post horses.

Steady Fire

Throughout that Friday the Boers concealed along the edge of the town directed a steady fire on the fort forcing the defenders to keep under cover. Restive animals sheltered in the ditch were hit by bullets as were some of their handlers who were attempting to quieten them. Leader Abram Class was killed and Driver Webb was wounded in the arm. However, quite early in the day an increase in the volume of rifle noise coming from the area of the square suggested that the Boers were beginning to concentrate their fire on the Landrost's office and the gaol.

The burghers had worked their way under cover through the surrounding gardens to positions within 100 yards of the gaol from where their short-range, accurate fire shattered the thin brick parapet sheltering the Fusiliers attempting to return shots. Dalrymple-Hay was forced to take his men down to the ground floor and knock loopholes through the main walls. From these new positions the Fusiliers had great difficulty in spotting the enemy, while the loopholes made excellent aiming marks for the Boers who sent shots whining through the apertures into the rooms. With the fort side of the gaol obscured from the enemy, Dalrymple-Hay was able to maintain semaphore communication with his commander. He obtained permission from Winsloe to allow the gaoler and his assistants to leave the gaol when it seemed safe, and to release the civilian prisoners for whom there was no food. One of the prisoners, a Swede named Anderson, was prepared to serve with the British and thinking he might be useful Dalrymple-Hay decided to keep him.

As the afternoon wore on it was apparent that the Boers, satisfied that they had effectively neutralised the gaol, were developing an attack on the Landrost's office and the adjacent buildings occupied by the British. Winsloe decided that despite the risk of engaging targets in the town he must retaliate by shelling likely Boer positions around the square, the Cape Commercial Bank and the gardens around Schikkerling's store whence the enemy could fire on the front of the Landrost's office. He also targeted the house belonging to the Reverend van der Hoff standing on the corner of Potgieter Street and the square, which gave covered access to the gardens between the office and the gaol. None of these sites was visible from the fort and the accuracy of the Gunners was due to Lieutenant Rundle having measured the ranges before hostilities began.

Never happy about the decision to occupy the Landrost's office, Winsloe became progressively more anxious about Clarke's situation. He sent a signal via the gaol advising Clarke to withdraw that night and assuring him that his retirement would be supported by the Fusiliers in the gaol and troops deployed from the fort. Whether this message reached Clarke is not clear. Only an erratic signal contact was possible owing to Boer snipers. Not until evening when a Fusilier signaller appeared through a hole in the roof of the Landrost's office was communication briefly re-established. Well-aimed shots quickly forced the signaller to duck back into cover, but not before he had passed the sad news that Captain Falls had been killed.

The fight for the Landrost's office was now well and truly on. Boer bullets sent chunks of brick and plaster flying off the walls of the building but their main targets were the loopholes in the sandbagged windows and doors through which the Fusiliers and Raaff's men were shooting. Casualties began to mount and the defenders looked around for anything that could be used to reinforce the barricades. Letters were emptied out of the mail sacks, which were filled with sand dug from the floor. Raaff, risking enemy fire, ventured outside to fetch some corrugated iron sheets from outhouses at the rear of the building. Other defenders quickly followed his brave example bringing in several more invaluable sheets. By dark there were nine wounded men lying around the rooms inside the building. Without a doctor little could be done to alleviate their suffering other than bind up their wounds.

The stifling summer heat inside the powder-smoke-filled rooms, the snatched meals of dry ration biscuits and salty bully beef aggravated everyone's thirst almost beyond endurance. In desperation perhaps more than hope, a well was sunk through the court-room floor and to the relief of all water was found after sweating, weary Fusiliers had dug down 11 feet. The interior of the Landrost's office was now a shambles, the walls pitted by bullets. The furniture, including the judge's bench, the dock and sundry other pieces of furniture not incorporated in the defences, had been thrown in a pile in the corner of the court-room.

At the gaol Dalrymple-Hay waited for dusk before sending the gaoler and his assistants to safety and releasing the dozen civilian prisoners. Only Anderson, the Swede, remained and he was about to perform an invaluable hazardous service. Dalrymple-Hay committed to writing the message intended for Major Clarke recommending withdrawal, which Winsloe had signalled earlier in the day. This was entrusted to Anderson, who was to make his way through the enemy lines to reach the Landrost's office. The risk taken by Dalrymple-Hay, presumably with the blessing of Winsloe, to entrust such a vital message to an unknown foreigner just out of custody seems surprising to say the least. Had Clarke somehow been warned to expect Anderson? Surely a stranger messenger materialising out of the dark claiming to have penetrated the Boer pickets would be very suspect. Anderson not only delivered the message but returned with a reply for Winsloe, reporting in to Dalrymple-Hay at the gaol on his way back.

In his reply Clarke assured Winsloe that his situation was not bad enough to justify a withdrawal and asserted that abandoning the government offices would have an adverse effect on morale. Presumably he meant the morale of loyalists in the town as later events showed the troops as being in good heart. Clarke confirmed the death of Falls and also requested the services of a doctor and some stretchers for the wounded. Winsloe reluctantly decided that it was impractical to try to send the medical aid.

A Brief Respite

When Boer fire tailed off at twilight the British in the fort were able to move about more freely and preparations began for another expedition to the Willows, to refill the water carts and take the horses and mules to drink. Scanning the surrounding country, observers realised that their oxen, which had been straying further and further away from the protection of the fort in search of grazing and water, had finally disappeared. They had been surreptitiously rounded up and driven off by the Boers: 120 oxen had been lost including slaughter cattle meant to provide the fresh meat ration.

Uncertain whether the Boers had moved out to the Willows, Winsloe decided a larger escort was necessary. Twenty-five Royal Artillery drivers were detailed to act as cavalry to reinforce the Mounted Infantry under Lieutenant Lindsell, who was placed in command of the whole operation. Once again a company of Fusiliers was deployed outside the fort ready to intercept any attempt by the Boers to interfere. The inevitable noises made as the animals were led out of their cramped lines in the ditch to be saddled and harnessed surprisingly did not attract any fire from the enemy. The removal of the animals allowed the Commissariat drivers to clear the stinking dung and rubbish from the insanitary ditch left after the cramped confinement of frightened animals throughout a long, hot day. The apprehensive women and children refugees were gently shepherded out of their tents to stretch their legs in the shelter of the ditch at the rear of the fort, but only until the watering party departed in case the Boers opened fire again.

The animals were watered and sufficient water brought back in the carts to give the garrison and refugees 2 pints a head for the next two days. The noisy and prolonged task had been successfully completed without any reaction from the enemy. Again a vital breathing space had been won, for none of the wells being sunk had yet produced any water.

Meanwhile at the gaol Dalrymple-Hay and Dunne took stock of their situation. Having been driven off the roof, the Fusiliers had spent the remainder of the day in stifling heat, temperatures in the upper 20s centigrade, cooped up in little rooms and cells. Their ears were ringing from the crack of their own shots in the confined spaces, and they were choked and blackened by the acrid powder smoke. Enemy bullets had continually thumped into the building. Some had shattered the glass in barricaded windows and ricocheted around the rooms inside. Miraculously no one had yet been hit. Every effort had been made to suppress Boer fire when the signaller was sent outside to semaphore the fort, and when the signaller in the Landrost's office made one of his perilous attempts to break cover and communicate. Unable to relax their vigilance all day, their only respite had been to snatch a few mouthfuls of bully beef and dry biscuit washed down with precious, tepid water. In the lull at the end of the day the two officers decided that the coolest and safest place to spend the night was on the roof. Most of the weary Fusiliers again went up aloft hoping for some rest; only the sentries remained alert at their posts.

Capture of the Landrost's Office

During the early hours of 17 December, 300 more burghers arrived at Potchefstroom from the north-west districts of the Transvaal bringing the republican strength to over 1,000 men, outnumbering the British by nearly five to one. The document printed by Borrius proclaiming the Republic was circulated in the town while copies were carried to the Triumvirate at Heidelberg and dispatched to other parts of the country. Despite the heavy firing by both sides all day the Boers had not suffered any more casualties and they were beginning to lose their fear of the British 9-pounders. However the Union Jack still flying defiantly from the pole at the corner of the Landrost's office was an irritating reminder of the determined resistance being offered by the special commissioner, Major Clarke, and his men.

At nightfall the Boer leaders resolved to capture the Landrost's office the next day. During the night a group of about twenty of the most intrepid and enterprising Boers prepared for the attack. They worked their way forward through the gardens of Butner's canteen and the Buskes house to break into the stable next door to the post office on the end of the Landrost's office. The leaders of this assault party were youngsters: Jan Kock, junior, the son of Brigadier-General Jan Kock commanding the Boer right flank, and Daniel van Graan. The gap between the stable and the back of the Landrost's office was no more than 10 yards.

The sound of 'tremendously heavy firing from the direction of the Landrost's Office' greeted the rising sun at 6 am on Saturday 18 December 1880. The British standing at their guns and lining the parapet of the fort at dawn were powerless to help. Unable to see the enemy and unsure where innocent civilians might be taking cover, Winsloe was not prepared to use his artillery. The Boers had in fact opened a withering fire on to the three open sides of the building, those in the stable firing at the point-blank range of 8 to 10 yards. Two natives sheltering inside with the British were immediately wounded.

In the excitement van Graan recklessly showed himself outside in the square and was shot down by one of Raaff's men posted in the Schikkerling store. Although hit in the side, van Graan managed to crawl to safety in Butner's canteen. Jan Kock, now the leader, decided he needed reinforcements and made his way back under heavy fire to see General Cronje at his Kerk Street headquarters. He told the general they almost had the Landrost's office in their grasp, and he needed twenty-five more men to ensure success. The required men were quickly assembled and Kock led his party, which included one, Du Plessis, who was to write an account of these events, back to the heart of the fighting. Heavy fire from the gaol whenever the Boers broke cover forced the burghers to use all their stalking skills to crawl through the orchards and gardens to reach the rear of the stable safely. Indicative of the Boers' lack of organisation, half-way through this hazardous journey Du Plessis discovered he was short of ammunition. He returned to the rear to fetch more, and then risked the British fire for a second time to catch up with his comrades.

Eventually forty or so Boers were hidden in the stable and behind garden walls at the rear of the Landrost's office, firing on the building. When the British realised that the enemy was concentrating on this side they switched men from posts overlooking the market square to man the loopholes in the barricaded windows and doors facing the new threat.

After an hour when it became clear to young Kock that they were no nearer breaking the British resistance with rifle fire alone, he, Advocate Buskes and others discussed possible alternatives and came up with the idea of burning out the 'rooi batjes' by setting fire to the thatched roof. Kock and

Buskes, aided by the latter's womenfolk, rolled up balls of rag and soaked them in turpentine. These were set alight and then hurled up on to the thatch. They were frustrated to see the round balls roll straight off the steep roof without igniting the thatch. After several attempts this method was abandoned and the ingenious pair devised a new plan. They got hold of some long 'Spanish' reeds, cutting points on the ends. They then wound a ball of turpentine-soaked rag round the shaft. It was hoped that, like a fire arrow, the reed would stick in the thatch enabling the burning rag to start a blaze.

Finding a ladder the daring young Kock climbed on to the roof of the stable and flung his first flaming 'assegai' on to the roof next door. The flames began to catch and as he was about to hurl a second missile urgent excited shouts from Boers firing from the church told him to wait. A white flag was being waved from a window in the front of the office. Raaff, realising that a corner of the roof had burst into flames, had told Major Clarke that if they did not surrender they would be burnt alive. Accepting the inevitable, Clarke authorised Raaff to put out the white flag. Not all the Boers could see the flag and firing continued for some minutes.

Inside the building not everyone was happy with Clarke's decision. Lance-Corporal Binnie, 2/21st, stated in his official report:

> Major Clarke came into the room where I was and said 'Men of the 21st the building is on fire and unless we surrender we shall all be burnt. I have therefore hoisted the white flag in token of surrender.' The men replied they would sooner die under the Union Jack than give themselves up as prisoners to the Boers. Major Clarke said this would be a foolish sacrifice of life. 'You have fought bravely and we can do no more, but I intend to demand security for life and civil treatment.'

When the shooting eventually stopped, Boers began to emerge in considerable numbers from their fire positions all around the square to stand and stare at the Landrost's office. Raaff and another defender stuck their heads out of a window; they were invited to come out and were assured that no one would harm them. Raaff accepted the potentially dangerous offer and stepped outside to be greeted by Brigadier-General Kock who was in command of the sector. Kock, standing with Buskes in front of the latter's house in company with several other burghers, was informed by Raaff that the special commissioner wished to speak to General Cronje in person. The triumphant younger Kock was sent hurrying off to fetch Cronje, who quickly arrived on the scene. As the fighting had stopped, they were able to take the short route across the square.

Major Clarke came out of the battered Landrost's building where the fire had been extinguished, to join Raaff, and together they accompanied Cronje, Brigadier Kock and Buskes into the sitting room of Buskes's house next door. Du Plessis stood guard at the front door to prevent the entry of any curious intruders. Clarke agreed to surrender but on the understanding that the lives of all his men would be spared. He was obviously very concerned for the safety of Raaff, his constables and the civilian volunteers; subsequent happenings were to prove him justified. Cronje wanted to know if Clarke was also surrendering the fort. Clarke replied that he could say nothing about the fort or what Winsloe would do. In any event he would not tell Winsloe to surrender. The terms for the surrender of the Landrost's office and the adjacent British-occupied buildings were eventually agreed and written down in duplicate. One copy was to be sent to Winsloe at the fort. Clarke requested that he be allowed to signal the news of his surrender to Winsloe but Cronje refused.

The surrender document was simple and to the point:

I Major Clarke, Special Commissioner of the District of Potchefstroom, finding the position I hold untenable, whereas a portion of the buildings are practically in the possession of the enemy, hereby undertake to surrender and to quit the premises which I now hold, namely, the Landrost's Office of Potchefstroom, and a certain building called 'de Algemenen Boerenwinkel' unarmed, and this I undertake to do with all the Garrison therein and to give free possession of the said buildings to the enemy and to send a duplicate of this document to the camp.

And I, the undersigned Pieter Arnoldus Cronje, General in command of these my troops, hereby accept the surrender unconditionally of the said Major Clarke and the men under his command within the said buildings promising that every man so surrendered will and shall be civilly treated and his life secured as long as they are my prisoners.

This done and passed at Potchefstroom this 18th day of December AD 1880 at nine o'clock in the morning.

Witnesses

M Clarke Major S Commissioner Potchefstroom

P. Raaff

J. H. M. Kock

P. A. Cronje

True copy was made by O. N. Forssman JP

Temporary Truce

Although the noise and smoke coming from the area of the Landrost's office made it obvious to the British in the fort and the gaol that Major Clarke and his men were under heavy attack, they had no clear idea of what was actually happening. When a lull in the firing was followed by an ominous silence they saw a white flag appear, being run up above the Union Jack that was flying over the government buildings. They were stunned and then more disconcerted when some minutes later a republican Vierkleur replaced the Union Jack, unbeknownst to them hoisted by the ubiquitous Buskes. With two such redoubtable characters as Clarke and Raaff in charge, what could possibly have happened?

Standing at their battle posts in the unnerving, even menacing, silence the British saw a single horseman riding through the peach trees towards them. Immediately suspicious and unaware that this was a peace emissary and that an accompanying Fusilier carrying a white flag was still hidden in the trees, someone opened fire wounding the Boer's horse. The indignant messenger turned tail and fled, racing back to Generals Cronje and Kock in the market square, where supported by his equally incensed comrades he threatened to shoot the British prisoners. Raaff as the Afrikaans speaker intervened attempting to calm the situation. He pointed out that the shooting would never have occurred if Major Clarke had been permitted to send a signal to Colonel Winsloe. He added that when the emissary had emerged from the trees, the white flag being carried behind would not have been visible from the fort.

The next time observers in the fort saw any movement it was a white flag coming through the trees between the Landrost's office and the gaol. This time the envoy paused cautiously when he broke cover, uncertain of his reception, but reassured by the sight of several white handkerchiefs being waved from the fort he continued on past the gaol from where Dalrymple-Hay recognised him as Erasmus the Commissariat contractor. Erasmus was intercepted at the Grootvoor by Lindsell and Sergeant Wall of the Mounted Infantry to whom he handed over a copy of the surrender document, saying he would wait for a reply. Winsloe, requiring time to read the document and consider his reply, ordered that Erasmus should be blindfolded before being brought closer to the fort, where he was to be given a chair and a glass of brandy. Winsloe took his time. Not until 1 o'clock did he speak to Erasmus to tell him that the British would agree to a cessation of hostilities until 4 o'clock that day. He also handed over a written reply to be taken to Cronje. The reply read:

I, Major and Brevet Lieutenant Colonel Richard William Charles Winsloe have read a letter brought to me by Mr Erasmus under a Flag of Truce, from which I understand that Major Clarke, Special Commissioner, Potchef-stroom, has surrendered the Landrost's Office and the store adjacent, with the Garrison thereof.

Such surrenders in no way concern other positions occupied by Her Majesty's troops under my command.

I agree on my part, however, to abstain from hostilities until 4 p.m. this day, in order that the due completion of the agreement between Major Clarke, Special Commissioner, Potchefstroom, and Pieter Arnoldus Cronje, styling himself General in Command, may be carried out.

Signed at Potchefstroom, Transvaal this 18th day of December, 1880 at one p.m.

R W C Winsloe Major
Bt Lt Colonel
Royal Scots Fusiliers in command of H Majesty's Troops at
Potchefstroom Transvaal

Witness
(a) P Browne Lt 2/21 R Scots Fusiliers
(b) Kenneth E Lean 2nd Lt 2/21 Royal Scots Fusiliers

Making his way back, Erasmus rode past the gaol again watched by Dalrymple-Hay who, being unaware of the nature of the negotiations, called out in a friendly way, 'How are you getting on, Mr Erasmus?' He received the surly reply, 'Oh! You will be under two fires presently.' Erasmus was no doubt feeling piqued by the apparently patronising and disdainful attitude that Winsloe had adopted towards him. The young officer had no idea what Erasmus meant but before the contractor had disappeared from view, despite the white flags hanging all about, he found himself the target for a number of shots fired from Jooste's house. Signal flags frantically waving from the fort informed an annoyed Dalrymple-Hay of Clarke's surrender and that a truce had been declared until 4 o'clock that afternoon. Commissary Walter Dunne recorded: 'We hoisted a white handkerchief as a flag of truce. The Boers then showed themselves freely in large numbers – big, clumsy, farmer like men, dressed in their ordinary sombre garb, without any attempt at a uniform, all wearing the wide brimmed soft felt hats so common in South Africa.'

Beneath the calm, urbane manner admired by his officers when he was dealing with Erasmus, Winsloe was extremely angry. In his opinion the surrender had been unnecessarily brought about by the obstinate refusal of Clarke to accept the advice offered by Winsloe to withdraw on the night of 17 December, while there was still the opportunity. Winsloe was to make his annoyance abundantly clear in his original manuscript report from Potchefstroom, dated 23 March 1881. Addressed to the AAG at Pretoria, this report somehow arrived with the adjutant-general, headquarters, at Mount Prospect from where it was sent to the War Office by Sir Evelyn Wood on 7 May 1881. The report reads:

Captain Falls 2/21 Royal Scots Fusiliers whose death I deeply regret to have to announce, having fallen in the discharge of his duty two days before. The command of the party at the Landrost's office was at this time in the hands of Major Clarke, R.A., and I much regret this officer should have found retirement to the Jail to be impossible.

I have not measured the distance but believe it to be 400 yards.

By signal I suggested retirement at night and promised support from the jail and from this position. At the time I believed retirement to be possible and what I have heard since has not shaken that belief. I had made all the necessary arrangements for carrying it out and communicated them by signal to the jail and to the Landrost's office.

These sentences are among those which at the 'desire' of HRH the Duke of Cambridge were expunged when the final revised report was resubmitted by Sir Evelyn Wood on 31 October 1881 and accepted by the duke as now 'being in a proper form for publication', on 19 November 1881.

Winsloe had just cause to be annoyed. Falls had been killed and, as a consequence of Clarke ignoring the military judgement of a senior officer, twenty Fusiliers were prisoners in the hands of the enemy, to say nothing of the loss of a quantity of ammunition and most of ten days' rations for forty men.

CHAPTER 6

Refuge in the Fort

18 and 19 December 1880: Days 4 and 5

The sudden and unexpected surrender of Major Clarke brought home to the British in the fort the full realisation of their predicament. In forty-eight hours the whole situation had been transformed from a complacent wait for the Boer commandos to remove their presence from the town, to one in which they had become a hard-pressed, thirsty garrison encumbered with numerous women and children, crowded inside an almost untenable, insanitary earthwork. Isolated from the outside world they pinned their hopes on a relieving column arriving from Pretoria.

The jubilant Boers had not been in such a position of superiority over the British since Pretorius had besieged Captain Thomas Smith and his men in their fort at Durban in May 1842. Inexperienced in handling European prisoners, they had some sympathy for the 'rooi batjes' of the 21st, but were unsure as to how to treat Major Clarke. Was he a political government official or a military commander? However, they had no doubts about a suitable fate for their *bête noire*, Commandant Raaff, and his civilian volunteers.

Perhaps it was indicative of the depth of feeling against the British that the Boers were to show little compassion towards the women and children who had taken refuge in the fort or towards any civilians in the town who did not openly support the Boer cause. There is well-authenticated evidence that among the Boers, both men and women, there were unscrupulous individuals ready to exploit the situation to repay old scores or for personal gain, even stooping to looting. Prominent names among those accused of these reprehensible activities were Advocate Buskes and Pieter Bezuidenhout.

Prisoners in the Town

The surrender document formally signed, the Fusiliers, hot, tired and none too happy at being ordered to surrender, came out into the sunlight to lay down their weapons in front of the burghers drawn up in a rough line outside the Landrost's office. The soldiers were accompanied by Raaff's men and the Landrost's staff including Moquette, known as the 'Flying

93

Dutchman' since being thrown off Bezuidenhout's wagon at the abortive sale in 1880. Other volunteers also emerged from the Algemenen Boerenwinkel and Schikkerling's store to join the assembled soldier prisoners. With the rifles and bayonets collected up by the Boers was the sword belonging to Captain Falls.

Very soon several 'Dutch ladies' appeared bringing blankets and stretchers for the wounded, whom they wanted to send back to the fort. However, the wounded men protested that they would rather stay with their own company comrades. This was a matter of indifference to the Boers who readily agreed to the request. The assembled prisoners were marched 'in a regular procession' through the streets to the house and store belonging to Chevalier Forssman, which were to be used as a prison. On arrival they found other prisoners awaiting them, nine taken from the Criterion Hotel and four from Impey's house.

Before the prisoners moved off from the market square, Cronje had ordered that a horse be brought for Major Clarke. Du Plessis, seeing that the major had only one arm, led the horse by the bridle and on arrival at the prison kindly helped Clarke to dismount. Despite the circumstances he was courteously thanked for his consideration. Clarke was immediately separated from his men and incarcerated in a small, hot bedroom that was part of a suite on the front of the Royal Hotel commandeered by the Boers. The handsomely furnished drawing-room was occupied by a guard comprising half a dozen burghers who treated the place as if it were a roadside canteen, smoking their evil-smelling rough tobacco and spitting on the floor.

All the other prisoners, including Raaff, who was to be kept handcuffed for two months and five days, were locked up in the Forssman store. Landrost Goetze was arrested at his house and brought to the Royal Hotel where he was seen by Bishop Jolivet. The news of his arrest soon circulated among the Boers and a crowd gathered outside Cronje's headquarters and the hotel demanding that the unpopular official be confined with Raaff and the soldiers and not given any privileged treatment. The war council found a compromise solution, deciding to put Goetze in the Forssman house, but the unfortunate Landrost had to suffer the indignity of being forced to walk between two rows of derisive burghers as he crossed the street to his new prison.

The elegantly furnished Forssman house, containing family heirlooms, silver from Sweden and even a Stradivarius violin, together with the next-door business premises, had been forced open and occupied by the Boers. The store contained all the accounts, records and archives of the family business since its inception. The Portuguese consular flag, which should have given the property diplomatic protection, was contemptuously hauled down and left lying in the mud for days. The fact that the chevalier had vacated his home and with his family taken refuge in the fort with the British was used by the Boers as sufficient justification for occupying these buildings and to make the adjacent central chambers, also owned by Forssman, the headquarters for Cronje and the war council.

What happened to the valuable contents of these buildings is not recorded, but after the war Forssman made a claim against the British government for lost assets amounting to £287,000 sterling, an enormous sum in 1882 equating to £15,000,000 at 1998 prices. The portion of the claim specifically related to the buildings commandeered by the Boers and the missing contents was £160,000. The claim was eventually discussed in the British House of Commons in 1882 when Gladstone himself was questioned during the debate. No doubt the property suffered the same fate as that from several other private houses in the town and surrounding countryside with furniture, pianos, carpets and in fact everything movable of value being stolen. The house belonging to Dr Sketchley was stripped of its contents except for a stove, one table and a bedstead.

Truce and Renewed Attack

When Erasmus rode away from the fort carrying Winsloe's refusal to surrender but agreement to a truce, the British knew they had a bare three hours in which to improve their defences and prepare for another attack. A shortage of tools had slowed the original construction of the redoubt. Now there were even fewer: some had been lost in the Landrost's office and others were inaccessible, cut off in the gaol. The ditch that had been dug out to build the parados was now crowded with animals and the tiny interior of the fort filled with soldiers, refugees, tents, carts and stores. All the useful Commissariat sacks and boxes had already been used to raise the height of the parapets, which were still too low to give protection to the defenders when moving about unless they were crouching down. Any items likely to stop a bullet – tents, blankets and personal clothing – were gathered up, rolled into tight bundles and then stuffed in between the mealie sacks and supply boxes, which were rearranged to give added height. Nothing was spared; every officer and soldier gave up all his clothing except for one shirt and a pair of trousers; ranks were indistinguishable.

Up to this time the 9-pounders had been standing practically in the open. The height of a gun to the top of the barrel was just over $3\frac{1}{2}$ feet, and therefore when standing in pits only 2 feet deep the entire working parts of the gun were exposed. Loading entailed Gunners standing completely without cover in front of the muzzle ramming home first the cartridge and then the shell. Before reloading, the barrel had to be sponged out and the vent cleared to ensure the cartridge could be ignited. The only protection for the Gunners was given by some hastily built piles of sacks containing mealies laid on the lip of the gun pits, and sandbags draped over the axle boxes of the guns themselves.

Given the intensity of the Boer fire and the number of casualties subsequently suffered by the Gunners, it is inexplicable why none were hit during this early stage of the siege. The opportunity was there for the Boers to neutralise the guns by systematically picking off the gun numbers as they were to do so successfully in the later battle of Ingogo. Well aware of their vulnerability, the Gunners lost no time in setting to, deepening the pits and resiting the guns to fire through makeshift embrasures between the mealie bags to cover likely targets. One covered the magazine, the cemetery and the Poortman and Jooste houses. The other covered the front from Jooste's house across to the gaol and then beyond over to the open ground extending to the western edge of the town, scene of the first abortive mounted Boer charge.

In the gaol there was little that Dalrymple-Hay could do except reinforce some parts of the parapet round the roof with sandbags. Communication was maintained with the fort by semaphore but there was no attempted movement of personnel between the two places.

The Boers, having satisfied their curiosity by emerging from cover to look at the British, disappeared again to strengthen and consolidate their own positions among the buildings, walls and gardens on the fringes of the town facing the gaol and the fort. Jooste's house became an important strong point. Because the Landrost's office no longer threatened the rear of those Boers around the gaol they could concentrate their attention on this building, which was the only obstacle between them and the fort. During the attack on the Landrost's office the Boers had been troubled by accurate fire from the gaol, leading them to believe wrongly that the gaol housed 'traitor volunteers' who were skilled shots, rather than the despised 'rooi batje' riflemen.

A commando led by Commandant Wolmorans occupied the empty Landrost's office, discovering quantities of ammunition and 'a gratifying abundance of tinned meat', obviously regarded as more palatable than tough, freshly slaughtered ox. However, they were not so enthusiastic about the stale bread and broken biscuits strewn over the floor. The burial place of Captain Falls and Volunteer Woods was found in the 'stinking fowl pen' behind the building but left alone. Butner's canteen provided a welcome supply of liquor for the triumphant burghers. Others, hungry after the fighting, took shelter in the ruins of the shell-blasted Cape Commercial Bank. Sitting around fires grilling lumps of meat on their ramrods, they were amused at being where only a few days before they would have entered, overawed, hat in hand, to do business with the bank manager.

That afternoon as 'we worked like fiends in strengthening our fort',

Winsloe decided that it was now too dangerous to attempt to hold the isolated gaol. He planned that Dalrymple-Hay and his men should withdraw that evening under cover of darkness at about 9 pm. A lighted lantern placed on the parapet of the fort would be the signal to move out.

Dalrymple-Hay and Dunne with a couple of Fusiliers were standing on the roof of the gaol absorbed in watching their signaller receiving the message that proved to be the order to withdraw when, without warning, at 3.40 pm a Boer volley shattered the truce twenty minutes early. Lance-Corporal Davidson dropped, shot in the arm and a thigh. Thankful not to have been hit themselves but livid that the Boers should have fired at them while the white flags were still flying, the group scrambled for cover carrying Davidson to safety. Dalrymple-Hay fortunately had some surgical knowledge and attempted to stop the blood spurting from Davidson's wounds using a silk handkerchief proffered by Dunne. When this proved insufficient Dalrymple-Hay took off his own shirt, tearing it into strips to make bandages. His prompt action and skill undoubtedly saved Davidson's life since the corporal was still the worst hospital case among the survivors when they eventually reached Ladysmith in April 1881.

The shots fired at the gaol also took the British in the fort by complete surprise as they moved about in the open, confident that they were protected by the white flags flying everywhere. The ordinary soldiers were particularly outraged by what they regarded as an act of Boer treachery. What caused some maverick group of Boers to violate the truce may never be known: too many 'soupies' in Butner's canteen, suspicion as they observed the British passing semaphore signals they could not understand, or simply a defective timepiece. Whatever the reason the remaining tense minutes of the truce ticked away slowly until at precisely 4 pm the Boers marked the end by opening fire on both the gaol and the fort from all their positions along the edge of the town.

During the day Cronje had been reinforced by 600 volunteers from the 'neutral' Orange Free State and 800 Transvaalers from the republican headquarters at Heidelberg. Other small groups had gravitated towards the town and by their own reckoning the Boers mustered some 2,500 men, enough to man an extended firing line nearly three-quarters of a mile long. A large number were concentrated in the houses and gardens on the town side of the gaol from where they directed a continuous accurate fire at three sides of the building. They were clearly hoping to repeat their earlier success at the Landrost's office and compel Dalrymple-Hay to surrender.

Simultaneously the Boers attempted to neutralise any support from the fort by sniping at the British Gunners, making it difficult for them to work the 9-pounders, and sweeping the parapet with rifle fire aimed at preventing any retaliation from the infantry. The length and dispersion of the Boer positions made it impossible for the British to silence anything more than one small sector of the Boer line at one time. Their technique was to use one or two well-placed shells, shrapnel among the trees or common explosive on buildings, followed up by an infantry rifle volley on the same target. The Boer strong points in the Jooste and Poortman houses came in for particular attention. Both buildings were soon in ruins.

Conditions in the gaol became increasingly uncomfortable and dangerous as the short-range Boer rifle fire kept the Fusiliers confined within the hot building, only able to return shots through the loopholes and windows that the Boers were using as aiming marks. One bullet coming through a loophole hit Private Leishman in the head. There was a rush to help him; Dalrymple-Hay tried to pour brandy from his own flask between his lips, but Leishman was dead. Ironically he had been one of the prisoners released from custody when the fighting began. Later Lance-Corporal McCluskey received a severe wound in his left wrist as he was firing through a loophole. By any standards this was a tight corner. The 22-year-old Dalrymple-Hay in his first action behaved with exemplary coolness, controlling his men quietly and firmly as he moved around the rooms giving encouragement and finding time to share out what was left of his own tobacco. Unable to be everywhere in the divided building, he was ably supported by Walter Dunne, who must have wondered how after Rorke's Drift he could have found himself in such a situation.

Doggedly the two officers and their men hung on in the confined space, enduring thirst, heat, smoke and the ear-shattering noise of their own weapons. Darkness brought relief as the Boer fire petered out and the defenders were able to go out into the cooler yard. Leishman was buried and preparations to evacuate the gaol began. Dalrymple-Hay, whose skill in tending the wounded had been invaluable, now showed the Fusiliers how to make a stretcher out of rifles and a greatcoat so that they could carry the dangerously wounded Davidson. McCluskey, although badly hurt, would have to walk.

The defenders of the gaol now had to wait anxiously in silence for what must have seemed an eternity, watching the fort for the signal to withdraw. At last, on time at 9 o'clock, a speck of light appeared. Quietly the wooden gate was opened and the Fusiliers stole out into the darkness, equally softly closing the gate behind them, leaving no sign to the enemy that they had gone. They carried their remaining ammunition but abandoned the equivalent of 150 precious rations. Forming up in skirmishing order, they moved off across the rough tussocky ground towards the fort. Movement was slow, and they were hampered by the wounded and the difficulty of keeping contact and cohesion in the dark. At any moment they expected to be hit in the back by a storm of bullets. None came.

In less than twenty minutes after the signal had appeared, Dalrymple-Hay reached the fort. He had led his men with the wounded safely across 400 yards of open ground and negotiated the deep Grootvoor water furrow under the very noses of the Boers. They were warmly welcomed by their comrades who had been anxiously looking out for them, ready to sally out to cover the retreat if the Boers attempted to intervene. How the evacuation eluded the Boers, who had been so close to the gaol all day, is a matter for conjecture. In their unmilitary fashion it is likely that only a few scattered pickets had remained on the firing line after dark, most of the burghers having made their way back into the town to rest and eat.

Back in the Fort

Sunrise on Sunday, 19 December 1880 was greeted by the Boers opening fire on the gaol. Despite their traditional reluctance to fight on a Sunday it seems that on this occasion the need to press their advantage overcame religious scruples. When no shots were returned, the burghers, realising the British had flown, advanced to occupy the building but were driven back by well-aimed shells from the fort. After this incident all shooting stopped and a general quiet settled over the Boer and British positions for the rest of the day. An unofficial cease-fire during daylight hours on the Sabbath was to be observed throughout the rest of the siege. Winsloe and his company commanders read morning prayers for their men on the parapet, while Commissary Dunne read the Roman Catholic service to the men of that Church.

With the return of the party from the gaol there was now a total of 296 military and civilians crammed into the main redoubt of the fort, which was about 30 yards square, and the adjoining gun pits, which added only a few extra square yards of space. Apart from the five bell tents and the Commissariat marquee there was no shelter from the weather. Under a beating sun, daytime temperatures reached the upper 20s centigrade while a sticky humidity and clouds gathering above the surrounding hills were a sign that the heavy seasonal rain storms would soon arrive.

The critical need was water, without which it would be impossible to hold out for any length of time. If coming days were to test the resolve of the military, they were to be an unrelieved nightmare for the thirsty and frightened women and children forced by the sun to shelter huddled in the stuffy tents. Their fears intensified when they were showered with splinters from the tent poles as they were hit by bullets, which riddled the tops of the tents that showed above the parapets. The wounded enjoyed little comfort or peace lying on the floor in the two hospital tents, which had been dug down two feet in the hope of protecting the unfortunate patients from being hit again.

The insanitary smell and general miasma was largely due to the frightened animals herded into the ditch. Some had been wounded and others
killed; carcasses had to be left swelling in the sun until darkness made their
removal possible.

During the afternoon there was a sudden shower of rain, which caught
the garrison unprepared. Consequently they only managed to catch a little
in containers and a tarpaulin to add to their dwindling stock, which if
carefully rationed might last another day or two. Puddles that collected on
the ground provided enough dirty water to give the animals a drink, but no
more.

Once safely back in the fort there was an urgent need for Walter Dunne
to assume his proper Commissariat duties and discover what had occurred
during his absence. The ASC supply sergeant, Freeman, explained how
every box and sack containing food and forage had been used to shore up
the defences and much had already been damaged by enemy fire. Many days
were to elapse before enough sandbags had been made to replace even the
most perishable items, by which time 1,000 pounds of preserved meat and
3,000 pounds of biscuits had been ruined by bullets, weather and damp. A
major part of the original reserve was lost.

Staff Sergeant Garside, ASC and civilian Conductor Klein, responsible for
the transport animals and beef cattle, made an equally depressing report.
All the trek oxen and beef cattle had strayed and been captured by the
enemy while the mules sheltering in the ditch were suffering great hardship
from lack of water, standing among dead animals or even tied to a wounded
beast. Dunne, who already enjoyed a reputation as 'a man of very excellent
judgement', realising that they could be facing a long siege and that his
supplies were already seriously depleted, asked Winsloe to approve an
immediate cut in the daily ration – the first of many more to come.

When darkness fell after a day without shooting, the British were
tempted into activity. Dalrymple-Hay with twenty Fusiliers escorting some
Commissariat drivers attempted a desperate foray down to the Grootvoor to
obtain water. They had managed to fill two barrels before they were
detected by the Boers who drove them back with several volleys. Caught in
the open, Fusilier Young was wounded in the neck and chest. Despite the
Boers now being on the alert, Winsloe ordered that the dead animals be
taken out of the ditch and dragged 500 yards away from the fort. This
heavy, unpleasant and dangerous work was done by the Commissariat
drivers and leaders, who came under fire from the enemy. Drivers Class and
Anthony were both wounded.

Inside the fort, men digging the well slaved all night with no result. The
remainder of the garrison and their 'guests' passed an uncertain and
uncomfortable night, disturbed by the fretful animals, the work going on all

around and the sporadic bursts of shooting. The need to go outside the fort for sanitary purposes added to the general misery particularly for the women and children, who had not had a change of clothes or a proper wash for three days. Such water as there was tasted of tar, making it hard to swallow and prompting Dunne to write: 'Who that has not experienced the pangs of thirst in a hot climate can fully realise the value of that cup of cold water spoken of in the Gospel.'

CHAPTER 7

Order and Disorder

19 and 20 December 1880: Days 5 and 6

Even if there was no more fighting after the Boers attempted to occupy the gaol on Sunday, 19 December, other activities were not curtailed. Men were organised to root out any British or their sympathisers who might still be hiding in the buildings around the square. One such mounted patrol caught a townsman, Edward Smith, and the barman Collins, one of Raaff's volunteers, at the back of the Criterion Hotel. When Smith was struck with a whip by one of the patrol, he and Collins ran to escape, followed by shots. Smith got away while Collins dropped to the ground, feigning death until the Boers rode away. Collins made good his escape only to be captured again later by Boers who were delighted to crow over a prisoner who had accompanied Raaff on the abortive attempt to arrest Cronje before the war.

A large party numbering twenty loyalists together with a number of African servants was brought out of the Hollins and Holder store in which they had been barricaded for three days since being given the option by Commandant Scheepers to join the Boers or go to the fort. The Boers, satisfied that these men had not taken any part in the fighting, allowed them to go free before occupying the building themselves.

There being no fighting and only sentries needed to watch the fort the remaining Boers gravitated into the town where many started drinking to celebrate their success against the British. As the day wore on many became truculent and unruly. Those who had searched the Criterion Hotel and Schikkerling's store had freely helped themselves to the contents; other search parties broke into a number of commercial premises on the pretext of obtaining blankets and other stores needed by the commandos. Despite a war council (Krijgsraad) notice declaring that all 'persons and property of the inhabitants would be protected', many private houses were also entered even if still occupied. Furniture, clothing, boots, valuables and saddlery were all taken. Although these goods were ostensibly being requisitioned for the Republic, no suggestions were made as to payment. Credulity is stretched to the limit by including among the 'war' stores commandeered the silks and other fabrics to which it was subsequently alleged certain Boer ladies helped themselves from Scorgie's store. Even the dandy Bezuidenhout was seen wearing a pair of stolen trousers.

The townspeople irrespective of faction became increasingly fearful as the rowdy armed men roamed the streets offering threats to all and sundry. Eventually, seeing the men were becoming insubordinate and out of control, the war council banned the sale or gift of alcohol to the burghers without an order from a commandant. Calm was ultimately restored by the end of the day.

Disorder in the Town

Before dawn the following morning, 20 December, the burghers had made their way back to their fire positions and at daybreak swept the fort with a barrage of rifle fire as though to make up for the truce on the previous day. Almost the first shot killed Driver Unsworth RA, a Zulu War veteran, who was hit in the head. The British had expected such an onslaught but had no inkling of the shenanigans that had gone on in the town, which exposed various Boer weaknesses, or the problems confronting Cronje and the war council to which the Hollander Buskes had been appointed secretary.

Never before historically had such large numbers of Boers come together for a war: perhaps a thousand had joined the demonstration against Britain, which culminated in the battle at Boomplaats, and the famous victory at Blood River was achieved by just 464 burghers. They certainly had never been involved in fighting disciplined troops supported by artillery in and about a town of such size and sophistication as Potchefstroom.

The command and control of the commandos and the organisation of civil affairs in these circumstances was completely outside the Boer experience. Although the commando system gave a limited cohesion, there was no established command structure or discipline. *Esprit de corps* such as that displayed by the wounded Fusiliers at the Landrost's office, who put remaining with company comrades before all else, did not exist. Although they currently had a common bond in their desire to be rid of the British, the traditional Boer individualism and instinct for self-preservation was very evident. With some notable exceptions like the young Kock and van Graan, most burghers were not prepared to take unnecessary risks or expose themselves to enemy fire. Despite his bellicose remarks to Winsloe after the surrender it is questionable whether, after their experience of British fire power during the first day's fighting, Cronje could have persuaded the Boers to assault the fort again over open ground.

Cronje himself was widely respected as a competent leader, just and fair in his dealings. However, he had a notorious short temper, which flared up when he was confronted with what he considered a trivial complaint, upsetting the ordinary burgher who approached him with a grievance.

There was discontentment among men who considered that they had been given an unfair share of the arduous tasks, resulting in their getting little rest since the fighting had begun. Dislike grew for some of the self-important local leaders of doubtful competence, among them Piet Bezui-denhout, who were believed to favour their friends and numerous relatives when it came to apportioning duties.

The loose informality of the commandos allowed men who took a dislike to their field cornet merely to transfer their allegiance to another leader who might suit them better. Importantly, when no general fighting was in progress there appeared to be very little control over the movement and activities of men not detailed for a specific guard or picket duty. In addition to the general thinning out of the forward positions at nightfall, many individuals moved between the firing line and the town much as they pleased.

The Free State volunteers had been given a surprisingly cool reception by the Transvaalers and after just one day at Potchefstroom many decided to leave for home. Possibly some were disenchanted by what they had seen on Sunday, but many may have had second thoughts about the wisdom of becoming involved in the war without the approval of their own government. Of those who stayed, most came from the area close to the border and had family or other interests in Potchefstroom.

Problems with the civilian population began to develop during the morning of 20 December when a substantial number of townspeople who had remained in the safety of their own homes for the three days since fighting began were forced to come out into the town in search of supplies. Although the sight of these people scuttling across side streets to avoid bullets fired from the fort caused the Boers some amusement, all the shoppers were treated with a great deal of suspicion. Particular attention was given to any British who were discovered, some of whom tried to avoid trouble by ingratiating themselves with the Boers who accosted them.

Many arrests were made and the accused taken to the Boer headquarters for questioning as to where they had been hiding and why. The war council was at this time very anxious to prevent communication between British sympathisers and the outside world. After deliberation the council authorised the issue of a limited number of passes permitting the applicants to move between specific houses within a restricted area. No one without a pass was allowed on the streets. The council shrewdly levied a charge of sixpence a day for a pass. A bizarre consequence of the system was that pass holders who were established customers of the Royal Hotel descended on the place expecting to be fed, much to the consternation of Dixon Young, the manager. Short of food he was already committed to feeding the officer prisoners and the wounded, for whom he drew a meat ration from the Boer commissariat. Somehow he contrived to meet the demand for up to a hundred meals a day, but insisted that the wounded and prisoners were always fed before anyone else.

Order in the Fort

The ordered routine with which the British faced this Monday was in sharp contrast with the disorganised state of Boer affairs. Under the watchful eye of Winsloe, who had given himself the most difficult duty watch, from 2 to 4 am, the garrison had manned their positions before dawn to await any Boer attack. When the Boers opened fire killing Unsworth they were ready to reply. However, staring into the rising sun they found it almost impossible to pick out targets for the guns, so skilfully were the enemy concealed. After a while when the Boer shooting began to diminish, the troops were stood down leaving only sentries to watch the enemy front. While the men attempted to get a little more rest the cooks lit fires to boil up some of the precious water to make coffee. At 7.30 a bugler sounded the breakfast call and everyone was issued with a mess tin of coffee and a handful of hard, dry biscuits. To the Gunners and Fusiliers this was normal campaign fare but such a meal must only have added to the misery of the women and children.

Already Winsloe was beginning to evolve the routine that was to become the daily way of life for the next three months. After breakfast, which the men had eaten sitting wherever they could find a space, each having left his rifle and ammunition at his appointed place at the parapet, the soldiers returned to their posts. Winsloe then made a tour of inspection, taking care to keep below the top of the parapet and avoid the attention of any watching Boer marksman. The inspection completed, a number of riflemen were detailed to remain at the parapets to fire on any enemy who showed himself. By this means Winsloe hoped to reduce the harassing fire that hampered work and movement in the fort. With the present difficulty of spotting and indicating targets, the full value of Lieutenant Rundle having had the foresight to measure various key ranges before hostilities began was appreciated.

The remaining officers and men were assigned to all the inevitable tasks and duties. Lieutenant Lean was made responsible for the building and repair of the redoubt; his priority was finding sandbags to replace the bags and boxes of foodstuff that had so hastily been used for the parapet on the first day. Under fire, some of the bundles made up of tents and tarpaulins were pulled out of the wall and given to a jovial Irish sergeant who was instructed to make sandbags. A great character, he assembled a fatigue party and began to cobble the assorted material into bags. By the end of the siege he had produced hundreds of sandbags, his labour force coming mainly from the wounded and those too sick for other duties. Other weary fatigue parties took over from the men who had been digging the well throughout the night; they had reached a depth of 30 feet and still not struck water. When he saw a man too tired to dig, Lieutenant Browne would take over his tools and set to with his men.

In the oppressive heat the sweating, thirsty soldiers prayed for rain despite knowing that they had no change of clothes or any prospect of shelter if they were soaked. Uppermost in everyone's mind was that vision of a simple cup of cold water. The Royal Artillery drivers and the Mounted Infantrymen had more than their own discomfort to worry about, as they looked on powerless to alleviate the suffering of the horses that were an integral part of their lives. The horses, which had been so short of water for days, stood abjectly in the ditch, heads drooping, until one reared up, wounded, or fell dead, hit by a Boer bullet.

Surgeon Wallis busied himself caring for the increasing number of casualties, all veterans of the Zulu War, and those reporting sick. Commissary Dunne organised his ASC supply men to bake some bread in an improvised oven, which was no more than a hole dug in the parapet, sufficient to give the wounded and the women and children some sort of treat. How the women and children passed the monotonous hours in the hot, crowded confines of their tents other than by sewing sandbags must be left to the imagination, as they left no record. It was realised that their presence was a grievous mistake, but when they had claimed protection Winsloe had had no alternative other than to accept them.

The daylight hours passed slowly by, interrupted by sporadic rifle fire from both sides. Without enough water to spare for cooking, the main meal at midday was again tinned beef and biscuits. At 5 pm, before the night guard was mounted, the last food of the day was issued, a mess tin of sugared tea together with the balance of the day's ration of biscuit. The officers gathered together with Colonel Winsloe to 'dine' off their meagre ration and to discuss the day's events and the hope of relief arriving from Pretoria or elsewhere.

Having eaten, the night work was begun as sentries looked out into fading light for any sign of enemy activity. Work on the parapet recommenced under the direction of Lean. The well diggers continued their backbreaking task. When darkness fell the Commissariat drivers began their unpleasant and dangerous task of dragging the dead animals out of the ditch and away out on to the veldt. After dark only the doctors were allowed a light and no one spoke above a whisper for the rest of the night. After labouring all day in the heat menaced by bullets thumping into defences or ricocheting away overhead, those not on duty hoped that darkness would bring some peace, giving the opportunity to sleep. They were to be disappointed. Probably attracted by the noise created by the well digging and dragging out of carcasses, Boer snipers kept up a well-directed fire on the fort all night. This made the task of retrieving the vital boxes and sacks of supplies from the parapet and replacing them with the new sandbags particularly hazardous.

So ended the sixth day of the siege.

CHAPTER 8

The Search for Water

21 December 1880: Day 7

Ready to face a new day, the seventh of the siege, Winsloe took up what was to become his accustomed position for the dawn stand-to, sitting on a chair in the middle of the fort with a bugler beside him.

Alone with his thoughts, Winsloe knew he was in deep trouble. Drinking water for the troops and the civilian refugees was almost exhausted; the horses and mules had not drunk for thirty-six hours. Despite the continuous backbreaking work with inadequate tools by day and night, the well had produced nothing. Unless water was found within the next few hours the future looked bleak. This would be a day of agonising decisions. There were the thirty-five women and children, tired, dirty, thirsty, hungry and frightened, crowded into two tents throughout the heat of the day with little relief at night. They had come to him for protection; he could not turn them out. The alternative of negotiating a safe conduct for them with the Boers would expose the precarious condition of the garrison. The distress of the animals, which continued to be hit by enemy fire, was painful to see. How much longer could they humanely be kept in these circumstances?

The officers and men standing by the guns or lining the parapet gripping their rifles as they waited for whatever the Boers were going to throw at them each had their private thoughts. The officers and men of the Mounted Infantry worried about the suffering of their individual chargers; Lieutenant Lindsell was especially attached to the thoroughbred mare that was his private property. Major Thornhill, Lieutenant Rundle and the artillerymen were unhappy at being unable to alleviate the hardships being endured by their battery animals and were concerned that without fit horses they would be immobilised. These were mostly splendid beasts brought from England for the Zulu War, which they had taken over with the 9-pounder guns from N/6 Battery after Ulundi. Remounts had replaced casualties over the ensuing months and included what Winsloe described as 'magnificent black Australians'. All were valuable animals, far superior to the general run of horses found in the Transvaal. Such animals were indispensable to the Royal Artillery, which was world-renowned for the quality of its teams and the care lavished upon them.

When only a few shots instead of the usual barrage from the Boer lines began the day it was something of an anticlimax, which was greeted with suspicion by the soldiers, but the situation did nothing to lessen the dilemma facing Winsloe.

There was no particular reason for this reduction in Boer hostility other than the fact that from the Boer viewpoint affairs had reached a stalemate and ammunition was not plentiful. The commanders needed to reappraise their tactics and bring order to civil affairs in the town where 'commandeering' of property and liquor continued unabated. Brigadier-General Jan Kock, grandly styled adjutant-general of the Burgher Force, Potchefstroom Division, called a meeting of the local people for 12 o'clock that day. Meanwhile the war council had decided to move Major Clarke out of the Royal Hotel, taking him to join Landrost Goetze imprisoned in the Forssman house. With an increasing number of civilians using the hotel this was a prudent move but the Boers did not know that Clarke had already contrived to pass his account of events in a note to de la Hunt, which was eventually received by Evelyn Wood, asking that it be sent to the British authorities as soon as possible.

In the fort following the breakfast bugle call that announced the frugal meal the daily routine began all over again. The troops lined the parapet while Winsloe made his morning rounds; then except for the marksmen left in place to watch for any Boer target the remainder set about their appointed chores. The well diggers were now hacking at solid rock 35 feet down and still finding no trace of water. Those making sandbags cut and sewed while others shovelled up soil from the well and floor of the fort to fill the completed bags. As they worked the men sucked their pipes, eking out the last remains of their tobacco.

During the morning the Boers only fired the occasional round but one found a mark, mortally wounding Private Bedford of the Mounted Infantry; he would live only for a few days. Surgeon Wallis, assisted by Dr Sketchley, was now caring for ten wounded men, some seriously injured. Once the men had been set to work Winsloe held a conference with his officers to discuss the general situation and in particular the fate of the animals. After much heart-searching it was unanimously agreed that unless sufficient water was found in the well by late morning the horses and mules must be turned loose to find water for themselves.

Events in the Town

The town meeting called by General Kock was intended to organise law enforcement and civic affairs, which had broken down or been disrupted by the removal of the Landrost and his staff. A large number of townspeople assembled at the central chambers, all having been affected in some way by the events that had taken place. The major complaint concerned the loss of running water through the town sluits resulting from the Boers cutting the main Grootvoor to prevent the fort obtaining water from this source. The meeting became noisy when it was understood that the war council proposals were tantamount to martial law, Boers as well as British being obliged to display a pass on their hats that showed their movements were officially authorised. Only Boer sympathisers were allowed to speak or vote at the meeting, and consequently those excluded were left feeling very uneasy about the future.

There was wide mistrust of some of those appointed to take charge of affairs in the town: Advocate Buskes to be secretary of the war council, Steinhoble, sometime counter-hand in a store, to be commandant of police and Piet Bezuidenhout to be district commandant of Potchefstroom. There was some reassurance when a popular and literate man, D. Petersen, was elected field cornet. With an assistant, Franz Joubert, he was to be responsible for granting passes and permission for stores to open, albeit subject to confirmation by the war council. There was general relief when it was announced that the water supply would be restored into the town as far as the market square. While the meeting was still in progress news arrived that the British had turned their horses loose and forty-nine had been captured. The word was that this had been done to save forage. The Boers did not realise the severity of the water crisis confronting the British. Despite the onset of pouring rain, jubilant Boers spent the rest of that day testing the paces and qualities of their prizes by riding round the streets of the town.

For the War Council, fully occupied with besieging the British and attempting to bring order to civic affairs, the British prisoners were an inconvenient side issue. Various individuals and groups were treated differently according to the degree of antipathy felt by their captors. Major Clarke, the special commissioner, was kept segregated and prevented from having any unauthorised contact with the outside world. The detested Raaff was kept handcuffed, for the first two days in the same room as the Fusiliers and then transferred to a damp earth-floored room without furniture or proper bedding. The volunteers and other civilian prisoners were kept in the Forssman store, and the officers among them were permitted to purchase supplies from the Royal Hotel. The Fusiliers were kindly treated and well fed, being given pipes and tobacco together with bottles of brandy and wine. Their sick and wounded were attended by a doctor four or five times a day and given anything they requested.

On the first Sunday after their capture the soldiers were visited by Bishop Jolivet who, although establishing they were not Catholics, decided to preach to them and made them say a few prayers. In the official report on his captivity Lance-Corporal Binnie, 2/21st, does not record the response of the soldiers to this spiritual experience.

The Animals are Set Free from the Fort

Winsloe made the crucial decision to release the animals at around midday. Set free at the rear of the fort they must have presented an extraordinary spectacle as some 150 horses and mules instinctively bolted towards the Willows in search of water. They were promptly rounded up and carried off by the Boers. At the start of the siege the British had a total of seventy-six horses; one subsequently killed in the fight outside the cemetery had been replaced by a captured Boer pony. The Boers reported capturing forty-nine horses; therefore, allowing that some might have escaped, upwards of twenty must have died in the ditch. No known records survive of the number of mules captured at the Willows; consequently it is not possible to estimate how many of the original 121 brought into the fort may have been killed by Boer rifle fire. However a considerable number lay among the putrefying carcasses outside the fort, attracting literally hundreds of vultures. Disgusting as they were, these scavengers probably saved the garrison from other pestilence.

Lieutenant Lindsell was allowed to keep two horses that were his personal property. His favourite, a valuable racing mare, Intombe, which he had ridden during the first encounter with the Boers, had previously been owned by Lieutenant Scott Douglas, 2/21st, killed in the Zulu War. Intombe survived the siege, being wounded twice, only to die after the war breaking her back when being thrown to remove a bullet received during the siege.

The loss of the animals was keenly felt by those who had taken so much pride in their care, but life went on, morale was good and the various activities made the inside of the fort resemble an 'industrial school'. Thunder and lightning over the surrounding hills warned of an approaching storm with the prospect of replenishing the stock of drinking water. This time the garrison would be prepared; every container and piece of tarpaulin was made ready to catch the rain if it came. During the afternoon the heavens opened and enough water was collected to last another three days. This would prove the wettest summer season for thirty years. The fact that the water was lukewarm and had a nauseous taste of tar made no difference to the feeling of sheer relief that prevailed.

Inevitably there was a penalty to pay; everyone was soaked to the skin and there were no dry clothes. The soldiers could tolerate the situation but it meant added misery and discomfort for the women and children and the wounded, who found little protection in the bullet-torn tents. The Commissariat marquee was so full of bullet holes that Dunne had problems keeping the perishables dry: tea, coffee, salt, pepper and the precious rice saved up for the hospital patients. Winsloe knew that the downpour had only provided a very temporary solution and that a well giving a continuous supply of good water was essential if the garrison was to hold out until relieved. He gave impetus to the search by offering a reward of £25 to the first party of diggers who found a spring.

CHAPTER 9

Noel

22 to 25 December 1880: Days 8 to 11

Having stopped the departure of the Kimberley coach on 16 December and impounded the mail, Cronje attempted to prevent any unauthorised communication with the outside world. Joe Green tried to dispatch the Kimberley coach on 20 December and told Bishop Jolivet to be ready to leave, but he failed to obtain permission. Three more days were to pass before Green was allowed to take a post cart to Kronstadt and then only because the Transvaal government wanted their proclamation delivered to the Orange Free State. Quite incidentally he was permitted to carry some ordinary mail.

Green was pledged by the War Council to return to Potchefstroom in three days. However, once at Kronstadt he refused to go back or allow the post cart to be returned. His behaviour infuriated the Boers and disappointed the townsfolk in general, all of whom were desperate for news. In the absence of reliable information, rumours began to spread like wildfire across the Orange Free State, south to Kimberley in the Cape and east to Pietermaritzburg in Natal, fanned by reports such as that from Webster's Agency:

The Boers in Potchefstroom. – Exciting proceedings and bloodshed. – One hundred Boers killed.

[Per Webster's Agency.]

Kimberley, December 24.

'Diamond News Advertiser' publishes statement of post driver from Bloemhof, who states that Clarke, son of Commissary, arrived before he left, and reported wildest excitement prevailed at Potchefstroom, throughout the Transvaal. When Boers took possession of Potchefstroom, and on proceeding to hoist the Republican flag, the Boer hoisting the flag was shot through the arm by the Captain of the regiment on duty, who is stated here to be Captain Lambart of the 21st, and who was immediately shot dead. J. Collins (believed to be W. Collins, Kimberley detective), Captain Raaf, Joseph Green (Transvaal coach manager), Reed (of Reed & Co.), were murdered in the midst of an assembly of 3,000 Boers, who actually fired three shots at

their own minister, the Rev. Jooste, who was most likely remonstrating with
them at their folly.

A post-cart driver has been shot.

Road beyond Bloemhof dangerous, as Klensdorp, one of the hottest beds
of rebellion.

Post driver to Kimberley had the greatest difficulty in inducing Kaffirs to
accompany him, for fear of the farmers on the road. No post arrived from
beyond Bloemhof. Nothing heard of coach to have started with Bishop
Jolivet and the passengers. Last coach which arrived had 22,000*l.* in specie.

Another version states that the Boers gave notice that on a certain day
they will take possession of Potchefstroom. Colonel Bellairs thereupon took
the distance of several buildings, when the Boers rushed on the Commercial
Bank. They were shelled out, retreating to a large store, and from that to a
church, from both of which they were shelled out, losing about 100 killed,
and many wounded.

General Colley at Pietermaritzburg telegraphed such stories to government
ministers in London quite dispassionately, reporting the capture of Major
Clarke, Boer threats to shoot Commandant Raaff and claims that the Boers
had been ejected from Potchefstroom suffering a hundred casualties. Only
when news reached him that the town of Kimberley was planning to raise a
force to march to the relief of Potchefstroom did he add an opinion. He
disapproved on the grounds that such an intervention could spark off an
uprising by the Boers throughout South Africa. Even at this early stage
Colley declared that he would not employ Natal volunteers against the
Boers so as not to provoke racial animosity. However, the rumour relating
to intervention by forces from Kimberley may have been one of the factors
that caused the Free State burghers to return home from Potchefstroom
after only one day in the field.

In reality the situation at Potchefstroom was very different from that
spread by the rumours. Once the rain arrived, the storms continued
unabated for days on end bringing equal discomfort to those in the fort and
the town. It was rain, rain, mud and water everywhere.

Conditions in the Fort

The departure of their draught animals brought home to the garrison the
stark reality that they were stuck in this mud bowl of a fort until relieved
from outside, ironically provided they could find sufficient water to drink.
Several parties of sodden, muddy soldiers began to 'prospect' for water,
encouraged by the promised reward of £25, a substantial prize to men who
seldom had more than sixpence a day left to spend after routine stoppages
from their pay.

Accounts vary as to exactly when, but sometime during the next two days a group of Gunners digging in the gun pits just outside the main parapet facing the cemetery struck a gushing spring at a depth of 12 feet. The excitement and relief of everyone can be imagined as water soon filled the well to the brim. A barrel filled with sand and charcoal was sunk into the well as a filter; their lifeline was secure. The old well, which had absorbed so much backbreaking effort, was abandoned but soon became an invaluable drainage sump for the filthy surface water that accumulated from the continuous rain.

The persistent storms brought fresh problems. The earth parapet began to crumble away and was further weakened as it became an urgent necessity to remove the boxes and sacks of supplies that had been used to shore up the defences before the contents were completely ruined by enemy fire and weather. The bundles of clothing also had to be recovered from the parapet to provide some additional garments, which could be dried and any surplus material such as flannel shirts used to make sandbags. A priority task after dark was to clear the remaining animal carcasses out of the ditch and bail out the stinking water that had accumulated in this midden.

The troops stoically went about their endless chores during these days and nights, getting what rest was possible lying silent in the open with no shelter from the elements. They had little tobacco left for the pleasure of a smoke to ease the monotony but plentiful water meant they could at least look forward to a hot meal of sorts. Winsloe ordered one dead horse to be kept to provide a special dinner on Christmas Day. However the strain of the appalling conditions was beginning to tell on the refugee women, fearful for their children, who were all under twelve years old. There were mur-murings of discontent among the Commissariat drivers and leaders, who could see little purpose in their remaining in the fort particularly when they saw another of their number wounded by Boer fire.

The plight of the wounded became even more wretched as racked with pain they lay on the floors of the dug-in tents with water washing around them as it spilled in from the surrounding ground and down through the bullet holes overhead. They still wore the blood-caked clothing they had been wearing when shot; any spare articles remained bundled up, stuffed into the parapets. Surgeon Wallis and his orderlies were hard pressed to find even a few pieces of towel to bathe the faces of men who were dying.

On 22 December there was noticeably less firing than usual although one shot killed Private Jones of the Mounted Infantry as he was working in the very centre of the fort, demonstrating once again the weakness of the defences. Sentries curious at the absence of enemy activity reported seeing numbers of Boers riding out of the town in the direction of Pretoria. Immediately the hopes of the garrison were raised that the Boers were deploying to confront a British relief force approaching from the capital. This proved to be wishful thinking, as the Boers kept up sporadic but effective fire by day and night from all along their line. Initially their main positions were in the ruins of the Poortman and Jooste houses but now a new strong point was manned in Steyne's house, which stood on the opposite side of the gaol, bringing fire on the southern side of the fort. When the fire from Steyne's became particularly troublesome and Bombardier Ganly was killed, Winsloe ordered precious shells to be used to silence this post.

Not until 29 December would the garrison learn why there could be little hope of relief from Pretoria. On 20 December the 94th marching from Lydenburg to reinforce Bellairs had been halted by the Boers and then destroyed in a fight at Bronkhorst Spruit, 40 miles from Pretoria. The entire column comprising 263 officers and men had been killed, wounded or made prisoner.

Civilians Attempt to Leave the Fort

During the morning of 23 December 1880 the Commissariat drivers and leaders told their employer Dunne that they had had enough and wanted to leave the fort. They were referred to Colonel Winsloe who readily gave his permission; the departure of over fifty unarmed men would not lessen his defensive capability but would assist greatly by reducing the number of mouths to be fed. Winsloe was at great pains to make it clear that their departure was their choice; there would be no compulsion.

At noon during a heavy thunderstorm, twenty of the transport men bolted out of the fort. They did not get far before they were spotted and pursued by Boer patrols who regarded them as 'vagabond volunteers' and showed them no mercy. Some were killed, others taken prisoner and only seven managed to escape and make their way back to the fort. Come nightfall, another party of twenty-one, undeterred by the failure of the first group, made their attempt to get away. They too were soon intercepted and this time only three evaded the Boers and regained the safety of the fort. The skeletons, picked clean by vultures, of those who were killed remained lying on the veldt as a grim reminder to anyone else tempted to try an escape through the Boer cordon. One among those leaving the fort had been entrusted with a dispatch for Pretoria. Winsloe could only wonder as to his fate.

By the following day, Christmas Eve, the refugee mothers had become so desperate they could think of nothing else but getting their children away from the unbearable conditions in the fort. Despite knowing what had happened to the Commissariat drivers it seemed they were prepared to take any risk. When they had fled into the fort on the evening of 16 December expecting to stay overnight and perhaps into the next day, they had brought nothing with them. For the last eight days they had been huddled with the other refugees, twenty to a leaky tent. They had been under constant rifle fire, wet and dirty, without any proper food for the children, some only babies. The sanitary arrangements were primitive; there was no hope of privacy. Towards the end of a singularly wet and dismal day all except the Forssman family including the married daughters and the two lady schoolteachers told Winsloe they wished to leave. They would escape under cover of darkness and make their way to a friendly farm outside the town. The plan was agreed as no one thought for one moment that the Boers would harm them. Surgeon Wallis recorded: 'Everything in the Fort and about within hearing was as still as death at 9 p.m. when the dangerous exit was commenced.'

The party that assembled in the ditch at the rear of the fort comprised four adult ladies and seventeen young children, the majority of whom were far too young to understand what was happening and that complete silence was imperative.

Lieutenant Browne gently lifted the bewildered little children out of the ditch to be gathered together in the dark by Lieutenant Dalrymple-Hay. Then the two officers began to lead their charges away from the fort to set them on their journey to safety. The group had only gone about 10 yards when terrified by the dark the infants began to cry and scream. Alerted by the noise, Boer pickets sent two volleys crashing into the hapless little band. Ten-year-old Herbert Taylor dropped dead at the feet of his mother and a small girl from the Anderson family was hit in the hand, while a baby in the arms of its mother was severely wounded. Continued firing by the Boers persuaded the horrified women that it was safer to go on rather than go back; happily they escaped without further casualties. Browne and Dalrymple-Hay carried the body of the dead boy back to the fort, having promised the heart-broken mother before she left that they would mark his grave for her to find after the war.

Christmas Day

The heart-rending events of the previous night set the scene for a depressing atmosphere on Christmas Day compounded by the weather, which was cold, wet and dreary. After some early shooting by the Boers everything went quiet. Sensing an opportunity Winsloe set the garrison about the urgent task of repairing the defences, which showed every sign of 'tumbling down like the walls of Jericho'. The continuous rain had caused the earthworks to sink and slip down while the reinforcing mealie and kaffir corn sacks had begun to burst as the sodden contents swelled up and started to rot. There was an immediate need for sandbags to revet the walls and construct more stable defences. As they sewed and shovelled, the troops grumbled at the lack of tobacco and tried smoking any substitute they could find: tea-leaves, coffee grounds, mealies, bits of paper and grass. To add to their vexation, the 'chef' declared the horsemeat intended for the special roast Christmas dinner to be rotten.

One can only imagine the thoughts and feelings of the refined, sophisticated Forssman family and the lady schoolteachers as they sat together in the leaking tents sewing sandbags. Try as they might to keep clean personally, they had not changed their clothes for ten days. How humiliating it must have been for these young ladies who had taken such pride in their looks to be seen in this dishevelled state by the officers who had been their admirers.

The Boer War Council

After the fight at Bronkhorst Spruit on 20 December, wiping out the reinforcements bound for Pretoria, Lanyon and Bellairs had withdrawn their troops and the civil population into a defensive enclave on the outskirts of that town. The Boers were effectively in control of the Transvaal. They would soon have blockaded Pretoria by establishing a ring of laagers six to ten miles outside the town preventing any contact with General Colley in Natal and the surviving little British garrisons at Potchefstroom, Rustenburg, Lydenburg, Marabastadt, Standerton and Wakkerstroom, all of which would soon come under siege.

Cronje knew he was not threatened from within the Transvaal but he had not been prepared for events as they evolved after the initial clash on 16 December. Coming to Potchefstroom with orders not to fight unless attacked he had allowed his commando to become embroiled in a seemingly stalemate situation, besieging heavily armed British regular troops holding a fortified position.

By the beginning of Christmas week his men were running short of ammunition: Kruger was to claim that the Boers started the war with only fifteen rounds a man. The Triumvirate having no military supply system, the provision of ammunition was always to be a problem. In January 1881, Boer forces were ordered not to take offensive action against the British garrisons unless they were attacked. Perhaps because of the proximity to the Orange Free State, Cronje's men did not seem to remain short of ammunition for long and indeed the force at Potchefstroom was made responsible for procuring cartridges and powder for the headquarters at Heidelberg.

The immediate shortage, which accounted for the slacking of fire observed by the British, could only be overcome by scouring the country around for any stocks held by traders in their stores. The horsemen seen leaving the town were on this errand. One party forty strong headed for

Klerksdorp and the store owned by Thomas Leask. Leask was an important licensed dealer in arms and ammunition, and was already under surveillance by the Boers who suspected him of being pro-British because once in the past he had entertained the high commissioner, Sir Bartle Frere. The burghers who descended on Leask's store were all old customers or friends, and most were in debt to him, but this did not prevent them from commandeering his entire stock of cartridges and gunpowder plus 2,000 pounds weight of lead. He was given a receipt but it was years before he received any payment. The Boers also began to remove a quantity of dynamite but with curious morality refrained when Leask protested that it did not belong to him.

Vice-President Paul Kruger arrived from Heidelberg on 23 December 1880. This was the first of the periodic visits he made to Potchefstroom during the war. Although spending most of his time at Heidelberg, he sometimes went to his home at Rustenburg and also made journeys to Majuba Hill and Standerton to consult leaders and encourage the commandos at those places. This time he brought with him the second proclamation issued by the Triumvirate, which he required to be printed by Borrius and then distributed via the Orange Free State to the world. This proclamation set out the Boer version of events since their restoration of the Republic, including the fighting at Bronkhorst Spruit and Potchefstroom, placing responsibility for the war firmly on the British. The final paragraph read: 'We hereby charge before the whole world Sir Owen Lanyon (1) with having commenced war without notice; (2) with carrying on this war against all rules of civilised warfare; and (3) particularly with the barbarous cruelties at Potchefstroom, bombarding an exposed town without warning.'

Kruger also needed to discuss with Cronje and his war council the military situation and plans for future operations at Potchefstroom. After the departure of Piet Joubert to the Natal frontier, the overall direction of operations around Pretoria and within the Transvaal including Potchefstroom was entrusted to acting Commandant-General H. P. Malan, who remained at Heidelberg. Clearly there was the patriotic, emotional reason for capturing what was widely regarded as the true capital of the Transvaal. Additionally the town housed the only printing press available to the Republic and was the main commercial link with the Orange Free State, the only outside source of ammunition and supplies.

Strategically, however, there was no reason for the Triumvirate to commit 2,000 men, 25 per cent of their total fighting strength badly needed elsewhere, to defeat a couple of hundred British troops in an out-of-the-way town unless there was some special prize. That prize was the possession of the two Royal Artillery 9-pounder guns. The guns were essential to neutralise the British artillery if the Boers were to have any

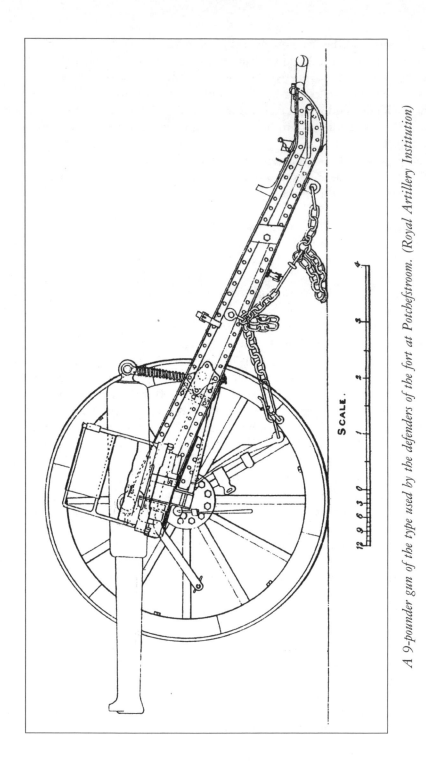

SCALE.

A 9-pounder gun of the type used by the defenders of the fort at Potchefstroom. (Royal Artillery Institution)

realistic hope of an early successful attack on Pretoria. If the Boers could gain control of Pretoria and Potchefstroom, they would be able to reinforce Joubert with captured artillery and a substantial number of men.

From his behaviour throughout the war, Cronje seems to have become almost obsessed by his determination to seize the 9-pounders intact. He defied orders by persisting with attacks on the fort when men were needed elsewhere. He threatened Winsloe with reprisals should the guns be deliberately damaged before a surrender. Most seriously he attempted to mislead Winsloe into capitulating by withholding the news of the armistice signed by Joubert and Wood. When the guns finally fell into his hands it required the personal intervention of the commandant-general to make Cronje return them to the British in accordance with the wishes of the Triumvirate.

The British were equally anxious that the Boers should not gain possession of the Potchefstroom guns. It was the fear of this happening that would persuade Colley to make the fateful premature attack on Laing's Nek at the end of January without waiting for the arrival of reinforcements. Even after the peace agreement the failure of the Boers to return these guns brought General Evelyn Wood to within days of invading the Transvaal and restarting the war. If the Boers learned one lesson from the war of 1880–81, it was the value of artillery.

His business completed, Kruger returned to Heidelberg, leaving Cronje to stamp his authority on affairs in the town and prepare the surprise he was planning to spring on the British intended to force their surrender. The second proclamation having been printed, copies were immediately sent in the charge of Joe Green to Kronstadt for world-wide distribution.

During the week before Christmas the Boers conserved their ammunition and unless alerted by some unusual noise or movement restricted their shooting to sniper fire by day and night, which inflicted casualties, harassed the British and hampered their efforts to repair the rain-damaged walls of the fort. At night only the main positions located in the Poortman, Jooste and Steyne houses were manned by pickets. Although partially wrecked, the buildings offered the Boer sentries more cover against the elements than their blankets alone.

While this spell of relative inactivity continued, some of the younger men, hardly more than boys, still regarded the siege as something of a game. They irritated their seniors when on picket duty by passing their time between taking pot-shots at the fort and in bragging and telling smutty yarns. Only when the British were provoked into retaliating with shell and rifle fire that sent the Boers diving for cover did they grasp that they too were targets in a deadly contest.

On Christmas Day, the war council issued instructions signed by Cronje aimed at bringing to an end the random commandeering and looting that had been rife. A Commissariat officer was appointed to take overall control of all the food, clothing, fodder and bedding required by the commandos. He was ordered to maintain proper accounts of everything that was received, whatever the source, and of all issues. The system of issues was to be rigidly controlled, only taking place between fixed hours each day and then only to meet written requisitions from the field cornets in charge of sections. Exceptions could only be authorised by Cronje or one of his commandants. The war council warned that any violations would be dealt with severely. In an attempt to discover what transactions had already taken place and counter any claims and complaints, the Commissariat officer was ordered to prepare a report for Cronje detailing all the acquisitions and disposals of stores to date.

On the same day new regulations appeared supplementing those already in existence, which governed the movement of individuals in and out of the town and the carrying of passes. These rules, which were resented by the Boers, were designed to prevent burghers wandering in and out of the firing line on a whim, or returning home to their farms without authority. Other new rules forbade the burning of a light after 9 pm that could be seen from the fort, obviously an attempt to prevent any loyalist signalling to the British to give information about the unusual Boer activities now taking place such as digging trenches and building emplacements. Another made it an offence to graze any livestock west of Kruger Street (Berg Street) or in the hills west of the town; any animals found in these areas would be killed or forfeited. This measure was to ensure that no fresh meat came within reach of a sortie from the fort.

The Boers Punish their Prisoners

The disposal of the prisoners was another problem that taxed the war council. While the Boers were generally well disposed towards the 'rooi batjes' they had captured, they were determined to punish any civilian who had taken service with the British. So began a series of courts martial that dispensed draconian punishments ranging from death to hard labour.

The first to be summarily shot in disputed circumstances was one of Raaff's scouts, Carolus, the coloured man who had warned Thomas Leask of the Boers' imminent entry to Potchefstroom. Local contemporary accounts reported that Major Clarke and Commandant Raaff were both tried for treason against the Republic and would have been shot if Kruger had not refused to confirm the findings of the court and ordered a new trial. He directed that the two accused were to be found not guilty and treated as ordinary prisoners of war. However, Clarke was kept segregated and never given the consideration usually accorded to one of his governmental status.

Others such as Hans van der Linden and Christian Woite would be executed in due course. A dozen of Raaff's volunteers were sentenced to periods of three to twelve months' hard labour and forced to join conscripted local Africans digging trenches under British fire. One, Trooper Findlay, was killed, as were four Africans, and several others were wounded. Landrost Goetze and his clerk Richard Impey were eventually released on bail requiring securities of £5,000 and £3,000 respectively, enormous sums for the times.

All the Fusiliers captured in the Landrost's office remained imprisoned in the Forssman store until Christmas Day, being well fed and the wounded receiving proper medical care. In the evening of 23 December, Attorney Buskes visited the prisoners on the pretext of discovering where they had buried Captain Falls, something he already knew. He asked if anyone had any property belonging to the captain and was given two rings by Sergeant Ritchie who had recovered them from the body. Subsequently the Fusiliers saw Buskes wearing these rings on his fingers. Buskes also asked them if they would like to be released and allowed to cross the Vaal into the Orange Free State. On receiving a unanimous 'yes', he said he 'would see what he could do'.

Early on the morning of Christmas Day, the Fusiliers were marched across to the central chambers where Cronje was presiding over a court martial with Buskes as his secretary in the presence of about 300 Boers. The proceedings of the court were read out to the soldiers, once in Dutch and twice in English. They were told that to be released they must on oath sign their names to a document agreeing not to take up arms or serve the British government in any way while the war lasted. They were warned that if they were found in the Transvaal again they would be shot without compunction. There is no record of whether most of the non-commissioned officers, two sergeants and three lance-corporals, refused to sign or whether they were detained by the Boers because of their rank, but they together with three wounded men were kept in captivity.

The party to be freed, comprising two lance-corporals and fourteen privates, were marched off under escort to a laager three miles south of the town where their uniforms were taken from them and replaced with old Boer clothes except curiously each man was given a brand-new hat. Again they were asked if they wished to remain prisoners or go across the Vaal. When the whole party elected to go they were marched under escort to within four miles of the river where they were set free. Lance-Corporal Binnie in charge of the Fusiliers asked the escorting field cornet for a written pass and food or money for the journey. Although the Boer officer promised to refer the request to Cronje, nothing more was heard. It was said in the town that Dixon Young of the Royal Hotel and the post contractor,

Coulson, gave the Fusiliers 'comforts' for the road although the nature is not recorded: perhaps these were the new hats. There was also a story that the Boer authorities gave each man a sovereign but they made no reference to this present in their official report.

Once across the Vaal, the Free State Boers in the frontier area shut their doors against the British soldiers, refusing them food and water. Not until they had walked several miles and crossed the Rhenoster River were they treated more kindly. Eventually they encountered a British businessman, Mr Atkins of the firm Baring, Gould and Atkins, who gave them money and hired a wagon to carry Binnie and his men to Kimberley. The prisoners arrived at Cape Town on 8 February 1881 and made their report. Two days later they were on the way back to Natal by sea. Lieutenant-General Smyth, Commanding Troops Cape Colony, lost no time, believing they could provide General Colley with valuable information, particularly concerning the amount of provisions held in the fort at Potchefstroom.

Christmas at the Royal Hotel

Another facet of that extraordinary Christmas at Potchefstroom in 1880 was portrayed by the happenings in the twilight world of the Royal Hotel. Standing across the street from Cronje's headquarters, it was patronised by Boer officers and dogged customers of every persuasion who braved the rain and bullets to reach the hostelry where Bishop Jolivet and his fellow coach passengers were still housed virtually as prisoners. Requests from the bishop to leave the town had received a courteous reply from Cronje, which promised nothing more than a safe passage at the first opportunity. Dixon Young the manager, who was obviously not his usual jovial self, was doing his best to make some festive arrangements for his guests and provide some special meals for the prisoners held in the Forssman buildings. The traditional Christmas Eve gathering fell flat; after dreary guests had drunk a toast to absent friends in silence they drifted off to bed at the unprecedentedly sober and early hour of 10 o'clock.

Christmas morning was dull, wet and depressing, but when the company assembled and sat down to dinner their spirits were lifted for a while despite some disappointment that Cronje had refused a request from Bishop Jolivet for Major Clarke to join the party. After dinner the atmosphere became more subdued as inevitably the conversation turned to the war and the anxieties created by the lack of news. Quietly the bishop reflected on the sadness of Christmas without Mass.

CHAPTER 10

Ou Griet: The Boers' Secret Weapon

26 December 1880 to 1 January 1881: Days 12 to 18

As if giving notice that the Christmas lull was over, the Boers raked the fort with fire at daybreak the next morning despite it being Sunday, wounding Corporal Tull ASC and Lieutenant Lindsell's precious mare Intombe. Undeterred by the bullets the British held their customary morning prayers.

Cooped up inside the fort, hot under oppressive overcast skies by day and drenched by rainstorms at night, the garrison was becomingly increasingly conscious of their isolation. They were constantly reminded of their parlous position by the republican flag flapping over the Landrost's office and the steadily growing number of casualties being inflicted by the Boer snipers. The gun pits were particularly vulnerable; an artillery sergeant was killed one day, a couple of days later another Gunner was wounded together with a Commissariat mule driver hit for a second time, and then next day another Gunner was wounded. Private Bedford of the Mounted Infantry died on 27 December having lingered for six days after being wounded, lying in the squalid conditions being endured by the wounded.

From the day fighting began, the garrison had received no news from outside to relieve their uncertainty and give any hope of relief. Except for one of the Commissariat transport men who had been entrusted with a message when he and his companions tried to escape on 23 December and who had crept back four days later having failed to find a way through the encircling Boers, none of the messengers dispatched by Winsloe had returned.

The Women in the Fort

For the present nothing could be done except consolidate their position and await events. A first priority was to improve the sanitary arrangements, which in the confined space offered by the fort and the ditch were primitive and a health hazard. By 28 December sufficient sandbags had been made to take the place of the boxes and sacks of perishable foodstuffs, principally biscuits and tinned beef, which had been used to heighten the parapet. Commissary Dunne assessed that he recovered sufficient undamaged to last no more than thirty days on full rations.

The refugee women and children, although reduced in number, posed an acute problem and were in constant danger from enemy fire. There were the two lady schoolteachers, and Mrs Forssman with her seven daughters, eight-year-old son and two infant grandchildren. It was imperative that they were given some safer shelter than the bullet-torn tents they occupied. Space and material were at a premium but a little 'stronghold' 9 feet square and 5 feet high was built from bags of mealies piled up on top of earth-filled boxes. A small hole 2 feet square was left at the bottom for the ladies to crawl in and out, no mean feat wearing the cumbersome clothes of the 1880s. The stronghold was covered with a wagon tarpaulin propped up on tent poles; this soon became riddled with bullet holes through which the rain poured in, drenching everyone and everything inside. The ladies were to live in this hovel for the remaining eighty-four days of the siege, only coming out when given permission either for the exercise upon which the doctors insisted or to join the officers in a nearby shelter for meals.

The hardships suffered by these sophisticated, fastidious ladies possessing nothing but the clothes they were wearing when they took refuge in the fort beggar description. Personal cleanliness and hygiene was a task that required all their ingenuity as they became increasingly more ragged. They passed the time in the gloom of their shelter sewing sandbags and making bandages from the officers' shirts until this material ran out. Often they would lead the soldiers lining the parapets in the singing of part songs for hours on end accompanied by the buglers playing their flutes.

In the early days of the siege the women together with the wounded received a small ration of flour, which Mrs Forssman baked into bread. She was to remember how she found bullets in the mixture as she kneaded the dough, bullets which had lodged in the flour sacks on the parapet. The heat in the stronghold could be almost overpowering and this, combined with the ever-present smell of wet sacking and mosquitoes, to say nothing of Boer rifle fire, made sleep nearly impossible. These brave ladies never complained and won the lasting admiration of the soldiers. Their one respite was the time spent with the officers who gathered together for their evening meal and to talk over the events of the day. Their return home assisted through the hole by the solicitous young officers drew a laughing comment from Winsloe on the length of time it took to say good night.

Plan of Attack

At 3 am on the morning of 29 December 1880, the fifteenth day of the siege, the Boers brought down a barrage of rifle fire on the fort such as the

British had not previously experienced, causing them to remain in their alarm positions waiting expectantly for an assault. The firing persisted although less intensely until 12 o'clock midday when a white flag appeared emerging from the edge of the town carried by a solitary native. The British responded by hoisting a white flag and sending out Lieutenant Lean to meet the messenger. Lean brought back an envelope addressed to Winsloe and as the messenger returned to the town the Boers broke the truce by opening fire while the white flag was still flying over the fort. Hauling down their flag, the British answered with a shell aimed at the Landrost's office.

This first news from outside was far from encouraging. The envelope contained copies of the republican gazette, the *Staats Courant*, giving a Boer account of the ambush of the 94th at Bronkhorst Spruit and details of the second republican proclamation, which put the blame for the war on Sir Owen Lanyon and the British. Since the gazette also implied that all the British troops in the Transvaal including themselves had either been killed or surrendered, they were not convinced by what they read. They were amused by Boer expressions of pity for the poor 'rooi battjes' who were being forced to fight for such an unjust cause. As though rubbing in their triumph, the Boers kept up their fire until darkness, when a thunderstorm broke over the area.

That night the Swedish ex-convict Anderson crept out from the fort attempting to reach Kronstadt in the Free State with a dispatch from Winsloe reporting the true state of affairs at Potchefstroom. He returned several days later, half-starved, having been unable to cross the River Vaal only twelve miles away.

The British were now on the alert for any unusual enemy activity and when next morning Lieutenant Rundle saw that the Boers had erected some sort of sandbag redoubt near the gaol he promptly knocked it down with a well-aimed shell. This was supported by a volley from forty Fusiliers directed by Lindsell, which drove the surviving Boers out of the wreckage. Throughout that day and the next the Boers, invisible except for the flashes from their rifles, kept up their sniping, but the British were not tempted to waste ammunition on unseen targets as they waited and wondered what the New Year would bring.

The British garrison were not to know that the Boers had been planning a major attack on the fort since Kruger had visited Potchefstroom on 23 December. Kruger and Cronje discussed Boer strategy as a whole with the need quickly to capture the fort with its guns and ammunition, which could then be used for an assault on Pretoria. Having disposed of Potchefstroom and Pretoria, the guns captured at these places could be sent with commandos released from both sieges to reinforce Joubert on the Natal frontier. The British forces under General Colley were already marching up to Newcastle and an attack on the Transvaal would not be long in coming.

Cronje knew that the Boers had a strong sense of self-preservation born of numerous native wars as they had fought to carve out their country. They were unlikely to repeat the mad rushes over open ground so unsuccessfully attempted on 16 December unless they were satisfied that the British fire had been neutralised.

To achieve his aim, in addition to 1,500 riflemen Cronje had a surprise for the British, a cannon that he hoped would breach the earth and sandbag walls of the fort. This cannon, affectionately known by the name 'Ou Griet', had been buried near Potchefstroom in 1877 at the time of the annexation. Dug up, it had been mounted on a wagon axle and wheels. The origins of the old gun were obscure. It was 24 inches long and the barrel had a 3-inch bore. It had been cast at Falkirk in Scotland in 1762 and was of the type of naval Carronade intended to fire case shot rather than solid balls. Boer legend had it that Ou Griet had been used in several native wars including the historic defeat of the Zulus at Blood River in 1838. During one of the Transvaal civil wars of the 1850s and 60s it had been used by Kruger against a rival at Potchefstroom where 'it had inflicted untold damage knocking down a stable and killing a mule'. Foraging parties such as that which commandeered powder and 2,000 pounds weight of lead from Leask's store at Klerksdorp had scoured the countryside for ammunition. An old stonemason was tasked to carve a mould and cast usable round shot. He produced lethal lead balls 3 inches in diameter and weighing 5 pounds.

To the townspeople the very presence of so many fighting men was ominous. Following the continuous rainstorms the streets were barely passable, having been churned up by the mounted burghers as they moved between their billets around the town and their positions in the firing line. The sanitary state of the town was deteriorating rapidly, owing to lack of latrines and the accumulation of offal from the beasts slaughtered for rations. An unpleasant sickly smell pervaded the whole area. Amidst all the warlike activities on the Sunday after Christmas, the Boer authorities permitted a group of the British businessmen to exhume the body of Captain Falls from the chicken run behind the Landrost's office and after placing him in a proper coffin bury him in the garden of the Standard Bank.

The frequent arrival and departure of officers at the Boer headquarters and activities such as the digging of trenches, loopholing walls and building sandbag emplacements among the houses at the southern end of the town gave rise to all sorts of rumours and speculation among the loyalists who gathered in places like the Royal Hotel. They were starved of news and blamed the mail contractor, Green, who had refused to return from Kronstadt.

1. Open rebellion by the Transvaal Boers during the darkest days of the Zulu War was only averted by a meeting between Sir Bartle Frere and the Boer leaders outside Pretoria, 12 April 1879. Behind the British flag stand members of the Boer committee, with ex-president M. W. Pretorius second to right of pole. The group on the right of the picture *(right to left)* are: Sir Bartle Frere, Sir Owen Lanyon and their staff. *The Royal Archives © 2001 Her Majesty Queen Elizabeth II*

2. The 'covenant cairn' at Paardekraal, where, on 12 December 1880, every burgher present laid a stone and made a solemn vow to fight for independence. *Author*

3. Commandant P. E. Raaff, c.1879. *Ron Lock*

4. General H. M. L. Rundle, c.1899. *Author*

5. Major M. J. Clarke, RA, c.1883. *Royal Artillery Institution*

6. Major C. Thornhill, c.1857. *Royal Artillery Institution*

7. Trumpeter N. H. Martin, RA, c.1882. *The Royal Archives © 2001 Her Majesty Queen Elizabeth II*

8. Second Lieutenant J. R. M. Dalrymple-Hay, c.1880. *Royal Highland Fusiliers Museum*

9. Captain A. Falls, c.1880, from *The Graphic*

10. Deputy Assistant Commissary-General W. A. Dunne, c.1879. *Author, from the Illustrated London News*

11. (*above*) The Right Reverend
Charles Jolivet, Bishop of Natal,
c.1880. *Roman Catholic Archives,
Natal*

12. (*above right*) Lieutenant-Colonel R.
W. C. Winsloe, c.1882. *Royal Highland
Fusiliers Museum*

13. (*right*) Lieutenant C. F. Lindsell,
c.1881. *Royal Highland Fusiliers
Museum*

14. General P. Cronje, c.1880.
Transvaal Archives

15. Pieter Bezuidenhout,
c.1880. *Transvaal Archives*

16. Boer commanders, c.1880. *Top row, left to right*: General F. Joubert, General N. Smit, General P. Cronje. *Second row*: Commandant H. Erasmus, Comdt J. de Beer, Comdt H. Pretorius, Comdt H. Botha.
Third row: Comdt D. Muller, Comdt J.S. Joubert, Comdt General P. Joubert, General J. M. Kock, Field Cornet Bezuidenhout. *Fourth row*: Comdt S. P. Grove, Comdt J. Weilbach, Comdt C. Engelbrecht, Comdt J. Fourie. *Bottom row*: General M. Schoeman, General J. P. Steyn. *Transvaal Archives*

17. Chevalier O. Forssman and his wife, c.1880. *Transvaal Archives*

18. Christian Woite, c.1880. *Author*

19 (*left*) and 20 (*above*). [19] Gunners of N/5 Battery, RA, and [20] men of the 2/21st, in Pretoria during the siege, 1881. Men of both units at Potchefstroom were of similar age and appearance. *Transvaal Archives*

21. Cape Commercial Bank on the corner of Market Square, looking towards the church and Schikkerling's store.
Potchefstroom Museum

22. Sir Owen Lanyon, c.1880. *John Young*

23. The Royal Hotel, looking south down Kerk Street towards Market Square. *Potchefstroom Museum*

140

24. (*right*) The Kimberley mail coach standing outside the Royal Hotel. *Author*

25. (*left*) Winsloe concluded that a general attack on the fort was developing from both flanks and realised the vulnerability of the 9-pounders, which were standing all but unprotected in full view of the Boers. *Pen and wash drawing by David Bennett, 2000*

26. (*left*) Finding a ladder, Johannes Kock daringly climbed on the roof of the stable and flung his first flaming assegai on to the roof next door. *Pen and wash drawing by David Bennett, 2000*

27. (*right*) The Landrost's office after the surrender. *Transvaal Archives*

28. (*below*) Reid's store on the corner of Market Square, looking north up Kerk Street towards the Royal Hotel. *Potchefstroom Museum*

29. The interior of the fort after the surrender. The town magazine can be seen in the distance. *Transvaal Archives*

30. The gaol at Potchefstroom, after the fighting. *Transvaal Archives*

31. *(left)* Scene outside O'Neill's farmhouse on the slopes of Majuba Hill, after the signing of an armistice, 21 March 1881. Front row centre, holding his helmet in front of him, stands Sir Evelyn Wood. To the immediate right are *(right to left)* President Brand, Paul Kruger, M. W. Pretorius and Piet Joubert. *Transvaal Archives*

32. The town magazine after the siege. *Transvaal Archives*

33. The monument in the graveyard at Potchefstroom, beside the remains of the fort, erected by the Royal Engineers in 1906. *John Young*

34. Ou Griet, photographed in the Voortrekker Museum, 1992. The wheels pictured are larger than those used in 1880–81. *Author*

When the ladies who had fled with their children from the fort on Christmas Eve and who had been sheltering at a farm for two days were allowed by Cronje to return to their homes, they were eagerly quizzed by the Boers and loyalists alike. The ladies gave little away, but the loyalists were pleased to know that the garrison was in good heart. They were shocked and saddened to learn of the death of young Herbert Taylor, the son of Ruth McIntyre, shot during the escape. The news of Bronkhorst Spruit had not yet circulated but the loyalists realised from the shooting and Boer preparations that something was afoot and could see the reasons for the war council regulations aimed at preventing any communication with the fort.

Persisting with his attempt to leave Potchefstroom, Bishop Jolivet sought an interview with Cronje on 29 December and was at last given a passport for the Orange Free State. Losing no time he took to the road at 12.30 pm. By so doing he missed being present during some dramatic events.

On 31 December 1880 Cronje and his officers resolved to attack the fort at dawn the next morning. Another decision was also made that day. The war council passed the sentence of death on Hans van der Linden, finding him guilty of treason. It was found proven that as a citizen of the Republic he had entered into an agreement with Raaff and some other British officer, presumably Major Clarke, that for the payment of 30 shillings a day he would spy on the Boer meeting at Paardekraal. He was accused of openly attending the meeting and deliberately deceiving his countrymen. Somehow his duplicity had been discovered.

At 3.30 pm that afternoon his wife was brought to his condemned cell. As she embraced him and made her distraught farewell, she was heard to whisper, 'I told you not to.' Promptly at 4 o'clock the old Reverend van der Hof arrived to conduct the religious rites. Six rifles were loaded, three with ball and three with blanks, which were then handed to six burghers who had been drawn by lot from among the large crowd of Boers assembled outside.

Commandant Lemmer was in charge of the proceedings, and a procession of some 300 people made its way to the riverbank on the edge of the town. When van der Linden came within 40 yards of his already-dug grave, he removed his hat, whereupon everyone in the crowd did the same. He then calmly walked up to the grave and the pastor said a short but moving prayer. As a hymn was sung, the prisoner was placed on his knees at the end of the grave, and a white hood trimmed with white lace set off with black was placed over his head and then pulled down to his knees. Commandant Lemmer moved to the side of the condemned man and, placing his left hand on the man's head, indicated with the handle of his whip held in his other hand where the firing party, now at a distance of 3 yards, should aim. Six shots rang out, three hitting van der Linden in the chest. The body fell backwards and the attending doctor declared he should receive another shot, whereupon on the order of an apparently dispassionate Lemmer a final shot was fired into the head of van der Linden.

When the reports of the execution reached Natal they had lost nothing in the telling. An extract from the *Natal Mercury* with the dateline, Orange Free State, 27 January 1881, read: 'Just prior to the execution the former [van der Linden] was taken to the Wesleyan Chapel, sang and prayed to, the worthy Buskes playing the harmonium.'

The Boer Attack, 1 January 1881

During the dark early hours of New Year's morning there was little firing to disturb the British as 1,500 Boers stealthily moved into their battle positions. The dispositions had been carefully planned for a co-ordinated attack on the fort. Twenty-five selected Potchefstroomers were to occupy the dangerous key position in the town cemetery only 350 yards from the British artillery gun pits. This was the place from which the British shells and Mounted Infantry had driven out the Boers led by Cronje himself during the first attack on 16 December 1880.

The role of the Potchefstroomers was to pick off the artillerymen when they emerged from cover to work their guns. By so doing, Cronje hoped to prevent the 9-pounders silencing Ou Griet. The gun pits were still protected only by a low parapet gapped by the wide-open embrasures necessary to allow the guns to be traversed across the Boer front.

Ou Griet was positioned in a sandbag emplacement near to Steyne's house towards the southern end of the Boer firing line. The old gun, partially screened from the British guns, was sited to fire on the southern side of the fort aiming to breach the wall facing the open ground, which was best suited for a mounted charge by the Boers. The burgher riflemen were deployed all along the edge of the town from Portman's house, past Jooste's, out to Steyne's. Crouching behind loopholed walls, on top of buildings and among the trees about the gaol they waited to deliver a devastating fire on three sides of the fort at ranges of 300 or 400 yards. Only the west side of the fort was safe from direct fire. Limiting the effectiveness of the British artillery was vital to the success of the Boer plan, and the small group entrusted with the task was led by the 'fighting' commandant, Jan Kock, himself.

When the Potchefstroomers crept into the cemetery they were accompanied by a number of black servants carrying water bottles filled with wine and brandy, plus a sack filled with biscuits and sardines, a real luxury. Once inside the cemetery they dug a shallow fire trench behind the wall through which they quietly made loopholes. Some eyed the gravestones as possible cover in an emergency.

At daybreak, Ou Griet fired the first round signalling the riflemen to sweep the fort with small-arms fire. The British retaliated immediately, engaging particularly the threat from the cemetery with both shells and rifle fire. Dust, smoke and flying stones obscured the whole area. Several Boers were hit before the British rifle fire abruptly stopped and the 9-pounders switched their attention to Ou Griet. The old gun fired twenty or more rounds before being silenced; whether it was dismounted by a British shell or whether, as derisive rumours that circulated in the town had it, it blew itself over is not certain. However, by this time it was clear to the Boer commanders that the gun had done little damage to the fort.

It remained to be seen if the riflemen had inflicted enough casualties to allow the Boers to charge without risking too much danger. For their part the men in the cemetery were convinced they had killed a number of the enemy. Cronje received a positive answer when the British rose up behind their parapets and fired volley after volley supported by the 9-pounders straight into the Boer positions. The Boers remained firmly behind cover and eventually the fire from both sides dwindled as though signalling that the Boer attack was at an end. A disappointed Cronje and his commandants were left listening to jaunty bugle calls sounding in the fort. The Potchefstroomers in the cemetery, who dared not attempt to withdraw in daylight, had to sit behind the wall, baking hot in the morning and rain-soaked in the afternoon, making the most of their brandy and sardines.

The British Response

The Boer security measures having been a complete success, the British were caught by surprise when at 4.30 am on New Year's morning a withering barrage from 1,500 rifles hit the fort on three sides. The startled defenders scrambled out of their wet blankets into their fire positions. Above the crackle of rifle fire the British heard the deeper thump of an explosion and as a succession of missiles, which turned out to be 5-pound lead balls, struck the parapet or tore through the tents they realised that the enemy had brought a cannon into action.

Initially the British attempted to return the Boer fire, in particular engaging targets in the town cemetery from where dangerous harassing fire was being directed at the 9-pounders in their gun pits, but Winsloe quickly appreciated the intensity of the enemy fire and decided to keep his men down under cover. Only sentries remained at the parapets keeping watch for a Boer assault. By this time the whole area was shrouded in a pall of powder smoke from the weapons of both sides.

Through this gloom Rundle and his Gunners, braving the rifle fire from the cemetery, attempted to pinpoint the enemy gun, which was located somewhere among buildings on the edge of the town a couple of hundred yards to the right of the gaol. The Boer gun was being reloaded with remarkable rapidity and managed to fire between twenty and thirty rounds, many of which hit the fort, before being silenced by the British 9-pounders. The Boer rifle fire lasted for nearly two hours and the Boers must have expended thousands of cartridges before the volume began to lessen and Winsloe, anticipating an assault, manned the parapets and in his own words 'let them have it'. Far from being cowed by the enemy fire, the troops had patiently sat at their posts, cheering the distinctive cannon shots or singing along with the intrepid ladies to ditties played by the buglers.

The Boers, who had been firing from the cover of loopholed walls, trees and rooftops, did not come out into the open and no attack materialised. After the garrison had been firing for about half an hour, everything went quiet. The Boer attack had plainly petered out. A triumphant Winsloe ordered a bugler to sound the breakfast call. It was now 8 am. Almost incredibly and certainly owing to the wisdom of Winsloe keeping his men under cover, the British casualties had been negligible, one killed and two wounded. Amid the turmoil and excitement of the shooting, the sad death of another man from the dreaded dysentery went almost unremarked. Major Thornhill had been too ill to take an active part in the fighting and consequently command of the guns had devolved on Rundle, who won the admiration of everyone for his skill and bravery under fire. Winsloe was convinced that the Boers had intended to rush the fort after the garrison had been softened up with rifle and cannon fire but had been deterred by the steadfast soldiers who had emerged from cover at the critical moment to return the enemy fire.

When the burghers all along the firing line realised that the attack had failed they began to filter back into the town. As the day wore on, instead of the crack of bullets, Winsloe and his men heard the sound of psalms being sung by the Boers gathered for New Year's Day worship at the Wesleyan Chapel and the Landrost's office.

CHAPTER 11

The Boers Attack the Magazine

2 to 7 January 1881: Days 19 to 24

Colonel Winsloe was pleased with the way in which his young soldiers had stood firm under a serious, sustained bombardment and felt it was testimony to the special affinity that had grown up between the officers and men of the garrison.

The Mounted Infantry Occupy the Magazine

The day following the attack was an anticlimax, being unusually quiet and uneventful even for a Sunday. The only sounds coming from the Boer lines were singing voices carrying across from the various religious services being held in the town. The absence of sniping left Winsloe not knowing whether the Boers were still occupying the cemetery only a couple of hundred yards from the isolated magazine, which now took on a new importance because it overlooked both the cemetery and the rear face of the fort. Apart from the fact that the magazine was known to contain a considerable quantity of ammunition, its possession would give the occupier a vital tactical advantage.

Unwilling to risk men in crossing the open ground to the magazine in daylight, Winsloe decided to bide his time until dark. The garrison was kept busy all day repairing the damage done to the walls during the attack, and the now daily chore of scraping the slime and mud off the floor of the fort. The few remaining Commissariat drivers were given the unpleasant task of bailing stinking water out of the ditch on two sides where it refused to drain away.

When the evening light began to fade, storm clouds were gathering and it was soon dark enough for Rundle to lead a party of Gunners across to the magazine. Not having a key for the heavy iron door, they had to make a hole through the thick stone wall while trying to avoid drawing the attention of any Boers who might be in the vicinity of the cemetery. After an absence of several hours the party returned through pouring rain bringing with them ten boxes of Martini Henry carbine ammunition (6,300 rounds), seven boxes of Snider ammunition (2,100 rounds), fourteen boxes of Westly Richards ammunition (3,150 rounds) together with ten barrels

and two sacks of gunpowder. The gunpowder and Westly Richards
cartridges being of no use to the garrison were thrown down the abandoned
well in the fort. The Boers had been denied a valuable prize.

The Gunners were safely back, when at about 1 am a sentry peering out
through the rain spotted a light in the cemetery. Curious, Winsloe called for
volunteers to investigate. Two Fusiliers came forward and, removing their
boots so as not to be heard, crawled out towards the cemetery. They
reported back believing they had seen as many as thirty or forty men
digging in the corner of the cemetery nearest the fort and magazine. Major
Thornhill, back at duty, ordered a shrapnel shell to be fired at the area. The
ensuing commotion suggested that the Boers had been successfully
dislodged. Winsloe knew he must occupy the magazine as soon as possible
before the Boers could take possession.

The overnight storms continued unabated throughout 3 January, the
twentieth day of the siege. Heavy fire expected by the British did not
materialise, but all day through the rain they were subjected to accurate
sniping. First one man was wounded in the arm, and then another in the
chest; by afternoon five Fusiliers had been hit. It was clear to Winsloe that
any attempt to send men across open ground in daylight to occupy the
magazine would be suicidal. Patiently Winsloe kept his men behind cover.
Only selected sharpshooters kept watch at the parapets and returned the
enemy fire. Torrential rain made the long hours of waiting for darkness
utterly miserable; the ground was swimming with water, no one possessed a
single item of dry clothing and there was nowhere to sit except on the wet
earth.

When darkness eventually fell, Lieutenant Lindsell led twenty men from
the Mounted Infantry over to the magazine and, making loopholes in the
walls, turned it into a blockhouse. Winsloe knew that he was risking some
of his best men, putting them in a very dangerous position, but he had every
confidence in their ability and was relieved to have secured his vulnerable
flank. At daylight Lindsell discovered that from the loopholes in the gable
end of the magazine he had a clear field of fire down Potgieter's Street on to
Boers moving in the market square. When a tempting target appeared, the
Mounted Infantry opened fire, disclosing their position to the Boers. To the
surprise of the British there was no immediate response from the Boers
whose fire remained unusually sluggish through the morning.

At 4 o'clock in the afternoon everything changed as the Boers implemented the plans they had been evolving since discovering the British were
in the magazine. Heavy rifle fire once again hit the fort, much of it directed
at the gun pits in the hope of preventing the 9-pounders from once again
silencing Ou Griet, which began to bombard the magazine from a new
position beside Jooste's house. The Boer gun was partly hidden by the house

and was also protected by a substantial wall of sacks and bales. From 500 yards the old gun fired twenty-one rounds before being silenced by the British 9-pounders; three pierced the roof of the magazine and a fourth went through a wall. After each shot, the British saw a head adorned with a red cap pop round the corner of Jooste's house observing the strike of the ball.

Lindsell's men stood firm while the 9-pounders opened up on Jooste's house, their eighth round bursting inside the building, setting fire to the thatched roof. The burning material soon fell in, throwing up a fountain of sparks, which was followed by a series of flashes and explosions indicating that a dump of ammunition had been hit. Scattered burning debris set fire to nearby outhouses and wool sacks used for the gun emplacement, which was reduced to ashes. Surrounding trees were shrivelled and scorched by the intense heat. The Royal Artillery men had the satisfaction of having silenced Ou Griet for the second time. The Boer snipers, however, kept firing until late evening and nearly killed Lieutenant Dalrymple-Hay, a bullet going through the rim of his helmet as he incautiously looked over the parapet at the enemy positions.

The Boers Attempt to Take the Magazine

The Boers, having been encouraged by the news of the British defeat at Bronkhorst Spruit, had taken up their battle positions on 1 January 1881 fully expecting that the weight of their rifle fire supplemented by Ou Griet would force the British to capitulate just as their comrades in the Landrost's office had done. They had been disappointed, and the resilience of the defenders had demonstrated to Cronje and his commandants that a direct assault would prove a costly venture even if the burghers could be persuaded to charge into the open. New tactics were required. Hostilities were largely suspended for two days while the Boer commanders considered their options, and the burghers were left to congregate for the traditional New Year's Day religious services, which continued on into the next day, a Sunday. The doughty Potchefstroomers had been withdrawn from the cemetery the night after the attack and been welcomed back by Cronje at his headquarters with a congratulatory drink and given forty-eight hours' home leave.

Over the weekend, loyalists relishing the failure of the Boer attack exchanged stories of the ineffectiveness of Ou Griet and the incompetence of the Boer gunners. However, occurrences during the next few days quickly removed their smugness. On the morning of Monday, 3 January, several of their number were detained in the streets and then made to wait for hours at the office of the war council to obtain new passes. Without warning, the council had abolished the old system and introduced more stringent and restrictive regulations.

Before the victims had time to cease complaining, the war council dropped another bombshell on the commercial community, which was largely loyalist at heart. In a letter addressed to F W Reid & Co, Cronje demanded that the 'storekeepers' of Potchefstroom should collectively make arrangements to deliver to his headquarters within six weeks a large quantity of expensive commodities that were listed, including tea, coffee, sugar and the best-quality rice. The prices were stipulated in the letter and were to be charged to the account of the new republican government. The storekeepers would be held responsible if these demands were not met.

The townspeople were feeling the reactions of Cronje and the war council as they attempted to cope with the unfamiliar problems they faced in fighting what was becoming an extended campaign against entrenched professional soldiers in an urban environment. The civilian population, some hostile, had to be administered and kept under control. The combatants had exhausted the supplies they had brought with them to war and needed to be provided with food, ammunition and other necessities. Lacking any experience of such complicated matters and having no financial resources, the council sought simplistic solutions, demanding supplies from the storekeepers under threat and raising revenue from passes and fines under regulations altered to trap unsuspecting offenders.

Tactically the Boer command decided that the priority was the permanent occupation of the cemetery from where fire could be brought to bear on the British gun pits. Then the magazine could be taken, allowing marksmen to overlook the rear of the fort. How to hold the cemetery in daylight and maintain a safe link over 200 yards of open ground under British observation was the problem. Commandant Jan Kock offered a solution, which was to dig a communication trench from Jooste's house out to the cemetery. There was plenty of labour available, prisoners of war serving sentence of hard labour and the native servants of civilians in the town. If the cemetery was occupied, first by night only, digging could safely begin from both ends to speed up the connection.

Before their plan could be implemented, the British had stolen the initiative by occupying the magazine and opening fire past the cemetery into the market square. Appreciating that the British presence in the magazine would completely frustrate his plans, Cronje took immediate steps to eject them. The number of men already positioned around Jooste's house was increased to forty, enough to protect the construction of a parapet from wool bales beside the building. From this emplacement, Ou Griet would be able to fire directly on the magazine at a range of 500 yards while being partially screened by the house itself from the British guns. Several hours were required to complete this work and trundle the old gun along the muddy roads from the other side of the gaol where it had stood silent for three days. Ammunition was brought round and stacked inside Jooste's house, which although damaged in earlier fighting still offered some dry protection from the rain.

Until all was ready the Boers left the fort and magazine in relative peace. Then at 4 o'clock, as heavy rifle fire was directed at the British gun pits, Ou Griet commenced shooting at the magazine. The building presented only a small target and most of the cannon shots flew high or wide owing to a combination of untrained gunners and poorly cast unsymmetrical lead balls. The loader, son of Borrius the printer, bravely poked his head round the wall to observe the flight of each shot. After the early misses, Field Cornet Franz Joubert took over laying the gun and achieved several hits on the magazine before a British shell struck Jooste's house, setting both it and the wool bale gun emplacement ablaze. Having no love for the Reverend Jooste, the Boers made no attempt to rescue any of the contents of the burning house until a message arrived from Cronje that anything they could save might be kept as loot. Once again the British Gunners had defied the Boer rifle fire and thwarted another Boer attack.

Next morning all remained strangely silent until a white flag appeared at the fort, causing great excitement among the watching Boers, who immediately assumed the British were about to surrender. To their surprise it was a solitary sergeant who came down to the Grootvoor bearing a request for the two lady teachers to be allowed to leave the fort and return to their homes. Convention would have been to use an officer as emissary but on this occasion and right up to the final surrender negotiations Winsloe, who personally liked the Boers as a people, never treated them as other than rebels. He always denied Cronje any military status, addressing him as 'P A Cronje Esq Styling himself as General in Command'.

Winsloe had carefully chosen this sergeant whom he regarded as one of his best men and continued to use him for all subsequent contacts with the enemy. The sergeant, a cheery extrovert character, was better educated than most other ranks, being a product of the Army boarding school in Dublin, the Royal Hibernian Military School. He became quite a favourite with the Boers who enjoyed his waggish banter when they met. Typical of his kind, he wasted no time in scrounging a fill of tobacco for his pipe while he waited for the reply to come from Cronje. On this and later meetings he contrived to bring back tobacco, which he shared out among the men as he regaled them with highly embellished, amusing stories of his encounters with the enemy, proving a great morale booster.

Cronje gave his consent and the two ladies, Miss Malan and Miss Watt, walked from the fort to be taken to meet him at his headquarters. Here they were questioned before one was placed in the charge of the Reverend Maury and the other in the charge of Mr Cameron. An unsympathetic Boer observer commented that they 'gave a pretence of being distressed': not surprising after twenty-two days without a change of clothes, cooped up under fire in either a wet tent or the tiny 'redoubt', with little sleep and a diet of rough Army rations. In view of the later adamant refusal of Cronje to allow the Forssman womenfolk to leave the fort, it is interesting to consider his motivation on this occasion. Did he hope to obtain some vital information regarding conditions in the fort after the New Year's Day attack, or was it kindness towards the teachers, who were on the staff of the Ladies Seminary and whom he knew from his position as a member of the local school board? Whatever the reason, only two days later, after they had again been interrogated by the war council, the ladies were sent away from the town under guard, presumably to the Orange Free State, as they had been made to promise never to teach in the Transvaal again.

Curiously neither Winsloe nor the other regular diarists in the fort recorded the reason for the teachers asking to return to their homes, merely relating that they left with the permission of Cronje. Possibly this was because the departure coincided with a matter of importance to the stomachs of the garrison and a preoccupation with Boer activities in and about the cemetery. Sometime during the day when the teachers left, a party from the fort succeeded in capturing eight oxen and four goats that had strayed within their reach. Not only was this a welcome supplement to their diminishing stock of tinned beef, much of which had been shot through and ruined on the parapets, but the cows were found to be in milk, providing some much-needed nourishment for the wounded. In a not-so-happy consequence, one of the captured cows gored Private Flynn of the Mounted Infantry.

Work in the Cemetery

The attention of both sides was now focused on the cemetery, which was clearly a key position. Their attempt to drive the British out of the magazine using Ou Griet having foundered, it was imperative for the Boers to complete the trench from the town, which would allow them to occupy the cemetery by both day and night. After dark on 5 January, a dozen burghers made their way into the cemetery and began digging. Simultaneously others started a trench from the town end by the cattle pound that stood between the wreckage of Jooste's house and the gaol. Their noise soon attracted shells and rifle fire from the British, which was countered by Boer fire from the town. The next morning the British attempted to knock down the cemetery wall with gunfire. Undeterred by the loss of some of their cover, the Boers again occupied the cemetery after dark and continued digging their trench. This night the British left them alone.

Becoming more confident, the next night, 7 January, the Boers sent a larger party to work in the cemetery. Casually they laid down their weapons before starting to dig and, despite there being some moonlight, no one detected the British patrol that crept up behind the wall facing the magazine from where they opened fire. Realising that the shots were not coming from the fort, the surprised Boers panicked and were grabbing their rifles when someone shouted, 'Here they come', adding to the confusion. Having no idea of the number of their attackers, the next shout, 'Retreat to the water furrow', was enough to make the mostly young and inexperienced Boers take to their heels. Leaping over the Grootvoor, they kept running until they reached the safety of the positions around the Jooste house. They were met by Commandant Jan Kock who, having been alerted by the shooting, had come forward with reinforcements. Angrily reprimanding the runaways he sent thirty men back into the cemetery to drive out the British and get on with the trench. They found the British gone. Next day the shamefaced absconders were the laughing-stock of the other Boers, despite protesting they had been outnumbered and lacked ammunition.

The events that occurred between 5 and 7 January were seen rather differently from inside the fort. Relieved that the Gunners had saved the magazine from the attentions of Ou Griet, Winsloe and his officers soon had fresh cause for concern as they heard the sound of digging at night and then at daylight saw the piles of new spoil marking the progress being made by the Boers on the trench linking the pound to the cemetery. During the night of 5 January when the sound of wheels suggested that Ou Griet was being moved into the cemetery, Dalrymple-Hay and Browne each with twenty men prepared to attack the place. However, shells and volley fire seemed to have been enough to drive the Boers out. In daylight the next morning, without great success, the Gunners attempted to knock down the cemetery wall with shellfire, hoping to deprive the Boers of its protection. At 3 o'clock that night for the first and only time Winsloe tested the alertness of his men. Suddenly the duty bugler sounded the alarm. In thirty seconds, before the last notes had died away and without any excitement, every man was in his fire position. Congratulating the men on their performance Winsloe promised there would never be another practice; all future alarms would be the real thing.

Despite the parapets facing the enemy being progressively raised as more sandbags were made − 200 a day were being produced − the Boer marksmen were still inflicting more casualties each day. To protect the hospital tents and give safer movement inside the walls, Winsloe decided to build a traverse of wagons diagonally across the fort. In darkness four

wagons, which had originally been placed in front of the exterior corners of
the fort, were brought into the ditch and dismantled; the parts were carried
inside the parapet, reassembled, filled with earth and then topped with
sandbags. To complete the traverse one of the remaining thirteen wagons
that were still parked out towards the magazine was dragged into the fort
ditch by using chains. An ASC soldier crept out in the dark to a wagon and
attached a chain, and then crawling back linked chain to chain until they
reached the ditch where a waiting gang hauled in the vehicle.

The threat to the Gunners manning the 9-pounders by the Boer occupation of the cemetery presented Winsloe with a dilemma. Trying to stop
the sapping activities of the Boers with shellfire alone meant heavy
expenditure from his finite stock of gun ammunition. The artillery had
started the war with only 400 rounds, of which nearly a quarter had already
been fired. The common shell – fused high explosive – needed for engaging
targets such as Ou Griet had to be husbanded, while the shrapnel shells,
which seemed to be having only limited effect on the widely dispersed and
well-hidden Boers, would be vital in stopping any attempt to rush the fort.
To launch an infantry attack on the cemetery over open ground under fire
from the town could lead to the destruction of a large part of his force.
Before making a crucial decision, Winsloe needed to know what was
happening behind the cemetery wall. Late in the afternoon of 7 January he
called for volunteers to form a reconnaissance patrol. Twenty men immediately came forward and six were chosen by drawing lots. Major Thornhill
drew the name of the officer to command, Lieutenant Lindsell being the
lucky man.

The weather was still unsettled but there had been some moonlight on
recent nights, which added to the chance of the patrol being detected. At
7.30 pm, Lindsell led his men out of the fort with the words, 'It is very
bright but follow me', setting off on a circuitous route round behind the
magazine. Dalrymple-Hay with twenty men took up a position outside the
fort ready to cover the withdrawal of Lindsell and his patrol, while the rest
of the garrison stood to at the parapets.

After what seemed an interminable wait, in reality thirty minutes, during
which time Winsloe feared for his men, a volley rang out followed by the
distinctive sound of a British 'Bulldog' revolver. The patrol had reached the
cemetery unseen and opened fire over the wall at the Boers they could
clearly see in the moonlight. Some were digging; others were sitting about
smoking; all their rifles had been casually laid aside. Taken completely by
surprise, the Boers panicked and rushed towards the gate in the wall on the
town side. Caught in this bottleneck, they gave the British time to fire two
more volleys, Lindsell himself firing ten revolver rounds. As the retreating
Boers disappeared, Lindsell's patrol came under fire from the town and a

Boer counter-attack developed from the direction of Jooste's house. Lindsell decided the time had come to depart and the patrol, despite being under fire, made their way back to the fort without loss. They were convinced that they had inflicted a number of casualties and the next morning swarms of vultures could be seen descending on the empty cemetery. The Boers were to deny any losses, as was their wont throughout the war; perhaps the bodies of black diggers, regarded as of no account, had been left behind.

Still jubilant at the success of the foray by Lindsell, the garrison received another boost when a sentry saw Ou Griet being transported out of the town on a wagon. They hoped they had seen the last of the gun that, although as yet it had done little damage, was becoming more accurate and dangerous with the improving skill of the Boer gunners.

From the intelligence he had now gathered and the speed of the counter-attack mounted against Lindsell, Winsloe was convinced that Cronje was determined to occupy the cemetery permanently and capture the magazine. Confirmation of this threat seemed to come quickly when before midnight outlying British sentries fired shots at men who appeared to be advancing from the cemetery. Quickly and quietly the garrison manned the parapets and fired two volleys in the direction of the supposed enemy. Small patrols were sent out to intercept any enemy but none were found suggesting the scare had been caused by a Boer working party that had lost its way in the dark. Assessing the options Winsloe pragmatically decided that he had neither the manpower nor gun ammunition to take the offensive action required to prevent the Boers pursuing their aim; he could only try to keep them at arm's length.

The Execution of Dr Woite

To the background noise of constant gun and rifle fire being exchanged between the combatants, the civilian inhabitants of Potchefstroom were still coming to terms with the bewildering events that had disrupted their lives when they were stunned by the news of the execution of one of their leading citizens.

On 6 January 1881 after a secret trial the war council condemned Christian Woite to death, the sentence to be carried out immediately. He was found guilty of spying for the British and sending a report back from the Paardekraal meeting to Commandant Raaff. This report had been found in the possession of Major Clarke at the time of his capture. Immediately the sentence became public, other Germans resident in the town hastily drew up a petition pleading that the death sentence be commuted. The petitioners had little time in which to act; consequently only a few signatures were gathered and the war council refused to entertain the appeal. From his prison Major Clarke protested to Cronje that the executions of van der

Linden and Dr Woite were unjust and illegal. He maintained that it was impossible to call them spies because the meeting at Paardekraal was supposed to be public and open to anyone. Besides, the war had not started until days after the meeting. This protest had no effect on Cronje who said the decision to try the two men was his responsibility alone.

In heart-rending circumstances, his wife and family were allowed a short visit to Woite, incarcerated in the same room that van der Linden had occupied before his execution. At 2 o'clock, the handcuffed Woite was taken under a strong guard down behind the Royal Hotel towards the river where a large number of armed Boers stood waiting around a ready-dug grave. A previously selected firing party, eight strong, was in position. The Reverend Kohler of the Berlin Mission, a countryman of Woite, his next-door neighbour and friend, offered a short but poignant prayer. The order was given to the firing party and Woite gave one convulsive bound upwards, falling hit by three bullets in the chest and one in the head. So died the 42-year-old Christian Woite, leaving a widow and nine children. Despite being handcuffed he had managed to scrawl in German on the wall of his cell:

> I trust in Jesus. I have given myself into his hands. I am glad to die; in Christ I shall live. In a little while I shall be no more seen; I go to the Father.
> C O Woite

Young of the Royal Hotel with some other loyalists witnessed the execution and later helped the Reverend Kohler to recover the body and bury it again in Woite's own garden, which he had loved.

CHAPTER 12

The Noose Tightens

8 to 17 January 1881: Days 25 to 34

The fighting at Potchefstroom now entered a new phase as Cronje revised his plans and set out to capture the fort by old-established siege methods, reaching out to the fort and magazine with saps and then encircling the British positions with fire trenches. These operations were to display a degree of military engineering expertise that must surely have been beyond the knowledge of Transvaal farmers. Commandant 'Buffelshoek' Lemmer, who had supervised the execution of Hans van der Linden, was the official military adviser to Cronje, but one account alleges that the general was steered by an unnamed Canadian and there was certainly at least one German ex-soldier among the burghers.

Each night, guards were assembled in the positions around Jooste's house ready to support the working parties and their escorts who were to go forward to the cemetery and continue digging. There was a marked reluctance among some burghers to take their turn in the forward positions, and shirkers had to be rooted out of their billets by the field cornets.

Van Graan Takes the Cemetery

The intrepid Dannie van Graan, who had been to the fore in the capture of the Landrost's office, and was now an officer, set about putting some heart into the timid by his personal example. Fearlessly he stayed in the cemetery with only a servant for a companion all day on 12 January, keeping up a lively fire on the British. The next night he formed up men in the cemetery for what was intended to be a morale-boosting sortie, but when a bugle alarm sounded from the fort and the British opened fire, continuing to shoot all night, the Boers took cover, crouching behind the wall, fearing a British attack. Van Graan did not give way and when no attack materialised he divided his men into three parties, which would take turns to hold the cemetery by day.

By his positive leadership, van Graan had taken permanent possession of the fire position most feared by Winsloe and his Royal Artillery officers. Working by night through rain and sometimes bitterly cold wind, the conscripted black labourers watched over by guards joined up the two

159

trenches connecting the cemetery and the pound. The trench was only deep
enough to protect a crawling man and was full of water, but at last the
Boers had a safe covered link to their forward position.

Another sap was begun immediately, extending out from the cemetery
towards the magazine. The 9-pounders opened fire as soon as the British
spotted the spoil being thrown up from this new trench running parallel to
the fort and only just over 200 yards away. Five precious shells failed to stop
the Boer excavations for more than a few minutes. Simultaneously the Boers
were working on a second main sap, which began near Steyne's house at the
southern end of their line. This trench pointed towards the right rear corner
of the fort and was soon to reach within 400 yards of the British defences.
The Boers were not checked by several shells that landed on or about
Steyne's.

While these preparatory operations were in progress, Ou Griet in the
charge of Field Cornet Joubert and heavily escorted was sent up to Rustenburg where the company of 2/21st was still defying Boer attacks on their
little redoubt.

The Siege Takes its Toll

Even before 13 January when van Graan consolidated his grip on the
cemetery, Boer activities in the area threatened the safe movement of men
and supplies between the fort and the magazine, which was always a
hazardous business only possible after dark. The summer grass springing
up everywhere as a result of the warm, wet weather would soon hide any
Boers creeping up close to the fort. By the end of the siege the fort was
surrounded by waving grass the height of an English cornfield, which
stayed green and defied every effort of the British to burn it off. Other
cover was provided for the Boers as the mealies left from uneaten forage in
the old horse lines sprouted and grew into maize plants 10 feet high. To
solve these problems Winsloe ordered a communication trench to be dug
between the fort and the magazine, work being started from both ends.
Listening posts were to be made 75 yards out in front of each face of the
fort connected by a zigzag trench. The sentries in these posts, pits with a
raised sandbag lip, were intended to give early warning of an enemy
approach on dark nights. When there was moonlight, sentries were kept
in the fort to stare out over the flickering shadows on the waving grass,
always a source of false alarms.

The morale of the garrison had remained high, a strong bond developing between the men and their officers who shared equally every danger,
task and privation to a degree unusual in the Victorian Army. However,
the lack of sleep owing to frequent alarms, inadequate food and the rav-

ages from being constantly wet and dirty were beginning to take their toll on officers and men alike. In addition to the physically heavy work organised by Lieutenant Lean, building the new wagon traverses, and the never-ending task of humping heavy sandbags to reinforce the parapets, they were now faced with digging several hundred yards of new trenches by night.

The usually optimistic Surgeon Wallis was depressed when he counted the number of dead and wounded, already twenty after only twenty-seven days of fighting. He worried that the wounded in their debilitated condition were making only slow if any recovery. The daily toll of gunshot wounds, such as those to Sergeant Troy who was hit in the head, demanded delicate surgical operations by Wallis assisted by Dr Sketchley, done in appalling, unhygienic conditions, with the fear that gangrene might set in. A high proportion of the casualties were shot in the head while on sentry duty, looking through gaps in the sandbags. How unnerving it must have been to take over a post from a dead comrade, his blood and brains scattered all over the rifle still held in his hands.

With cooking kept to a minimum by the shortage of fuel, the proximity of the latrines and the stinking water lying in the outside ditch it was only a matter of time before a dysentery epidemic struck. The first widespread symptoms appeared around 10 January 1881 and the first man died on 14 January. From this time on, sudden changes in recorded duties and gaps in the journals of the regular diarists show when officer after officer became unfit for duty. Major Thornhill was frequently confined to his bed, such as it was, leaving the young Rundle with the responsibility for operating the 9-pounders.

Despite increasing difficulties, the disciplined, ordered way of life for the garrison continued, regulated by the customary bugle calls, reveille, meals and lights out. Such goings-on must have mystified the Boers, who were now close enough to shout taunts like 'Come out, you old women, and fight like men'. The British usually replied with rifle fire and on one occasion cut down the republican flag flying over the Landrost's office with a carefully aimed shell.

A shortage of food, mainly owing to the loss of 1,000 pounds of tinned beef and 3,000 pounds of biscuits ruined when on the parapets, was now being felt. On 11 January 1881, twenty-eight days into the siege, Dunne obtained authority from Winsloe to cut the ration again. From that day until 22 January, half the biscuit ration was replaced by mealies on three days in the week; tea was cut, only being issued on the same three days. The ration for each man from which the cooks were supposed to concoct three meals a day comprised:

Monday, Wednesday, Saturday

Tinned beef	$\frac{1}{2}$ pound
Biscuits	$\frac{1}{2}$ pound
Mealies	$\frac{1}{2}$ pound
Coffee	$\frac{1}{2}$ ounce
Tea	$\frac{1}{2}$ ounce
Sugar	1 ounce
Erbwurst	1 tin
Rice	2 ounces
Lime juice	$\frac{1}{2}$ ounce
Salt	$\frac{1}{4}$ ounce
Pepper	$\frac{1}{36}$ ounce

Tuesday, Thursday, Friday, Sunday

Tinned beef	1 pound
Biscuits	$\frac{1}{2}$ pound
Flour	$\frac{1}{2}$ pound
Coffee	$\frac{1}{2}$ ounce
Sugar	1 ounce
Preserved vegetables	1 ounce
Salt	$\frac{1}{4}$ ounce
Pepper	$\frac{1}{36}$ ounce
Lime juice	$\frac{1}{2}$ ounce

On a few occasions when the men had been particularly wet for days on end, Winsloe authorised an issue of grog from the carefully husbanded few gallons of rum held by the Commissariat.

Enemy rifle shots from the cemetery and nearby trenches on 14 January drew the attention of Fusiliers in the magazine toward two natives who seemed to be trying to reach the fort through the pouring rain. When one was recognised as the messenger sent to Pretoria way back on 16 December 1880 they were beckoned to come into the magazine. Safely inside, one produced a tiny scrap of paper from inside a quill hidden in his clothes that appeared to be a dispatch from Colonel Bellairs. This was immediately taken across to the fort by Private William Humphries, who risked his life crossing the open ground in daylight. This news from Pretoria, the first for thirty-one days, made far from encouraging reading:

Officer Commanding, Potchefstroom.
Your report of 17th received. 94th from Lydenburg have been cut off. Hold out, but do not take the field with so small a force. At last, should no assistance reach in time render guns and arms useless
December 22, 1880, 6 pm   W B

The messenger was interrogated by John Nelson, who remembered him as the man he had instructed on behalf of Winsloe to carry a dispatch to Pretoria on 16 December. Nelson, a loyalist farmer, was a capable interpreter and for this and his local knowledge Winsloe had put him in charge of intelligence when with his two brothers he had come to the fort on 16 December to offer their services. Prior to the outbreak of hostilities, John Nelson had come to an arrangement with Major Clarke to gather information for him concerning Boer activities. The messenger told how he had left Pretoria twenty-four days before but had been captured by the Boers and kept prisoner for eighteen days in a laager three miles outside Pretoria. He had escaped when put to work herding cattle. He regaled the eager listeners with the rumours he had picked up on the way: there was fighting at Rustenburg but none at Pretoria; relief was expected from Natal; volunteers riding up from Kimberley were only thirty miles from Potchefstroom where it was said the Boers had suffered many killed and wounded.

The next night in pouring rain the two messengers stole away again bound for the Nelson farm fifteen miles north-east of Potchefstroom, on their way back to Pretoria with a dispatch from Winsloe. There would be no safe haven for them at the farm. John Nelson did not know that his father, a justice of the peace, was held prisoner in Potchefstroom by the Boers, or that their farm had been looted, cattle, pedigree horses and wagons stolen, and valuable growing timber cut down and removed by neighbouring Boers. The brave messengers were intercepted by the Boers and treated as spies when a search uncovered what they were carrying. Hidden in a quill was a dispatch from Winsloe to Bellairs, and letters he had written to the London *Times* and to his home in Scotland. The dispatch contained reference to making the guns and other weapons unserviceable in the event of surrender, and reported the clearance of the ammunition from the magazine and also the destruction of the unwanted gunpowder and cartridges. Cronje was incensed by what he read and was to make use of the dispatch to threaten Winsloe at a later date.

In the early hours of 15 January while the messengers were still in the fort, Dalrymple-Hay had gone across to the magazine to replace Lindsell in command and carry out some new orders. Before daylight the roof had been removed and the gable ends knocked off to the same level as the side walls. A fire step was built up inside allowing men to shoot all round between sandbags placed on top of the walls. With stone walls 2 feet 6 inches thick and 6 feet high the magazine became a formidable little blockhouse confronting the encircling Boers.

After being under siege for nearly five weeks the continuous heavy rain that had been falling for several days considerably worsened conditions in the fort, especially for the women, the sick and wounded. Hot food and drinks were the only alleviating comforts and it was at this unfortunate moment that fuel for cooking ran out.

Life in the Town

The only things that the disciplined, ordered life of the garrison had in common with that of the commandos and civilians living in the town were rain, mud and low fever.

Cronje and the war council conducted the war and civil affairs, and dispensed justice from the central chambers in Kerk Street next door to the Forssman house and store where the prisoners of war including Clarke and Raaff were kept. Across the street beside the Borrius printing works an empty store and the outbuildings of the Wesleyan Church had been taken over by the Boer commissariat. The fighting men of the commandos lived in encampments and billets scattered about the town using buildings around the Landrost's office, the bottom of the market square and in and about the Criterion Hotel. After a turn of duty in the pouring rain, often spent in a trench barefoot and knee-deep in water, always fearful of British fire or an attack, most burghers could only return to their billet for a rest. The fortunate local Potchefstroomers were able to go to their own homes and families to enjoy the luxury of a bath and bed.

At some time all gravitated to the commissariat area, nicknamed the 'Grub Camp', there to draw supplies or be fed. The Grub Camp, which held all the commandeered provisions, was controlled by Jac Scheepers, one of the early promotions made by Cronje, his only claim to authority being that like Bezuidenhout he had been imprisoned by the British for an ammunition offence. He was soon abusing his unaccustomed power and plenty, indulging his family and friends while neglecting the fighting men. When discovered, he was promptly relieved of his post. The main feature of the Grub Camp was the butchery to which cattle were brought each morning for slaughter. Waiting burghers took all they wanted leaving the offal and other unwanted remains to fester right there in the centre of the town. Nearby under some mulberry trees numerous huge pots of food and kettles were kept continually on the boil, attracting a stream of people to the area between their spells of duty. The place was a haven for skivers who preferred to eat and drink rather than become too involved in the fighting.

Some of the more petty regulations being imposed by the Boer authorities on the townspeople suggested that not only were the Boers creating a dubious source of revenue but they were venting their animosity on the British and others regarded as having behaved arrogantly since the annexation. For example, a person found guilty of entering the war council offices or other official premises without doffing his hat or of replacing it too soon after leaving was fined for disrespect. Fines varied from 1 shilling to £37 10s. When African servants of loyalists were conscripted to dig in the trenches they were paying the price for having chosen to work for a Briton rather than a Boer. Some were being punished for insolence remembered by an individual burgher from before the war.

Responding to the threatening demand for supplies that Cronje had sent on 5 January 1881, fourteen leading members of the commercial community, mostly but not exclusively British, representing the majority of trading firms based in Potchefstroom, assembled in the offices of Reid & Co. on 7 January. After a general discussion the meeting was adjourned while representatives went to Cronje's office seeking to clarify certain points. Before long they returned under no illusions about trying to bargain with the war council. The meeting promptly agreed that there was no alternative but to comply with the Boer demands. However, as the quantities of provisions required did not exist in the town it was decided to reconvene the meeting next day to resolve how the stores, which would cost £3,000, could be obtained and how transport costs could be met. Transport contractors would require payment in cash, which was in short supply and could amount to another £3,000.

Next day after discussion and a vote it was agreed that each firm should individually order a proportion of the total requirement from their peacetime suppliers in, of all places, Natal. The minutes of the meeting were sent to the war council and included a request that delivery of the stores be accepted in three equal parts and the time allowed for the first delivery be extended. Hoping to persuade the council to make a prompt payment, the traders offered to deliver the goods without adding a profit margin and only charge for transport at cost if the government would reimburse them as soon as possible after delivery for the amount of capital they had laid out, plus interest at the current bank rate. The traders received an unequivocal reply signed on behalf of the war council by the now all-powerful secretary, Buskes:

[Translation from Dutch]

Potchefstroom, Jan. 14, 1881.
A. Borchards, Esq., Secretary of meeting storekeepers, Potchefstroom.
Sir,
I have the honour to bring to your notice the following resolution, No. 5 of the War Council, dated Jan. 12, 1881:

The Council of War having heard the resolution of the storekeepers of Potchefstroom, passed in accordance with the order of the War Council, dated Jan. 3, 1881, resolves thereby:

(*a*) That the goods as ordered by letter of the Secretary, dated Jan. 5, 1881, must be delivered by the storekeepers, at prices laid down therein.

(*b*) That the mode of payments for such goods shall be regulated hereafter, as soon as it shall become apparent that the orders have been properly carried out by the storekeepers, and that the goods have been delivered by them at the places specified, as after security or certainty had been given by them for the due performance thereof.

(*c*) That the delivery shall be made in two instalments. The first half of each order within six weeks from date where mentioned, the second half within eight weeks from present date; and that the said storekeepers shall individually and collectively (in solidum) be held responsible for the due performance of the above.

In default of which due penalty of such a fine to be determined upon by the War Council if the said goods be not delivered within the time specified. The place of delivery to be at the office of the General, or any such place in Potchefstroom as shall be pointed out.

I have the honour to be,

Your obedient servant,

By order of the Council of War,

(Signed) C. H. Buyskas, Secretary.

In its judicial role the war council, having passed the death sentences on van der Linden and Christian Woite, sat in judgment on several of the volunteers recruited by Raaff. Despite being prisoners of war they received sentences ranging from three to twelve months' imprisonment with hard labour, which entailed digging in the trenches under fire. The public servants of the British, Landrost Goetze and his clerk Richard Impey, were only grudgingly released from custody on the enormous surety of £5,000 each.

The Ruse

There now occurred one of the most bizarre incidents of the whole war, an attempt to lure the garrison out of the fort by subterfuge.

It began when Ben Palmer returned from a business trip that had kept him away since before the war, to find that his wife and two children had left his house, which stood behind Church Street, and taken refuge in the fort. His wife Catherina, aged twenty-three, was the eldest daughter of Chevalier Forssman, and in the absence of her husband had accompanied her father and family when they had taken refuge with the British. Palmer, whose brother was a member of the Cape parliament, enjoyed a good relationship with the Boers and Cronje permitted him to send a letter into the fort asking his wife to return home.

At 11 am on 16 January 1881 a native runner carrying a flag of truce came out of the town through the pouring rain to the customary meeting place by the Grootvoor. He was met by the usual Fusilier sergeant who accepted the Palmer letter, also taking an official-looking envelope addressed to Colonel Winsloe, which the messenger passed to him surreptitiously together with a piece of tobacco. The truce lasted only a few minutes but there was time for a former German soldier to jump out of the nearest Boer trench and shout that he hoped Winsloe was not wounded, adding 'Tell the Colonel he would never have held out for so long had he not been a German.' Winsloe was highly amused. Born of British parents at Innerleithen, twenty-five miles south of Edinburgh, he could not have been less German. He guessed that amazingly he was being mistaken for a brother who had served with the German army.

Opening the envelope, Winsloe noticed that unlike the letter for Mrs Palmer it had not been franked by Cronje and bore no signs of having been seen by the Boers. The enclosed letter, which with the exception of the date was written in Morse code, purported to come from Colonel Bellairs and when deciphered read:

Thorndale Park, January 14th
Colonel Winsloe, am ordered to come to your rescue with 400 men. Shall advance to Potchefstroom in four divisions – one by Ventersdorp, one by Klerksdorp, one by Free State and one by Pretoria road. Will be at Potchefstroom on Monday next at daybreak; signal of arrival night before, three rockets from Vaal Kop. Shall attack the Boer laager on Ventersdorp road; when you hear firing, then march out to Klerksdorp road. Boers following will be attacked in the back from all sides.
                                                    W Bellairs Colonel

The general consensus among the British officers was that this was a hoax – 'the language and the pretend dispositions are most unmilitary and foolish'. After the armistice, Winsloe learned that the message had been concocted in Kruger's headquarters at Heidelberg. This probably accounts for the date not being in cipher but left open to be added when the opportunity came to slip the message into the fort as though unknown to the Boers. Cronje created this opening by delaying the delivery of the Palmer letter for forty-eight hours. Having been assured of her safe conduct, Winsloe permitted Mrs Palmer with her two infant children to leave the fort.

No rocket signals were seen during the night and the garrison standing to before dawn on 17 January 1881 watched and listened, intrigued as to what might happen next. They guessed that out in the quiet, behind the surrounding houses, walls and trees, hundreds of alert Boers lay concealed, waiting to ambush any exodus from the fort. Their suspicions that the affair was a fraud were confirmed by the unconvincing noises that came from the direction of Vaal Kop punctually at sun-up. First were loud thumps, which sounded more like dynamite or blasting powder than 9-pounder shells. These were followed by two ragged volleys that appeared to come from about fifty riflemen who fired from one position and then moved a short distance before firing again. There was none of the spontaneous, dispersed interchange of shots that would have occurred in a real fight. After about thirty minutes the Boers accepted that the British had not taken the bait and called off the operation. The whole inept charade had taken place in a violent storm and pouring rain through which the amused British soldiers watched a couple of hundred sodden horsemen, some wearing red jackets, trot cross-country back into the town. In derision Winsloe ordered Rundle to fire two shells into the horsemen to speed them on their way. The burghers, in no way dispirited by the failure of the trick, fired back as they passed the distant fort.

The probability is that the idea of a ruse, like the bogus message, emanated from Heidelberg, and the diversion did not deflect Cronje from his main plan, the systematic encirclement of the fort with trenches, from which the sheer weight of rifle fire would make the British position untenable. Working mostly by night, prisoners and conscripted labourers dug tirelessly under the watchful eye of their Boer guards, undeterred by British shells and bullets. The skilful use of huge bales of tight-packed wool pushed ahead of the diggers gave them considerable protection, another indication of someone having a trained knowledge of siege tactics.

By this date Cronje had put the redoubtable van Graan in charge of operations at the cemetery, replacing Field Cornet Muller. Muller had been involved at the cemetery since the fighting on 1 January and it was he who had given the panic order for the retreat that had turned into a rout when Lindsell attacked on 7 January. Muller, a German, was now given overall charge of constructing the trenches and fortifications. It is interesting to speculate, on circumstantial evidence, whether Muller was the former German soldier who confused Winsloe with his brother and was the trained soldier with enough military knowledge to provide Cronje with advice on siege methods.

CHAPTER 13

The Sortie

18 to 23 January 1881: Days 35 to 40

A race now developed between the two sides for control of the magazine. For the British it was vital to complete the trench, which would give a safe link to the fort, before the Boers digging out from the cemetery came close enough to rush the little blockhouse. The increasing number of casualties, wounded and sick had forced Winsloe to reduce the number holding the magazine to an officer, one sergeant and nine men including a signaller. Sometimes the shortage of officers fit for duty caused the sergeant to be left in command. While the Boers could call on a large pool of labour in addition to their fighting men, Winsloe had only his soldiers and the remaining twenty Commissariat drivers, three already wounded, to meet all the work to be done. Digging in the trench at the magazine end was made increasingly difficult and dangerous by the need to bail out the rain that fell continuously, day and night. Despite being given strict orders not to show themselves, two Fusiliers throwing out the water were severely wounded in one morning alone. The Fusiliers in the magazine had some success in hindering Boer progress when their fire forced the enemy to change the direction of the straight trench they were digging and take a slower zigzag course.

The Boers Encircle the Fort

On 18 January the weather improved for the better, ending four days of continuous rain when there had been hardly a dry hour. This came as a great relief to the garrison, who had been struggling day and night to prevent the rainwater that accumulated in the stinking ditch from seeping into the drinking-water well. Everyone took pleasure in the chance to dry out their sodden clothing and what bedding they possessed, but a sharp reminder of their situation came with the news that Private Thornbeck had died in agony, having suffered torture from the scalp wound received sixteen days earlier. Even his burial at the rear of the fort after dark was not without danger, as vigilant Boers hearing some activity opened fire. The Boers also took advantage of the drier conditions to push ahead their digging with renewed vigour, giving the garrison an uncomfortable feeling that they would soon be completely hemmed in.

By Wednesday, 19 January 1881, the shallow trench between the fort and the magazine was complete although only deep enough to protect a crawling man. The ever-lengthening Boer trench from the cemetery seemed to be reaching out to pass behind and beyond the magazine. In an effort to stop their progress, Rundle trained his guns in daylight on to the trench area, ready to open fire when the labourers moved in to work after dark. Dalrymple-Hay and his men in the magazine stood ready, while Lieutenant Browne led a party of Fusiliers along the new trench to take up a fire position.

When in bright moonlight a large party began work in the enemy trench, the 9-pounders hit them with two shells and the infantry delivered several volleys. The enemy workers stopped for a short while but soon resumed, continuing all night despite fire from the magazine. By daylight they had progressed another 30 yards. Winsloe could see no alternative but to dig yet another trench out from the magazine towards the Boer works, attempting to keep them at a distance. In a couple of days a short trench with a dug-out fire position at the end was completed bringing the two sides within 40 yards of each other. Able to shout across, some of the young Boers were tempted even to throw stones at the Fusiliers.

The siege had now entered the thirty-eighth day, twenty-five days since Commissary Dunne had assessed that he held only enough full rations to sustain the garrison for one month. However, this had been only a basis for calculation, and supplies had been eked out by cutting the daily ration of basic items, beef and biscuits, by almost half on 11 January 1881. Now as flour began to run out and stocks of biscuit and beef looked pitifully small, the time had come for another reduction. From 22 January the remaining flour was to be reserved for the wounded, the sick and the women refugees. The officers and men would have to subsist on half a pound of meat, half a pound of biscuits and half a pound of mealies a day, with a little coffee and tea while these lasted. Wood fuel for cooking had all been used by 15 January, since when, in great danger from the listening Boer marksmen who fired at every rattle of a chain and rumble of a wheel, the wagons lying outside the fort had been dragged in one at a time to be broken up for firewood. The process that had begun with the hauling in of a wagon to complete the traverse inside the fort was completed in three weeks when all the wagons had been recovered.

After a suspiciously quiet night the British looked out at daybreak on 21 January to see that their worst fears had been realised. The Boers had dug fire positions on the rising ground in the rear of the fort completing their encirclement. There was a new trench 500 yards to the rear of the magazine and another 300 yards out from the right face, the southern side, of the fort itself. Until now the wide ditch at the back of the fort had been screened from direct enemy fire and been used for cooking, latrines and access to the magazine. This would no longer be safely possible in daylight. The parapet at the rear of the fort would also have to be raised considerably, needing even more sandbags to be made and demanding extra heavy manual work from the already tired men.

The enemy soon demonstrated their advantage by opening fire from the new positions and those in the town simultaneously, killing another Fusilier. The 9-pounders, which until now had faced the town, had to be reposi-tioned to engage the new targets, which were tactically well sited, being screened from the gun pits by the fort itself. Using indirect fire, Rundle sent several shells at the new trenches, eventually silencing one with shrapnel, time-fused to burst overhead. Under a galling fire the garrison was faced with the unpalatable truth that the Boers now commanded all four sides of the fort and significantly denied the safe use of the rear ditch, which was proving vital to survival. In what had become a process of move and countermove, the British had failed to prevent their encirclement and as darkness fell could only await the next development.

The Storming Party

Despite their predicament or perhaps because of it the garrison awaited the dawn on 22 January 1881 remembering that this was the second anni-versary of Isandhlwana and Rorke's Drift – a day of poignant personal memories for several of them. With daylight on a fine morning, the soldiers began to move about. Shots crashed in from another new Boer trench less than 300 yards from the rear ditch of the fort. One man was wounded, another had the cap on his head shot through and a third was severely bruised by a bullet that ripped open his shirt. To prevent even more casualties this Boer nest had to be cleared sooner rather than later even if it meant an assault over open ground in daylight. From the fort the enemy trench did not appear large enough to hold many men; therefore Winsloe with his limited resources decided that a storming party of one officer, one sergeant and ten men would suffice. Volunteers were called for, officers from the Fusiliers only but NCOs and men from all the corps that made up the garrison. Inundated, Winsloe ultimately selected Dalrymple-Hay, leaving the men to be decided by drawing lots. The 22-year-old Dalrymple-Hay was a popular choice, having proved himself a cool, brave young officer, who was idolised by his men.

A sudden attack in daylight would not be expected by the Boers and might achieve some surprise. With this in mind Winsloe devised a simple plan to engage all the main Boer positions with covering rifle and artillery fire while an assault was made from the trench leading to the magazine. A 9-pounder shell opening the bombardment would be the signal to commence the covering fire and the attack to begin.

Dalrymple-Hay positioned his men in the magazine trench and then sent word to Winsloe that he was ready. At 12 o'clock the signal shell was fired, and the walls of the fort appeared to 'vomit flame' as a barrage of bullets and shells tore into the unsuspecting Boers. The assault party with fixed bayonets led by Dalrymple-Hay, sword in one hand and pistol in the other, jumped out of the trench and and ran uphill towards their objective. The Boers recovered and responded immediately, catching the charging men in crossfire from wherever they could be seen.

Driver Walsh RA fell mortally wounded, his thigh shot through; then Private Colvin RSF collapsed, his arm torn apart by what seemed to be an explosive bullet; Private Banks RSF went down, hit in the thigh. The moment they saw their comrades wounded, two Gunners, Driver Gibson and Trumpeter Martin, who had saved his own life escaping from the Zulus at Isandhlwana, rushed out of the fort ignoring the enemy fire to carry the dying Walsh back to safety. This done, Gibson ran out again, this time accompanied by Driver Pead RA to bring in the wounded Colvin. Eventually Gibson and Pead, both in their twenties, and Martin, only just eighteen, were each awarded the Distinguished Conduct Medal for their gallantry.

Having run forward about 150 yards, Dalrymple-Hay halted his men for a moment to get their breath; then with an encouraging shout he led the final charge straight at the Boer trench. Before Dalrymple-Hay and his men reached the trench, a white flag came up on a ramrod. The delighted subaltern discovered he had captured four prisoners, two of whom were severely wounded, together with six rifles, a lot of ammunition, entrenching tools and some coveted waterproof coats. Handcuffing the fit prisoners and tending to the wounded, Dalrymple-Hay prepared to withdraw, taking the Boers with him. The position was far too isolated to be held; therefore the attackers must again risk enemy fire to regain the shelter of the fort.

When Dalrymple-Hay and his party were safely home, Winsloe sent a letter to Cronje inviting him to send out men to remove the Boer killed and wounded from the battleground. Straight away a figure appeared holding up a 'huge Geneva Cross Flag' and the British raised a white flag in reply. The flag bearer who approached, looking very uncertain and far from happy, was recognised by Winsloe as a Dr Mahler whom he had met at Standerton as a photographer. Surgeon Wallis and Dr Sketchley were already busy treating the Boer wounded, and Mahler was perfectly happy to let them continue their ministrations while he and Winsloe sat down and chatted under one of the wagons still standing outside the fort.

Enjoying his first smoke for a month from a handsome carved pipe handed to him by Mahler, Winsloe listened to the doctor's story. Mahler did not wish to fight and had been ordered against his will to Potchefstroom for duty as a medical officer. Told to approach the fort with his Red Cross flag, he was terrified that the British would open fire on him. After the fort surrendered, Winsloe met the friendly doctor again and learned that he had been put in irons by Cronje for fraternising. He showed Winsloe his left hand minus a finger, which had been amputated after being fractured by a British shell splinter.

Unfortunately for posterity, the British doctors did not record in the same meticulous way they did for their own the number of enemy casualties they treated. Winsloe claimed to have seen eleven Boers fall, but the Transvaal chronicler J. D. Weilbach differs; he states the number of wounded as two seriously, who were taken prisoner, and three others slightly, figures which were repeated in the final Boer casualty list for the war. However, immediately after being exchanged by the British, one of the Boers taken prisoner told loyalists in the town that he personally had seen fifteen of his comrades killed or wounded.

The British lent the Boers stretchers to carry away their casualties. Next morning these were returned with a present of fruit for the wounded and a small quantity of carbolic acid, lint and oil that Surgeon Wallis had requested. Winsloe, touched by this humane gesture, wrote a letter of thanks to Cronje. He also wrote the first of several letters he was to address to Cronje complaining about the use of explosive bullets from sporting rifles such as that which had torn apart the arm of Private Colvin.

During the afternoon an exchange of prisoners was negotiated; the four Boers captured by Dalrymple-Hay would be handed over in return for three Fusiliers and one of Raaff's volunteers, all taken prisoner at the Landrost's office. The Fusiliers had been wounded and unfit to travel when their comrades had been sent to the Orange Free State on Christmas Day. The war council still kept two sergeants and three corporals from the original batch of prisoners, and their reason for exchanging one of Raaff's detested volunteers is obscure. On their return, the British prisoners looked well and spoke highly of their treatment; similarly the four released burghers told of the courtesy of the British and their generosity in giving them a tin of beef and some biscuits on their departure. Tinned beef was regarded as a luxury by the Boers, who subsisted on the toughest of ox meat and no bread, but it is not unlikely that the British generosity owed something to a wish to impress the enemy that they were not short of food.

The prolonged truce lasted until nearly dark while the casualties were removed and the prisoners exchanged. During this time both sides moved about freely, enabling the British to count more than 300 Boers in the area of the cemetery and the adjoining trenches. Shortly after the white flags were lowered a shot rang out from the prison. 'Hostilities had recommenced, and we were enemies again.' The success of the sortie gave a considerable boost to British morale, which was further lifted when the released prisoners brought news of the large reinforcements that had already landed in Natal from England and India, adding to their hopes of being relieved.

Early next morning, 23 January 1881, the fortieth day of the siege, a Union Jack was hoisted over the fort to the loud cheers of the garrison. Since the capture of the Landrost's office in December, the British had not possessed a Union Jack they could fly in defiance of the enemy. Now the Royal Artillery men had remedied this deficiency by concocting a flag from the red and white linings of the cloaks belonging to Lieutenant Rundle and one of his sergeants and a blue serge coat offered up by one of the infantry officers.

CHAPTER 14

Holding On

24 January to 5 February 1881: Days 41 to 53

The resolve, determination and judgement of Winsloe were now to be severely tested. In a matter of forty-eight hours the Boers were seen not only to have reoccupied the trench cleared by Dalrymple-Hay but to have improved the position with sandbags. It had become a formidable strong point, which stood menacingly above the level of the rear parapet of the fort. Winsloe had two alternatives: another assault, which inevitably meant more casualties, or demanding extra backbreaking work from his tired men to raise the rear wall in an uncertain hope of providing adequate protection for the defenders. The strength of the garrison was already depleted by seventeen dead and upwards of thirty wounded, some dying in excruciating pain in the appalling conditions provided by the hospital tents or surviving scattered about by their posts at the parapets.

Enemy fire criss-crossed the fort from their encircling positions; British sentries standing behind even the smallest loophole were in constant danger from snipers. Boer shooting remained consistently accurate even after dark, and not until after the war did the British discover their secret. Some inventive burgher had devised a rifle rest made from a thick log of wood about 2 feet long, which gave a prone marksman complete cover. Through the log was cut a hole large enough to admit a rifle barrel at the firer's end widening to 6 or 8 inches at the other; from this the rifle was ranged and aimed at a selected target in daylight and then wedged into position. All that was required to make an accurate shot in darkness was to squeeze the trigger. Nearly fifty of these 'fixed line' devices were brought into use, the principle of the aperture resembling an arrow slit in the wall of a medieval castle.

As the number of wounded continued to rise, among them one of the Nelson brothers, there were many eager for another charge at the enemy. Wiser counsel prevailed and Winsloe decided against this course, his judgement being vindicated when the Boers seemed to have abandoned their new vantage point. Any feelings of relief were short-lived as reports came in from the magazine of increased digging by the enemy at the end of their trench approaching from the cemetery.

Apart from the enemy, a new threat to the garrison appeared on 27 January when a case of enteric fever (typhoid) was diagnosed. Until now they had been relatively free of sickness other than diarrhoea brought on by the poor diet and general fatigue. Enteric gave the doctors, Wallis and Sketchley, great cause for concern. Victims of this highly infectious disease must be kept isolated, and they had to be fed from the inadequate rations, which were guaranteed to aggravate the condition.

Ou Griet Returns

The garrison was again taken by surprise at dawn next day, 28 January 1881, the forty-fifth day of the siege, when Ou Griet opened fire. The old gun had last been seen twenty days before being carted out of the town. It was now concealed at a range of 500 yards near the ruins of Jooste's house, from where it was to fire on the fort nearly every day until 10 March. All the British were ever to see of the gun was the flash when it fired and an occasional glimpse of a man who appeared to be observing the shots. The Boers had learned a lesson; this time the gun was well hidden among bushes and partly screened by a house. Rundle, who could not afford to waste shells, only returned fire when a flash was seen. The house protecting Ou Griet seemed unusually solid and impervious to the British gunfire; consequently the Boer cannon was never silenced for very long, continuing to fire on average ten rounds a day. The accuracy of the Boer gunners improved with practice until they were regularly hitting the fort although not doing a great deal of damage. When the defenders had seen sandbags displaced to fall and injure men, splinters fly off the traverse wagons and a rifle shattered they realised the danger of a 5-pound ball ricocheting around inside the fort. A sentry was detailed to watch out for Ou Griet and give the warning cry 'Down' the moment he saw a flash. Everyone was soon adept at falling flat on their faces to avoid the incoming balls.

The events of that last week of January 1881 gave the garrison little cause for optimism, but such was their faith in General Colley that once they heard from the exchanged prisoners that reinforcements had arrived in Natal they calculated that he must come to their relief any day now. On 1 February, Winsloe instructed Major Thornhill to organise a look-out party to keep all the surrounding hills under constant observation for flashing light signals by day and rockets by night. A home-made heliograph improvised from a mirror stood in readiness to reply.

Late one evening a look-out man called to Winsloe, reporting rockets over the hills in the direction of Heidelberg. Excited, everyone turned out to stare, including the ladies wrapped up in their ulsters. All were convinced they were seeing rockets and, fully expectant that relief would arrive in a matter of hours, they happily went off to try to sleep. Some dreamed or imagined they heard bagpipes coming down the Heidelberg road to the tune of 'The Campbells are coming'. Disappointment came next morning when a helmet hoisted above the parapet was promptly shot through.

Once again their hopes would come to nothing. Towards the end of January, Colley had concluded that Potchefstroom could not hold out much longer and decided to attempt its relief by breaking through the Boer positions at Laing's Nek using the limited force he had assembled. On 28 January a gallant attack by the 58th Regiment was driven back by the Boers. The British lost 197 officers and men killed and wounded. Colley had no recourse but to await the reinforcements on their way from India and Britain.

Events in the Town

Under the direction of Muller and van Graan and aided by the spell of better weather, the efforts of the Boers to complete their encirclement of the British had gained a new momentum. Commandant Jan Kock and van Graan devised a new plan. They proposed building a redoubt at the end of their cemetery trench that would overlook the magazine, enabling them to neutralise the place and fire down the British communication trench. Soil dug out of a huge hole would be used to fill barrels and sacks, which abounded in Potchefstroom. The barrels would form a solid base on which the sacks could be piled up. The extension of the trench and the new redoubt would require all the workers the Boers could muster including prisoners of war. There was outrage among the loyalists when this abuse of the prisoners became known but they had yet to learn the lengths to which the Boers would go in order to conscript the labour they needed.

When Ou Griet had arrived back from Rustenburg, where it had achieved nothing, it had been put in the charge of a new gunner and was again used against the fort. A position was carefully prepared near to the ruins of Jooste's house designed to give the gun and its crew the maximum protection. A small house was filled with sacks of earth to shelter the gun from British shells when being loaded or not in use. The firing position was next to the house among thick bushes that hid the gun mounted on its low carriage and gave cover to the crew pulling the gun into position using ropes. To reload, the gun was dragged back behind the house again. Pelser the gunner insisted on more carefully cast shot that would give greater accuracy, laying and firing the gun himself and observing each shot from among the bushes, dropping to the ground when he saw the flash of a replying 9-pounder.

In the midst of all the local military activity news began to filter through by letter and individuals coming from the Orange Free State of the rapid marches being made by the British reinforcements towards the main Boer commando under Joubert occupying a position on the Natal frontier below Majuba Hill. The rumours of an imminent British attack that circulated in the town were only partly discounted by the Boer authorities, consequently causing some disquiet among Boer sympathisers. When on 20 January two drafts of men, one of twenty-five and another of fifty, were ordered to Heidelberg there was open concern that the town was being exposed to a sortie from the fort. The drafts were slow to depart, blaming a twenty-four hour delay on the lack of transport. Some were reluctant to leave their families but many were relieved to be freed from the danger of fighting in the Potchefstroom trenches.

The men were hardly gone when the feared British sortie took place on 22 January. Despite the attack being on the trenches and not the town there was panic in the streets even among the burghers and it took threats and stern action by the officers to restore order. Two hundred men were brought in from outlying laagers to rebuild confidence and ensure that work was continued on the trenches, which included improving the one cleared by Dalrymple-Hay and his men.

This incident was only one of the many frightening and bewildering occurrences experienced by the ordinary people of Potchefstroom as they attempted to pursue their lives on the edge of a battle, in a town under military occupation and a primitive form of martial law. Not the least of the hazards were the stray bullets from the combatants, which occasionally hit people in the street, and British shells, which fell among the houses; one lodged in the roof of the Royal Hotel during a funeral but fortunately failed to explode.

The scare created by the British sortie had hardly subsided by Sunday, 23 January 1881 when thirty prisoners from the 94th Connaught Rangers, wounded at Bronkhorst Spruit, arrived in the town on their way to be released in the Orange Free State. While they rested and were being fed, and given tobacco and civilian clothes, the men were visited by some of the prominent loyalists led by Smart, the Standard Bank manager, and Young of the Royal Hotel. They had requested permission to send the prisoners some refreshments but this had been peremptorily refused by Buskes who, as secretary to the war council, had taken upon himself the authority to control everything he chose. Happily for the prisoners other more humane burghers intervened, allowing gifts of fruit and wine to be delivered. When it became known that one of the sergeants was a Freemason, members of the Potchefstroom Masonic lodge collected £17, which they gave to him. Other loyalists raised more money, which they entrusted to another prisoner, to

provide necessities for the party on their journey. The prisoners demonstrated their gratitude as they marched away by giving three cheers for
Potchefstroom and singing, 'For they are jolly good fellows'. As they passed
the Royal Hotel they shouted, 'We shall never forget Mr Young and the
Royal – God bless him.'

Since his detention on the night before the war began, Smart always
seems to have been in the forefront of any confrontation with the Boers, and
his bank, which he kept open, was often the focus of their attention. On one
occasion a drunken Boer with a loaded rifle entered the bank and then went
into the attached dwelling house where he terrified the lady occupants
before being overpowered by Smart and two other unarmed companions
who dragged the miscreant to the war council office. Next day when sober
the Boer was examined, and being unable to pay a fine was sentenced to
eight days' hard labour – remarkable as he was the first and probably only
Boer arrested by an Englishman during the war. Another time Smart was
arrested and questioned after it had been reported in the Kimberley
Diamond News that he had mined the bank with dynamite to prevent it
being plundered by the Boers.

About this stage of the siege Leask, the Klerksdorp trader, received 'a
kindly but pressing invitation' summoning him to the Boer headquarters at
Potchefstroom. Under escort and taking a circuitous route to avoid fire from
the fort he arrived to find himself in front of Cronje and a court attended by
200 burghers, most of whom knew him well. The atmosphere was not
menacing or unfriendly when the puzzled Leask asked what charges were
being made against him.

Cronje, who was an old friend, a fellow member of the Klerksdorp school
board and a regular customer of his business, handed Leask a letter that had
been intercepted by the Boers. This came from Christopher Bethel, a
business associate, innocently enclosing a banker's draft for £80 and telling
Leask that he was sending two wagons loaded with produce. However, in a
postscript Bethel asked Leask to inform Colonel Winsloe that he could
bring 5,000 tribesmen to assist against the Boers and the number increased
to 50,000 if required. Invited to offer his defence, Leask replied that he
could not be responsible for anything written to him by a hotheaded fool.
Bethel was well known as having been forced to resign his commission in
the British Army when caught cheating at cards. Such was his reputation
and standing that Leask easily persuaded the court of his innocence of any
complicity in Bethel's scheme, but under protest he was made to sign an
agreement that he would not aid the British. Addressing the court he said,
'You have a bond for my person and property; I suppose my soul is my
own', facetiously adding that perhaps they did not consider his soul had any
security value. This remark appealed to the Boer sense of humour, roars of

laughter restoring the friendly atmosphere to these extraordinary proceedings.

A far more embarrassing incident for the Boers involved the arrest outside the town of a young man named Cowell on suspicion of being a British spy carrying dispatches from Pretoria for delivery to Colonel Winsloe in the fort. Cowell had been brought up by ex-President Pretorius, now a member of the Triumvirate, and when questioned admitted having been in Pretoria. Not knowing what to do, the perplexed war council solved their dilemma by passing him on to Heidelberg for interrogation.

Hard-pressed for the manpower and finance needed to pursue the new ambitious plans to bring about a British surrender, the war council issued an autocratic order requiring most of the townsmen, irrespective of their sympathies, to report for service on Monday, 31 January 1881 or face a fine. It transpired that some would be given the alternative to service of paying a contribution of £10 or more on a sliding scale towards the cost of the war. The contribution would be decided by three commissioners appointed by the war council, one of whom was Erasmus, the erstwhile meat and forage contractor to the British, now despised and shunned by every loyalist. Incensed, the loyalists protested that as subjects of the Queen they would not take up arms against the British. Many wrote to the council pointing out that since they no longer had any business or employment they were unable to pay a levy or fine.

The protests were ignored and on the appointed day all those who were required to give service were told to report to the Landrost's office, and those who were to make the cash payment were directed to the war council offices. Outside the Landrost's office, Commandant Wolmorans faced a gathering of nearly 200 to whom he gave the choice of serving the republic or openly declaring their allegiance to the British crown. Seventeen courageously stepped forward, declining to serve the enemies of Britain. These staunch loyalists were told they would be permitted to stay in their homes provided they paid their fines and made no trouble, but were warned that in the event of their causing any disturbance they would be packed off into the fort.

Pressure was also brought to bear on suspected loyalists living outside the town. Roscher, the field cornet of Ventersdorp who had accompanied Raaff on one of his trips to meet Cronje before the war, was replaced by a Boer and sentenced to hard labour when he refused to take arms against the British. He was one of those made to work in the trenches, where he was wounded by British fire. Roscher subsequently complained to the British government that other young members of his family had been forced to serve with the Boers against his wishes.

On 2 February 1881 copies of the *Staats Courant* rolled off the presses in the Borrius printing works publishing the news of the British defeat at Laing's Nek on 28 January 1881. In addition to quoting verbatim reports from Commandant-General Joubert to Paul Kruger and to Cronje it contained a letter from Colley to Joubert requesting permission to remove the British dead and wounded from the battlefield. Quite reasonably the Boers assumed that if Winsloe was given such authentic information he must surely realise the futility of any further resistance.

However, Cronje felt he required the permission of the Triumvirate before passing the official gazette to the enemy. Communication with Heidelberg was tenuous and not rapid; the recently contracted weekly mail coach took twenty hours for the journey and consequently it took two days for copies of the gazette to reach the Triumvirate and their authority to come back to Cronje. During this hiatus all sorts of rumours regarding the battle circulated among the dismayed and disbelieving loyalists.

From the message intercepted on its way to the Nelson farm in mid-January, Cronje was well aware that Winsloe was under orders to destroy his guns, weapons and ammunition before surrendering, and that this must be stopped. The guns that the Boers had needed earlier to support an attack on Pretoria would be more important in any future fighting against Colley on the Natal frontier. To an extent Cronje had gone against the main Boer strategic policy in pursuing his single-minded efforts to capture these guns. Now his reputation would be at stake. When the gazette was finally sent into the fort it was accompanied by a threatening letter:

Commandant-General of H.M. Troops in the camp at Potchefstroom.

Potchefstroom,
4th February, 1881.

Sir,

We are informed by one of your spies caught on the road to Pretoria, that you are wantonly destroying powder and ammunition, and if the moment comes for surrender, that you will do so only after having nailed up your guns.

We remember you, Sir, that this is entirely against the usages and customs of civilized warfare to do so.

In the late Prussian-French war, when Metz surrendered, a few of the French prisoners commenced to destroy their arms, but they were stopped to do so by their own Officers, because such acts would make them forfeit all claims to a kind treatment.

We from our side wish to follow the line of warfare established amongst civilized nations; we adopt the principles laid down at Geneva and if therefore that we warn you not to commit the acts whereof you are accused, it will only make the conditions of the inevitable surrender harder.

Sir, I have the pleasure of enclosing herein our last *Staats Courant*, out of which you can read the latest battle which has been fought with H.M. troops under command of Sir G. Pomeroy Colley, and the Boer forces under command of Commandant-General P. Joubert.

I have &c.,

(Signed) P. A. Cronje, Commandant-General.

Winsloe Reproves Cronje

As the siege reached the fiftieth day, 2 February 1881, it was that family-like *esprit de corps* fostered in British Army units that sustained a garrison facing hunger, danger and unrelenting toil. Notwithstanding all the efforts to strengthen and improve the parapets especially the newly threatened rear wall, the interior of the fort remained extremely vulnerable to enemy fire and every day there were more casualties. The defenders of the isolated magazine, now reduced to eight Mounted Infantrymen in the charge of Colour-Sergeant Wall, had over time suffered more than their share of casualties but by some perverse logic the post was regarded by the troops as safer than the fort. The Boer trenches and the British weapon pits around the magazine were in such close proximity that the occupants would shout at one another with provocative bravado. Typically when opening fire at daybreak the Boers would taunt, 'Why don't you get up and fire a volley at us?', to which the Fusiliers would reply 'If you don't keep d—n quiet down there, two or three of us will go and charge you to — out of that.'

Death and the suffering of the wounded touched everyone in this close-knit community very directly. This was particularly apparent when a popular family man such as Corporal Gartshore died, shot through the head when firing at the enemy, with one word 'Heaven', or next day when Driver Pead who had risked his life rescuing wounded during the sortie was himself severely wounded in the leg. Within another twenty-four hours Driver Walsh, his thigh smashed to pieces during the charge, died after ten days of torture. Conversely there was general relief when Dr Sketchley made it known that Private Colvin, who had been hit by an explosive bullet, was recovering and would survive.

On 4 February Surgeon Wallis was shot in the thigh as he went about his duties, and it was later that morning, 11 am, that a white flag was seen being carried out of the town towards the usual rendezvous. Winsloe sent his sergeant to meet the Boer messenger, who only waited long enough to hand over a letter and a copy of the *Staats Courant*. Whatever Winsloe may have felt when he read the news of Colley's defeat he sent an intentionally facetious message back to Cronje saying that he would be pleased to receive the gazette regularly. He also sent a strongly worded reply to the threats from Cronje:

From Bt.-Lieut-Colonel R. W. C. Winsloe, Royal Scots Fusiliers, Commanding H.M. Troops, Potchefstroom, to P. A. Cronjé, Esq., styling himself Commandant-General of the Boer forces.

Potchefstroom,
4th February, 1881.

Sir,

I have the honour to acknowledge the receipt of your letter of this day's date.

(1) I beg, without wishing to be discourteous, to decline to enter on any subject which may have been raised by any messenger of mine.

(2) I thank you for the hints you give me as to the customs of civilized warfare and would ask to be allowed to assure you that I have been accustomed to none other, and that I have no intention of breaking these rules in the smallest particular.

(3) In the second paragraph of your letter I find the following, viz, 'We from our side wish to follow the line of warfare established amongst civilized nations; we adopt the principles laid down at Geneva, &c.'

I take leave, Sir, for the third time, to remind you of the fact of explosive shells from sporting rifles having been fired into my camp and that this practice is still continued.

This, I before stated and am still willing to believe is done contrary to your orders, and I again ask that it be immediately discontinued, being contrary to the provisions of the Geneva Convention which you wish to follow.

(4) If you will do me the favour of sending one of your doctors to my camp, I will show him the wound for your satisfaction.

(5) I have not yet thought of surrender and therefore think you will excuse my discussing that point.

(6) I shall feel obliged by receiving answer to paragraphs 3 and 4 at your earliest convenience.

(7) I enclose a letter from one of my surgeons for your information.

I have, &c.,

(Signed) R. W. C. Winsloe, Bt-Lieut. Colonel, R.S. Fusiliers,

Commanding H.M. Troops,
Potchefstroom.

The Officer Commanding Potchefstroom.

I hereby certify that Private Colvin at present in Hospital here, was wounded on the 22nd January by a rifle bullet, the said bullet or missile being in my opinion of an explosive character, as no kind of bullet whatever allowed by the Geneva Convention could have caused such a wound as the man is now suffering from.

(Signed) K. S. Wallis, Surgeon, A.M.D.,

(Signed) C. G. Sketchley, Acting District Surgeon of Potchefstroom.

Next day, 5 February, another letter from Cronje arrived at the fort, which Winsloe returned unopened. He took offence at the way in which it was addressed, regarding this as insulting 'to my rank in Her Majesty's Service', penning this reason on the outside of the envelope.

That same day Winsloe was himself wounded in a thigh.

CHAPTER 15

The Beginning of the End

6 February to 3 March 1881: Days 54 to 79

Now began weary weeks of attrition as the British garrison growing progressively weaker and exposed to unrelenting, harassing fire did what they could to prevent the Boer net drawing ever tighter. The weather continued to play a major part in their lives, whether dry and burning hot as it was during the first six days of February, or subsequently when the sudden violent thunderstorms returned bringing pouring rain that drenched everyone, leaving the floor of the fort and the gun pits inches deep in liquid mud.

Starvation Rations

The lack of food was already sapping the stamina of the otherwise physically fit young soldiers but as items of supplies ran out there was no alternative but to cut the daily ration even further. Sugar was all gone by 6 February, the day it became necessary to make salt issues only on alternate days. Biscuits were replaced by a daily allowance of 1 pound of mealies and 2 pounds of kaffir corn (millet). This grain was boiled up into a kind of porridge to which was added grass and young, green mealie stalks gathered outside the fort at night, to prevent scurvy.

There was insufficient fuel for the lengthy cooking needed to soften the hard kernels so men were set to making a kind of flour; some tried grinding with a pair of flat stones and others used an iron bolt as a pestle to pound the grain in a mortar provided by the hub of a wagon wheel. The wounded performing these tasks presented a bizarre picture; two men, both with one arm in a sling, worked as a team, each using his good arm. The badly wounded were given bread until the flour finally ran out, supplemented with such of the medical comforts as remained: beef tea, a little rice and a much-disliked gruel concocted from erbwurst.

There were now over thirty wounded and chronically sick crammed into the leaky hospital tents or languishing in dugouts cut in the rear ditch near the gun pits. These damp dark holes covered over with corrugated iron sheets recovered from the roof of the magazine were used to isolate cases of enteric fever, in some instances for many days until the unfortunate patient

185

died. The four most badly wounded were always given the only stretchers;
everyone else lay on the bare wet earth, their bedding a couple of blankets
worn threadbare after three campaigns, with a stone, a boot or a helmet for
a pillow. Still wearing the clothing in which they had been wounded, these
unfortunates shivered from a want of nourishment, a factor that further
lowered their chance of recovery.

Wallis, himself wounded, and Dr Sketchley, working round the clock,
were initially assisted by a corporal and three privates of the Army Hospital
Corps, but when one of these was badly wounded and all the others at
various times fell sick, artillerymen and Fusiliers were brought in to help as
medical orderlies. By 11 February all the surgical dressings and bandages
were exhausted, including those made up by the Forssman ladies from the
linen shirts given by the officers; the doctors were reduced to using any rags
or bandages they could recover and clean.

Being unmarked, the hospital tents were as vulnerable to enemy fire as
any other part of the fort. The light from the lamps used by the doctors at
night, which glowed in the tops of the tents, inevitably drew sniper fire,
filling them with holes. The officers were constant in showing compassion
and concern for their own men who were wounded. Rundle sought permission to care for his Gunners in shelters made from horse blankets in the
gun pits and, when this was refused as impractical, like Dalrymple-Hay he
gave up his own bedding to those in need. The sad end for many was
interment after dark in the ever-widening plot behind the fort where,
risking snipers, the officers insisted on dignifying every burial by at least
reciting some prayers or, when there was enough moonlight, reading the
proper burial service.

For a few days there was little to be seen of the Boers other than soil being
thrown up as they continued to strengthen and extend their trenches. Ou
Griet fired a number of rounds every day, most hitting the fort without
doing much damage, but the lethal threat was always there. One almost
spent ball struck a hospital tent and, becoming entangled in the folds, fell
on the startled wounded lying below. The enemy snipers were more
effective, curtailing British movements during daylight while regularly
inflicting casualties in both the fort and the magazine. A particularly
dangerous and unsavoury task was the nightly emptying of latrine buckets
and burying of excreta, which had to be done in the open as far from the fort
as possible to reduce the health risk.

The Boers Come Closer

Towards the middle of February the night sentries began to report Boers
unacceptably close as they moved between the trenches encircling the fort.
The British had tried without success to burn the surrounding grass and

self-sown mealies that were providing cover for the enemy, so Winsloe decided to send out patrols to deter the Boers and keep them at a distance. Owing to sickness among the infantry officers these expeditions, which went out on successive nights, were led by volunteers. Commissary Dunne, Lieutenant Rundle, who left his guns, and Lieutenant Lean were normally in charge of repairing the defences. These patrols penetrated up to 700 yards into enemy territory among the mealies growing south of the gaol, staying out all night from 7 pm until nearly daylight. They failed to waylay any enemy but their presence was known to the Boers with the result that rumours spread round the town that the British were out foraging for food. When the Boers attempted unsuccessfully to surprise and cut off a British patrol, Winsloe called a halt to this risky undertaking.

Sentries at daylight on 15 February saw that overnight a dozen large wool bales had been brought up by the Boers and positioned to screen the head of their trench behind the magazine from where the sound of hectic digging could be heard. When Winsloe ordered the 9-pounders to open fire on this new target there was an immediate response from Ou Griet with every shot being aimed at the gun pits. One ball came through an embrasure sweeping the head off one Gunner and severely bruising the shoulder of another. The ghastly sight of the headless Gunner Larkin filled his comrades with horror. Fearing that the Boers were preparing to attack the magazine, Winsloe sent over food, firewood and water together with ammunition and medical supplies to last a week if the post was cut off. He also ordered the men in the magazine to push out their sap towards the Boers, keeping them at a distance, but there were too few fit men to make any progress with this dangerous task.

The British never gave the Boers any inkling of their parlous condition; indeed Cronje was to tell Winsloe after the surrender that had he guessed the weak state of the garrison he would have stormed the fort. It was not in the nature of Victorian officers to be intimidated in adversity and typically those at Potchefstroom, enthusiastically supported by their men, did their outmost to irritate and frustrate the Boers. The usual round of jaunty bugle calls indicated that the disciplined daily routine was being maintained, while the sound of singing accompanied by trilling flutes hardly suggested the garrison was under pressure.

During some particularly boring and quiet spell at night the irrepressible Rundle would seek permission from Winsloe to give a 'screech'. Told he must first warn the sentries, he would clamber up on the parapet and let out a series of unearthly yells, much to the amusement of the soldiers, quickly dropping back into cover to avoid the fire that startled Boers returned from every direction. A favourite trick played by the troops was to hoist a lighted lamp on a pole, simulating signals being passed between the fort and the magazine; this always attracted a considerable amount of fire, causing the enemy to waste ammunition for no purpose. When the British raised their *ad hoc* Union Jack over the fort, the Boers, not to be outdone, took to flying three republican flags, two at the Landrost's office and another at the gaol. A well-aimed 9-pounder shell cut down one of those over the office much to the delight and satisfaction of the Gunners.

Among the stories that circulated in the town about the British patrols was one of a raid on the gaol, which drove out the Boer guard and led to the capture of a burgher whom they released having taken his rifle and umbrella, before their return to the fort with sheets of corrugated iron. Two days later, went the tale, the Boers were mortified to be confronted at dawn by a scarecrow standing between the gaol and the fort dressed in woman's clothes holding above its head an umbrella. Giving up some of their previous clothes to taunt the Boers would typify the spirit of the Forssman girls that so endeared them to the soldiers. Although this yarn does not appear in any British account, it is given credence by the fact that after the surrender a number of corrugated iron sheets were found in the fort by the Boers.

Regardless of all their stouthearted bravado, time was running out for Winsloe and his men. On 19 February 1881, the sixty-seventh day of the siege, two of the Nelson brothers volunteered to carry a message from Winsloe to General Colley in Natal, reporting that the fort could hold out only until 18 March, and that casualties to date were seventeen killed with thirty-seven wounded and sick in the hospital tents. Only the Nelsons had any hope of getting through. The soldiers did not know the country, while the coloured Commissariat drivers were either unwilling to try or considered too unreliable.

The brothers started after dark in a thunderstorm. Avoiding three Boer patrols they walked twenty miles to reach the River Vaal and swim over to safety in the Orange Free State. By the end of the next day they had covered sixty miles, having acquired horses, to reach Kronstadt, where they saw ex-President Pretorius. This member of the Triumvirate, accompanied by a staff, appeared to be engaged on two rather disparate tasks: trying to drum up volunteers from among the Free State burghers, and buying mackintoshes to take back for the Transvaal commandos. Finding the Free State Boers strongly anti-British and only being kept neutral by the firm hand of President Brand, the Nelsons pressed on, suffering considerable hardship. Their journey of over 200 miles took them past the townships of Bethlehem and Harrismith, over the Drakensberg Mountains, to reach the Natal Army headquarters at Newcastle on 8 March 1881, by which time General Colley was dead.

Back at Potchefstroom, the garrison was plunged into gloom on 28 February when one of the Forssman daughters, Mrs Sketchley, died of

enteric fever. A beautiful, vivacious young woman, a bride for a year, she
was only twenty-one years old. Pregnant and weakened by the privations
suffered in the fort, she succumbed quickly to the deadly fever despite all
the efforts of her doctor husband to save her. For seventy-six days the ladies
of the Forssman family had stoically endured filthy, insanitary conditions
without fresh clothes, undernourished by appalling food, cooped up in their
wet, murky shelter for most of every twenty-four hours. Their bravery under
fire and their complete faith in their protectors had become an inspiration to
the young soldiers, who were deeply affected by the death of Emelia.

Under a flag of truce Surgeon Wallis sent a letter to Cronje on behalf of
Dr Sketchley asking for a coffin to be sent into the fort and requesting
permission to bury his wife in the consecrated town cemetery. The reply
came back promising that a coffin would be delivered next morning but
saying that the burial must take place in the vicinity of the fort. Predictably
the Boers were not going to give any British attending the funeral an
opportunity to see the trenches and other works behind the magazine. Next
morning a fine coffin arrived, the inside filled with fragrant stephanotis
flowers and evergreens, the top covered with wreaths and flowers. Cronje
had allowed a truce for one hour for the funeral, which took place in full
view of the Boers. Lieutenant Browne, who acted as adjutant to Winsloe,
conducted the service.

The grave had not been filled in nor had the hour-long truce expired
when without warning Ou Griet opened fire. The British dived back into
the fort, and the Gunners brought the 9-pounders into action, ending on a
sour note what the garrison regarded as one of the saddest days of the siege.
Not until after the surrender did the British learn that Boers had searched
the coffin and wreaths for messages and callously thrown out a black dress
intended for Mrs Forssman together with mourning ribbons for her
daughters.

Disquieting Events in the Town

A constant rattle of musketry and the periodic thump of exploding shells,
quiet for only a few hours each Sunday, provided the disturbing background
to life in Potchefstroom as the days of February 1881 passed by. The Boers
concentrated on tightening their grip on the fort by improving their trench
system and constructing the redoubt to overlook the magazine. They
avoided unnecessary contacts with the British, even leaving their incursive
patrols alone. The main requirement was for labour, and consequently the
number of fighting men in and about the town was allowed to fluctuate,
sometimes dropping from around 1,000 down to only 400. Some were sent
for duty elsewhere; others simply drifted away without leave to visit their
homes and look to their domestic affairs. Only the occasional individual

seems to have been punished for insubordination or absence under the lax discipline of the commando system.

By contrast, the war council was relentless in putting pressure on the civilians, in particular loyalists, who were required to comply with regulations under the threat of heavy penalties. Their native servants were conscripted to dig in the trenches alongside prisoners of war and others under sentence of hard labour, employers being warned that they personally would be made to take the place of any servant who failed to report for duty.

Inevitably a succession of native labourers was killed or wounded by fire from the fort but the loyalists were outraged when on 24 February Trooper Finlay, a prisoner of war, was killed by a British shell while being forced to work in the trenches. Finlay had volunteered for Raaff's constabulary and, after being taken prisoner when the Landrost's office was surrendered, had been sentenced by the war council to twelve months' hard labour. His body was brought back into town at sunset where his distraught young widow waited with her two small children. Cronje authorised the Reverend Richardson to conduct a proper interment the next day in the garden of the English Episcopal Church but forbade the firing of the customary three volleys over the grave. At midday, the British community were joined at the graveside by Finlay's fellow prisoners of war who were brought down from confinement in the Forssman store under armed guard. The padre delivered an impassioned address, which evoked angry emotion among the gathering. Moquette, 'the Flying Dutchman', one of the prisoners, gave vent to everyone's feelings when he furiously accused the Boers of the deliberate murder of Finlay. Indignant at the allegation, the war council sentenced Moquette to three months' hard labour for his outburst.

The British officers, Major Clarke and Commandant Raaff, themselves segregated in prison and being treated indifferently, were impotent, unable to prevent the improper treatment of their men. Clarke, who had protested when van der Linden and Woite were executed, now objected to prisoners being put to work under fire, but his complaints were to no avail.

Isolated, Raaff was kept handcuffed from 5 pm each evening until 8 am the following morning for eight weeks and five days. This practice was only stopped on the recommendation of the doctor who attended Raaff when he became ill.

Thomas Leask left an account of how Major Clarke was treated when a prisoner. In late February 1881, not having seen his family since the previous December, Leask asked for a pass to leave the Transvaal to visit Natal. At first Cronje refused but later relented, even promising that Leask's property would be safeguarded while he was away. Leask then requested to see Major Clarke, whose wife Anne he knew. Mrs Clarke was living with her father General Lloyd near Bushman's River in Natal. After a first refusal Leask managed to persuade Cronje that if he saw Clarke he would be able to refute reports in the Natal press that the major was being brutally treated and kept chained to a fellow prisoner.

Accompanied by the ubiquitous Buskes, Leask visited Clarke, who was visibly affected by this kindness asking, 'Will you go and tell her personally I am well and being kindly treated?' Thinking a note would be better, Leask asked Buskes if Clarke might write his message on the scrap of paper he offered. When the officious Buskes refused, Clarke was philosophical saying, 'Never mind. Tell my wife I am well and have everything I require except my liberty, and that will come.' Yet again Leask was infuriated by the vindictive behaviour of Buskes, whom he described as that 'damned Hollander', believing that Cronje would have allowed Clarke to write to his wife.

Keeping well away from the fort, Leask left Potchefstroom in his trap, driven by a Cape boy. He crossed the flooded River Vaal and made his way over the waterlogged north-eastern Orange Free State veldt. Travelling was difficult and after several days, when making a halt at a farm for food and fodder, he was told that General Colley had been killed on 27 February in a battle on Majuba Hill. The excited farmer showed Leask a bloodstained Highland sporran that his son had brought back from Majuba. Nonplussed, Leask continued his journey to Natal, eventually arriving at the home of General Lloyd. He was rewarded with the look of sheer relief on the face of the incredulous Anne Clarke as she heard his message and began to comprehend that her husband was alive and safe.

The farmer's story was true. On 12 February 1881, Kruger had written to Colley offering to negotiate an end to the war. The letter reached London by telegraph on 14 February but it was 21 February before Colley was authorised to offer a suspension of hostilities if Kruger replied within forty-eight hours. No reply was immediately forthcoming.

Perhaps the idea that Boer resolve was weakening and that he might menace them into a bloodless retreat prompted Colley to occupy Majuba Hill, overlooking the enemy camp. The facts will never be known, as Colley had sent his deputy, Brigadier Evelyn Wood, back to Pietermaritzburg on 21 February and told no one of his plans. On the night of 26 February, Colley led a force of 400 drawn from various units on a precarious night march to the top of Majuba Hill. The tired men did not dig in. At first light, a ranging shot fired on the orders of Colley alerted the Boers to the British presence, causing panic in the camp. Quickly recovering, the Boers began an attack. Skilfully using ground and covering fire they reached the top of Majuba about midday. Once in close contact, the devastating Boer rifle fire drove the British further and further back until finally the soldiers broke and fled down the precipitous mountainside. Colley was shot dead in the midst of the fighting. The British lost 150 officers and men killed and wounded, and 56 were taken prisoner. Evelyn Wood rushed back from Pietermaritzburg to assume command.

The ever-increasing problems faced by the townspeople of Potchefstroom were further aggravated at the end of February 1881 by a shortage of food. The supplies demanded from the storekeepers by the war council in January had not yet arrived, causing the council to make an order on 2 March placing all edibles under the supervision of the commissariat officer for him to ration out to the civilians. Additional irksome pass restrictions and other regulations were introduced, which were strictly enforced by officious constables determined to extract fines for any infringement, particularly from the British. Refusal to pay a fine led to immediate imprisonment even for respected citizens such as the Wesleyan minister, the Reverend Cawood, who declined to pay when stopped while going about his parochial business without his pass. A native accused of attempting to carry a message to the fort was given twenty-five lashes after he tried to avoid punishment by implicating in the plot a number of businessmen whom he failed to identify when they were paraded in front of him. Dogs making a noise at night were shot and their owners fined.

A major cause of frustration was the dearth of authentic news, which was not satisfied by the arrival of the weekly mail coach from Heidelberg or intermittent post deliveries from the Orange Free State. Apart from a long-delayed copy of the *Natal Mercury* received on 11 February containing the British account of the battle at Laing's Nek, all other newspapers except those favourable to the Boers were shut out. In such a climate rumours were rife. Reports circulated among hopeful loyalists that massive reinforcements from Britain and India were concentrating on the frontier ready to attack. The Boers were heartened by stories that hundreds of Free State burghers had signed a petition exhorting their government to unite with their Transvaal cousins in their struggle against British rule.

Following the death of Emelia Sketchley it was no surprise when the word passed round the town on 4 March 1881 that Chevalier Forssman had asked Cronje for permission to bring his family out of the fort. When Cronje refused, a delegation of prominent ladies, which included Mrs Palmer and was led by Caroline Raaff, sister-in-law of the imprisoned commandant, attempted to persuade Cronje to change his mind. The ladies were received very coolly by the irascible Cronje, who not only turned down their request but to their astonishment launched into a tirade against interfering women in general, saying that they were at the bottom of all mischief.

There was, however, a hidden motive behind the apparently heartless refusal by Cronje. He believed that the British surrender was imminent and that the suffering of the Forssman family might induce Winsloe to make the decision more quickly. As early as 2 March the war council had passed a resolution allowing anyone who wished to leave the town to do so; at the same time it issued a notice to the effect that after 7 March the authorities would not be responsible for any loss or damage due to military operations until such time as the British capitulated. The council was anticipating that Winsloe might carry out his threat to fire off all his ammunition into the town before spiking the 9-pounders prior to surrendering. Cronje also thought Winsloe might consider the repercussions on the safety of the Forssman family before he embarked on destroying his guns and ammunition.

CHAPTER 16

The Final Crisis

4 to 17 March 1881: Days 80 to 93

From the early days of the siege Winsloe, his officers and the Forssman family had gathered each evening in the little mess area beside the ladies' redoubt for their main meal of the day. If the colonel needed any reminding that time was running out for the defenders the sight of his companions sitting round a communal three-legged pot being served with spoonfuls of mealie porridge to which had been added a few ounces of tinned beef and grass must have made the situation very plain. By 4 March the daily ration had shrunk to 4 ounces of tinned beef with $1\frac{1}{2}$ pounds of unground mealies and $\frac{1}{4}$ ounce of coffee. Illness among the garrison caused by the husks left in the badly ground mealie flour was another insoluble problem. Beef tea for the sick and wounded was finished and a substitute brewed from tinned beef contained little nourishment.

Warning of the Final Attack
The eightieth day of the siege, 4 March 1881, marked a resurgence of Boer activity after several relatively quiet days as they opened rifle fire on all sides of the fort, and Ou Griet fired twelve rounds, of which eleven hit the fort. One ball struck Corporal McClusky a glancing blow on the head without killing him. The fortunate McClusky was still recovering from the severe wound he had received during the fight for the gaol in the previous December. Lieutenant Rundle also had a lucky escape when he was only slightly wounded in the head by a bullet. With Major Thornhill often too sick for duty the loss of Rundle to command the guns would have been a catastrophe.

The magazine, once again under command of Lieutenant Lindsell, was menaced at a range of 30 or 40 yards by the Boer redoubt. Built as planned of earth-filled barrels and sacks, it was nearing 12 feet high and 6 or 7 feet wide at the top. From this close range the Boers were able to use buckshot effectively against the Mounted Infantrymen defending the position. Even with the trench, movement between the magazine and the fort during daylight was out of the question, and Dr Sketchley began to spend most days at the magazine ready to care for any casualties on the spot. Sniper fire

194

continued through the night and into the next day when Ou Griet opened fire again, scoring six hits out of seven shots fired, forcing the defenders to dive constantly for cover. The load on the overstretched doctors was increased by three men wounded at the magazine and several more cases of dysentery. One old soldier who died had served for twenty-one years without a day's sickness.

Soon after dark on 5 March a sentry on the rear parapet of the fort spotted a man crawling towards him. As he challenged, several of his comrades rushed out and captured the individual bringing him back into the trench leading to the magazine. Told that a Dutchman had been captured, Winsloe was taken along the sap where incautiously he ordered he be left alone to question the man, who he suspected was a spy. The prisoner seemed terrified and was trembling so much he could hardly speak. Baffled, Winsloe, on hearing a sound, peered into the darkness beyond the prisoner to discern a soldier, who unbeknownst to him had been detailed as an escort, holding his bayonet within an inch of the man's neck. Incapable of speaking and thinking perhaps actions would be better than words the prisoner stood up and, unbuttoning his coat, showed an astonished Winsloe that his body was wrapped around with an inch-thick rope of tobacco, while his pockets were stuffed full of the precious weed. Without any prompting the guard dropped his rifle and helped Winsloe to unroll the tobacco by spinning the spy around and around until the man was giddy. Swiftly they removed their man and his cargo into the fort where in less than no time the tobacco was divided into portions and distributed all around. The prisoner meanwhile was handcuffed to a wagon wheel to await further interrogation. He was given a large glass of Hennessy 'Three Star' brandy from the hospital supplies to loosen his tongue, and pumped for information by one of the Afrikaans-speaking civilians.

He gave his name as Hudson but offered no explanation as to why he had come to the fort, making Winsloe think that he must be an enemy agent paid to bring misinformation to the British. Surely the Boer cordon was far too tight for anyone to pass through without their knowing? The tobacco was meant to be proof of his friendly intentions as was the spoonful of salt in a screw of paper that he presented to Winsloe. Questioned, Hudson recounted how the Boers had been defeated in a battle ten days before with the loss of a thousand men; as a result the British relief column was expected to reach Potchefstroom in a fortnight. He went on to say that the local Boers were greatly disheartened by the defeat and were already starting to disperse but that they intended to make a final attack on the fort next Monday, protected by a screen of native allies. He told of how the British at Pretoria had defeated the Boers on 16 January, killing 150 and taking seventeen prisoners, and also that the company at Rustenburg was still holding out. Hudson said that all the British had been turned out of Potchefstroom and that one of the British prisoners had been killed in the trenches by a British shell.

Dubious as to what to believe, in particular as to the warning of an impending Boer attack, Winsloe remained convinced that Hudson was a spy and ordered that he be kept chained to a wagon at night, only being released by day under escort.

The following day being Sunday, both sides observed the unofficial cease-fire that had become the practice on the Sabbath. After prayers had been said, the garrison had much to mull over as the stories extracted from Hudson were passed around, while they enjoyed the luxury of a real smoke for the first time in over two months, taking the edge off their hunger at least for a while. However, there was apprehension that the next day would bring another attack.

Monday came and went without the assault predicted by Hudson materialising. The Boers kept up sporadic rifle fire all day while Ou Griet delivered another thirteen rounds without causing any real damage. The Boer labourers could be heard and occasionally seen as they worked on their redoubt and trenches undeterred by British shooting. The next two days, 8 and 9 March, were ominously quiet, the silence only broken by snipers on both sides when they detected a target. One of the remaining Commissariat mule drivers was wounded, lingering for days before he died. British marksmen would never know how effective they had been, specifically in mortally wounding Muller the German, who had charge of the siege works. Muller was busy supervising the building of the redoubt behind the magazine when he was hit.

Ou Griet Renews the Bombardment

When day broke on 10 March 1881, the eighty-sixth day of the siege, the absence of cannon fire during the previous two days was immediately explained when Ou Griet opened fire from a new position 600 or 700 yards to the rear of the fort. Overnight the Boers had dug a line of rifle pits on the rising ground that looked down on the back of the fort. In the centre of these trenches they had made an emplacement for their cannon. Since their sortie on 22 January this was the area the British most feared the Boers might occupy. The gun emplacement looked solid. It was built of sandbags, barrels and wool sacks, and more wool sacks had been placed at intervals in front of the rifle pits for their added protection. The Boer position was partly hidden from the Royal Artillery gun pits by long grass and a fold in the ground.

Ou Griet was at first invisible but came into view when raised up on planks by the Boers, seeking to improve their shooting. The Boers lashed the fort and magazine with cannon and rifle fire for twelve hours, from sun-up to sundown, with only periodic breaks lasting from thirty minutes to an hour. The British estimated that there were about seventy Boer riflemen occupying the weapon pits from where they kept up a 'smart' independent fire all day, the volume increasing when Ou Griet was being reloaded and the crew exposed. During this sustained bombardment, Ou Griet fired eighty-three rounds of which about forty hit the fort knocking sandbags out of the parapet and sending splinters flying off the wagon traverse. Thirteen rounds were aimed at the magazine, which was hit only once by a ricochet that damaged one wall.

Since 22 January when the Boers had first tried to establish themselves in the rear of the fort, Winsloe had made strenuous efforts to heighten the back wall and reinforce the traverse. The backbreaking work was now rewarded as the garrison was able to crouch behind much more substantial cover. For their better protection the ladies were brought out of their 'redoubt' and put into the Commissariat marquee where the floor, tucked under the rear parapet, had been well dug out and was relatively safe. Only a few selected marksmen were left to man the parapets and return the Boer fire while the remainder of the garrison stayed under cover. Bored, the soldiers soon began to amuse themselves by signalling the strike of each cannon ball as though they were the butt party on a rifle range. For a while everyone regarded this teasing of the Boers as great fun and good for morale but when the signal poles began to attract dangerously concentrated rifle fire Winsloe decided to stop the 'frolic', much to the disappointment of his men.

Throughout the long day the British 9-pounders stayed silent, only the British marksmen answering the Boer bombardment. The decision not to use the Royal Artillery guns was to prove contentious and after the war General Evelyn Wood was to censure Major Thornhill for this omission. Thornhill, who was too ill to get out of his bed that day, did not himself ever see the Boer positions but because he did not formally hand over command to Rundle, the subaltern had to accept his directions. From the confines of his bed Thornhill discussed the tactical situation with Winsloe, emphasising how little 9-pounder ammunition remained, thirty rounds a gun, only enough for two or three days' shooting at ordinary rates and hardly suffi-cient to stop a determined charge by the Boers. Thornhill advised Winsloe that shrapnel would be ineffective at so short a range, 600 or 700 yards, while the prospect of a direct hit on Ou Griet, 'a mere speck', using common shell with a percussion fuse, was nil. He contended that riflemen firing over the rear parapet would have as much if not more chance of silencing Ou Griet as a shrapnel shell. Winsloe disagreed but bowed to the professional opinion of Thornhill, looking on as his marksmen failed to stop the Boer cannon firing at will.

The improved defences of the fort proved effective and at the end of the day-long bombardment casualties were few, only Dalrymple-Hay with a piece torn out of an ear by a bullet and three soldiers wounded. One of these was Winsloe's servant who was hit above the wrist while holding a basin of water for the colonel to wash his hands before dinner. The defenders of the magazine, being more vulnerable, were less fortunate; two of the small band were killed and two wounded, one of whom was to die the day after the fort surrendered. When darkness fell and the bombardment died down, the first task for the weary, half-starved soldiers was to make good the damage done to the parapets, which were already subsiding under the heavy rain before taking the battering from Ou Griet. The work done, the men could settle down to get what rest they might, knowing they would be chilled to the marrow by a heavy dew if not sodden by one of the rainstorms that had persisted for days.

The bleary-eyed, tired soldiers were standing to at 5.45 am the next morning when Ou Griet began firing from the same position as the previous day, supported by an increased number of riflemen who looked to number about a hundred. The cannon and rifle fire was to continue all through that day until sundown, only interrupted very occasionally for about half an hour. The rifle fire proved extremely trying, coming from all four sides but in rotation and unusually for the Boers in volleys. These were being controlled in some fashion by signals to ensure the crossfire did not inflict casualties on their own men. The rifle fire from the trenches guarding Ou Griet was exceptionally heavy, clearly intended to prevent British marksmen interfering with the old cannon. Such was the sustained intensity of the enemy fire all day that Winsloe became astonished that the Boers had any ammunition left. Ou Griet fired over fifty balls, half of which were either direct hits or ricochets that ended up in the fort.

Fortunately the height of the parapet prevented too many of the hail of bullets striking inside the defences and only two more men were wounded, one of whom was Gunner Evans who had taken part in the defence of Rorke's Drift. One cannon ball flew low over the wall, penetrating a hospital tent where men were waiting for their wounds to be dressed. The ball carried away the previously wounded arm of Winsloe's servant, Cruikshank, below the elbow, and then hit Private Mullen, already severely wounded in the shoulder, shattering his pelvis. There was no alternative but to amputate Cruikshank's arm. Tragically Mullen was beyond help and died two days later. Dalrymple-Hay visited the two desperately injured men who both belonged to his company, and Surgeon Wallis watched as the compassionate young officer tried to comfort his men, offering them the only thing he had, his miserable ration of food.

Towards evening when the enemy fire began to die down, the British, thinking the day's bombardment was over, hastened to cook their evening meal. Winsloe and his usual companions had hardly sat down to eat when a ball from Ou Griet whirred through the air to hit the ground among them, covering the whole party with a shower of earth. Thinking this was a signal for the Boers to charge the fort everyone dashed to their battle positions. When nothing happened, all returned to their food believing this must surely be the last shot of the day. Having finished his meal, Winsloe, who had been sitting with his back to a wall of sandbags with a lady on either side, stood up to stretch his legs and moved away. A second later another cannon ball flew in hitting the sandbags where his head had been only moments before and missing the ladies by less than a foot. Scrambling back to the parapets the British opened fire. Winsloe wrote, 'We made it very unpleasant for the enemy going home just by way of saying Goodnight.'

The unfortunate Cruikshank had to wait until dark for his shattered arm to be amputated as Surgeon Wallis required the assistance of Dr Sketchley who could not get back from the magazine in daylight. The operation was performed successfully under chloroform while Boer bullets attracted by the light from the surgeon's lamp tore holes through the top of the tent overhead.

The Forssman family were all now suffering from the stomach disorders rife among the garrison, which must have been very difficult and embarrassing for the womenfolk. A crisis arose when the young son Alric, who was being nursed by his sisters, contracted enteric fever. As soon as the bombardment allowed he was put in one of the isolation dugouts where, lying on a bed of straw, he was watched over by his father until he died days later.

Desperate Days

Thankful to have survived another day, the whereabouts of the relief column promised by the spy Hudson was the main topic of conversation among the sodden soldiers as they braved enemy sniper fire to make good some of the damage to the walls caused by hostile fire and the persistent rain. The first glimmer of light next morning, 12 March, the eighty-eighth day of the siege, caught Lieutenant Browne and a working party in the open as they were shoring up a piece of wall near the gun pits, which had collapsed overnight. Alert watching Boers fired, slightly wounding Browne and three of his men, a lucky escape for Browne and a great relief to Winsloe who had come to rely on this steady company commander who also acted as his adjutant. For the first month of the fighting Browne had worked day and night, first digging wells and then on the defences, with little sleep eventually coming near to exhaustion.

When there was enough daylight to reveal the Boer positions clearly, observers in the fort saw that Ou Griet had disappeared together with the wool sacks that had been laid around the gun position and in front of the neighbouring rifle pits. This turn of events left the British guessing as to what plot Cronje might be hatching, speculation that increased as several relatively uneventful days followed.

Intermittent sniper fire continued to claim victims, one day a man in the fort and three at the magazine, and next day Driver Lewis, the second of the two N/5 Battery men to be wounded who had fought at Rorke's Drift. The next to be hit was an old soldier of twenty years' service who had not fully recovered from a wound he had received the previous January. This man, Private Noble, 2/21st, was to die after the surrender. Surgeon Wallis commented that men like him were worn out by long service in India and less able to survive than the young soldiers. Sickness added to the toll when Sergeant Thomas Quegan died of a burst blood vessel.

During this uncertain lull one of the youngest Forssman girls had a terrifying experience. For days the doctors had been badgering Winsloe to allow the ladies to take some exercise, which they considered was essential for their health. Against his better judgement Winsloe gave way, allowing them to walk about the fort with their father one afternoon when all seemed quiet. They had hardly left the mess area when Winsloe heard a scream at his elbow and looked round to see a young girl lying on the ground. His immediate thought was that she was dead. It was a great relief to discover only a slight wound, but the bullet that had grazed her neck had narrowly missed her spine. Understandably there was less enthusiasm for taking exercise after this incident. The tribulations of the Forssman family continued when Alric died from enteric fever on 13 March, just two days after his ninth birthday. The little fellow was placed in a rough coffin knocked up from brandy cases and laid to rest beside his sister Emelia. There was no solace for the stricken family when the danger of sniper fire forced the hurried burial of their son and Private Mullen at midnight with the barest of ceremony.

By 17 March 1881, after ninety-three days under siege the garrison was in a perilous condition and, despite flippant remarks from Dalrymple-Hay suggesting they might have a 'lively Saint Patrick's Day', Winsloe knew he was facing the final crisis. He could muster less than 150 men to man the guns and the defences, many of whom were weakened by diarrhoea and other stomach complaints or were recovering from wounds. The only other labour he could call on to help repair the parapets, which were crumbling fast under the rains that had lasted for weeks, or for menial tasks such as emptying the latrines were the remaining seventeen Commissariat drivers. Several of these had been wounded, one three times. All the men looked thin and worn; many of those who had been wounded were so frail that they fainted when taking their turn at even the light duty of cooking.

As Cronje had anticipated, Winsloe was much concerned for the safety and welfare of the thirteen civilians still in the fort, in particular the Forssman women. Of paramount importance were the twenty-eight seriously sick and wounded shivering in the unhygienic leaking hospital tents, their prospect of recovery lessening with every day through the lack of dressings and medical supplies, and the inadequate diet.

The remaining food consisted almost entirely of sacks of mealies and millet, all damaged and rotting as a result of being used for the walls; these could not last for more than a few days. The daily ration had been cut down again two days previously to 1 pound of unground mealies and $\frac{1}{2}$ pound of millet seeds, with 4 ounces of tinned beef on alternate days. Salt to make the unappetising gruel at all palatable was greatly missed. Other than the daily dose of lime juice there was nothing to drink but water. Only a few pounds of rice and some erbwurst were left to provide anything extra for those in hospital. That the supplies had been eked out for so long without the need for sudden and demoralising cuts in the daily ration had been due to the foresight and good management of the Commissariat officer, Walter Dunne, whose philosophy was always 'We must do anything rather than surrender to the Boers.' The only reserve, carefully guarded in the tattered Commissariat marquee, comprised seventy bottles of brandy and fifty bottles of port wine.

Faced with all these factors Winsloe concluded that it was absolutely vital to obtain some up-to-date information before deciding what action he must take. Though he did not trust Hudson, Winsloe saw no alternative but to risk using the spy and offered him £100 to get into the town and return with any newspapers or other information he could glean. Hudson agreed and pointed out his own house standing out on the far right of the town where he said his sister would appear next morning and show a white handkerchief if he had arrived safely. He assured Winsloe that the grass between the fort and the town, which had earlier given cover to the British patrols, was now so tall there would be no difficulty in creeping past any Boer sentries. The night passed uneventfully and as no one had much faith in Hudson there was considerable surprise at daybreak next morning when a woman came out of the Hudson house, walking about fifteen paces before turning back. As she disappeared again behind the wall she raised her handkerchief and then let it fall behind her on the grass.

CHAPTER 17

Cronje's Stratagem

7 to 20 March 1881: Days 83 to 96

Rumours that a general armistice was being contemplated began to circulate among the townspeople of Potchefstroom during 7 March 1881 while Ou Griet could be heard bombarding the fort and sharp exchanges of rifle continued between the combatants. The mail coach arrived from Heidelberg the next day bringing the dramatic news of the British defeat on Majuba Hill. The report told of General Colley being killed, 150 British dead and wounded, and forty prisoners taken and sent to Heidelberg.

While still trying to absorb these unbelievable tidings the loyalists were confronted with a war council notice which, while announcing they were free to leave the town if they so wished, also made it clear that anyone staying after 11 March could not expect any official protection. Previously not even sick loyalist women and children had been given permission to leave. The bewildered loyalists were not to know this was a deliberate ploy to rid the town of those who might be tempted to pass information into the fort before the next Boer attack, planned for 10 March. Within the next day or two most of the loyalist families fled, braving the interminable rainstorms that had been deluging the region for weeks. All soon found themselves stuck on the open veldt with only their wagons for shelter, unable to cross the swollen streams.

The news from Majuba and the rumours of an armistice did not deflect Cronje from his set purpose of mounting another attack, which he fully expected would finally force the British who must be at the end of their tether to surrender. According to plan Ou Griet opened fire at daybreak on 10 March. By dark on 11 March, when it was obvious that 140 cannon balls and a vast expenditure of small-arms ammunition had not achieved any tangible result and that cannon balls which overshot the fort posed a danger to the town, it was decided to abandon the attack from that front. That night under cover of darkness Ou Griet was to be repositioned, dragged up a ramp on to the top of the redoubt from where it could fire down on the magazine and the fort. While the new plan was being arranged the Boers contented themselves with sniping but had the satisfaction of catching one working party in the open at dawn.

Subterfuge

Within hours of deciding to change his plan of attack Cronje found himself confronted by an entirely new and complex situation, and his procrastination over the next four days would result in his being accused of deceit and dishonourable behaviour by tricking Winsloe into surrendering. The controversial sequence of events began with General Sir Evelyn Wood and Commandant-General Piet Joubert signing the deed of armistice at a place half-way between the British camp at Mount Prospect and Laing's Nek on 6 March 1881. The armistice, intended to allow time for Kruger to reach the frontier and join the negotiations, was to last for eight days, until midnight on 14 March. The conditions were that neither side would make any forward movement from their positions, although Wood was free to send eight days' provisions but no ammunition to the besieged garrisons (Pretoria, Potchefstroom, Lydenburg, Marabastadt, Rustenburg, Standerton and Wakkerstroom). Joubert undertook to inform the garrisons and the Boer commanders immediately.

Joubert sent details to Kruger with a letter that left Laing's Nek on 7 March. It travelled 111 miles to reach Heidelberg during the night of 9/10 March. At daybreak on 10 March Kruger dispatched a copy of Joubert's letter together with some other instructions by express post to Cronje, which arrived at Potchefstroom ninety miles away early on 12 March. The instructions from Kruger required Cronje to pass the details of the armistice agreement on to Rustenburg, Marico and Bloemhof. The second paragraph read: 'It is your duty to notify Major Winsloe of the agreement between Wood and Joubert; but the armistice at Mooiriver is not to commence prior to the arrival of supplies, and handing over thereof to you. Before such time be free to continue warfare.'

The letters that Kruger required to be sent to the outstations were still being written when two representatives from President Brand arrived at Cronje's headquarters in Potchefstroom. Mr G. P. Mollet, the Landrost of Kronstadt, accompanied by Mr Slymers had been sent by their president with a letter from himself and copies of a telegram from General Wood for delivery to both Cronje and Winsloe advising them that an armistice had been concluded to take effect at Potchefstroom on the arrival of supplies for the garrison.

Cronje claimed he was completely confused, believing the letters presented to him from Kruger and Brand were contradictory. Joubert's instructions received via Kruger indicated that he, Cronje, was responsible for informing Winsloe but the telegram from Wood sent by Brand requested that Brand should tell both Cronje and Winsloe. Faced with this dilemma Cronje chose to do nothing until he had received further instructions from his government at Heidelberg. In the meantime he prevented Mollet from contacting Winsloe in the fort. Surprisingly he allowed Mollet to visit Major Clarke in his prison on 13 March, when the erstwhile special commissioner was told of the armistice terms.

Two days passed before the war council met on 14 March and resolved to write to President Brand telling him that his letter had not been delivered to Winsloe because further instructions from Heidelberg were awaited. The next day, after again being refused permission to deliver their letter to the fort on the grounds that something had taken place at the Nek that Cronje was not at liberty to disclose, Mollet and Slymers gave up and returned to the Orange Free State to report to President Brand. Cronje let two more days pass after the war council meeting before sending by the ordinary mail coach his request to the government at Heidelberg for written instructions on how to act.

All the time Mollet and Slymers were in town only the snipers were active, picking off any opportunity target in the fort. Ou Griet, hidden behind the redoubt overlooking the magazine, was not brought back into action. The only loyalists left in the town were those who for some specific reason had been given special permission to stay. All others had finally fled under threat of being driven out if they did not go of their own accord.

The Spy Returns

At the fort, after having been agreeably surprised when the promised handkerchief signal was seen at dawn on 18 March, Winsloe and his men could only wait and wonder if and when Hudson would return. They were rewarded when at long last night fell and the spy came creeping back through the darkness into the fort, bringing a two-day-old copy of the *Staats Courant* published on 16 March. This spelled out in full the terms of the armistice signed by Wood and Joubert, which properly Cronje ought to have communicated immediately to Winsloe. Hudson also brought copies of President Brand's letter to Winsloe and Wood's telegram, which Mollet had been unable to deliver; these had been given to him by an anonymous person in the town.

From this information it was plain that there was no possibility of relief arriving before more of the wounded might die and the few remaining mealies and tins of beef were exhausted. Winsloe consulted his officers who unanimously agreed that 'the game was up' and that they must come to terms with Cronje and the local Boers, who manifestly had failed to comply with the armistice agreement. During the night Winsloe wrote a letter which was sent over to the Boer lines under a flag of truce at sunrise on 19 March 1881. This read:

From Brevet Lieutenant-Colonel R. W. C. Winsloe, Commanding H.M. Troops, Potchefstroom, to P. A. Cronjé, General Commanding Boer Forces, Potchefstroom Division.

Potchcfstroom,
19th March, 1881.

Sir,

It has come to my knowledge that an agreement in regard to an armistice for eight days has been entered into between Major-General Sir Evelyn Wood, V.C., in the name of the British Government and Commandant General Piet Joubert of the Boer Government.

In the second clause of this agreement I see that Sir Evelyn Wood, V.C., or his successor, has liberty to send provisions and firewood if he finds it necessary (but no ammunition) through the Boer lines to all his Garrisons in the Transvaal for the eight days.

I also see that the Boer officials engage to send provisions to such garrisons, and the British garrisons shall discontinue hostilities during eight days after the arrival of such provisions.

In article 3 I see that Piet Joubert engages to make known this agreement of armistice at once to the Boer Commanders at such places.

I am further informed that the provisions referred to are at present waiting entry into the fort.

I have the honour, therefore, to request that you will do me the honour of granting me a personal interview for the purpose of arranging for the carrying out of the terms of the agreement.

I have, &c.,

(Signed) R. W. C. Winsloe, Major, Bt-Lieut. Colonel R. S. Fusiliers, Commanding H.M. Troops, Potchefstroom Fort.

To this Cronje replied:

From P. A. Cronjé, General Commanding the Boer Forces, Potchefstroom Division, to Brevet Lieutenant-Colonel R. W. C. Winsloe, R. S. Fusiliers, Commanding H.M. Troops, Potchefstroom Fort.

Potchefstroom,
19th March, 1881.

Sir,

I beg to acknowledge receipt of your letter received this morning, and beg to state that I am fully prepared to carry out the terms of the agreement, referred to by you as soon as I receive intelligence of the arrival of the provisions, which I can assure you is not yet the case.

I also beg to inform you that I shall carry out the terms of the agreement according to my instructions from headquarters, and therefore address you on the subject again as soon as the provisions arrive here.

I have, &c.,

(Signed) P. A. Cronjé, General.

Winsloe immediately wrote again requesting a meeting with Cronje.

From Brevet-Lieutenant Colonel R. W. C. Winsloe, Commanding H.M. Troops,
Potchefstroom, to P. A. Cronjé, General Commanding Boer Forces, Potchefstroom
Division.

Potchefstroom,
19th March, 1881.

Sir,

1. I have the honour to acknowledge the receipt of your letter of this day's
date.

2. I again beg to request that you will do me the honour of an interview,
accompanied by such of your Officers as you may think fit, as I have papers of
importance to lay before you.

3. I shall bring with me a similar number of Officers (say two or three) to
those you bring with you and also an interpreter.

I have, &c.,

(Signed) R. W. C. Winsloe, Brevet-Lieutenant Colonel, Commanding
H.M. Troops, Potchefstroom Fort.

Finally Cronje agreed to a meeting at twelve noon that same day.

From P. A. Cronjé, General Commanding the Boer Forces, Potchefstroom Division, to
Brevet-Lieutenant Colonel R. W. C. Winsloe, Royal Scots Fusiliers, Commanding
H.M. Troops, Potchefstroom Fort.

Potchefstroom,
19th March, 1881.

Sir,

1. I have the honour to acknowledge the receipt of your letter of this day's
date, requesting me again to grant you an interview to lay before me certain
documents of importance.

2. Such being the case, I shall have the honour to meet you with three
Officers and an interpreter on both sides, between this town and your camp
on the bank of the town water-furrow 12 o'clock at noon to-day, where I
shall arrange for that purpose.

3. It must be distinctly understood that from the receipt of this letter till
the interview is ended, the hostilities will be discontinued on both sides, and
that during this time the position on both sides shall not be removed, but
remain occupied as they are at present, and that no one shall be allowed to
come or speak to the men of the opposite side.

I have, &c.,

(Signed) P. A. Cronjé, General.

The Negotiations

Some time before the hour appointed for the meeting a white flag appeared above the Boer lines and the British hoisted theirs in return. Able for the first time in three months to put their heads above the parapets without fear of being shot, the curious soldiers watched as a party of mounted Boers brought a loaded scotch cart down the Kimberley road to the Grootvoor. They unloaded a small marquee, which was pitched about half-way between the gaol and the fort. The hungry soldiers quickly spied a hamper being lifted out of the cart and immediately began to fantasise as to the contents; according to taste they imagined French brandy or 'Square Face', the Hollands gin beloved of the soldiery.

All morning the servants of those officers going out to meet the Boers had been frantically mending, brushing and polishing. For appearance's sake, Winsloe bargained with one of his officers for a pair of fashionable 'Peel's patent boots'. Winsloe described their departure: 'When the time came to leave the Fort; we turned out in a way that would have done no discredit to St James' Street; even cigarettes were not wanting, our spy having brought us some the night before.'

At noon Winsloe, Surgeon Wallis, Rundle, Browne and their civilian interpreter, Nelson, dressed in military uniform, sauntered the 150 yards down to the Boer marquee. Major Thornhill was too ill to accompany them. They were determined by their manner to conceal the true state of affairs in the fort. They were awaited by Cronje, two of his commanders, Jan Kock and Coos Wolmorans, with a member of the war council and Secretary Buskes to interpret. All the Boers appeared scruffy and unkempt and as they were shaking hands one asked Winsloe in astonishment, 'How are you all so clean when you come out of that hole?'

Introductions over, Winsloe pointedly remained standing outside the marquee while he read to Cronje from the papers he was holding, first details of the armistice agreement from the *Staats Courant* and then the contents of Wood's telegram to President Brand. He asked Cronje outright why he had not complied with Article 3 of the armistice agreement, which required the terms to be passed on to all garrisons. The Boer Commander was evasive, replying that something had occurred that compelled him to seek further instructions from his government. Winsloe then said he had information that the provisions sent by Wood had already arrived at Potchefstroom. When Cronje vigorously denied this, Winsloe asked if alternatively it was true that the supply wagons had reached the Free State bank of the Vaal. Cronje responded, 'If you will believe me as a man of honour, then I must assure you that I positively have no information thereof.'

There is no means of telling how much either knew of the movements of

Captain Anton, 94th, who had left Mount Prospect on the afternoon of 7 March with a convoy of four mule wagons destined for Potchefstroom and four ox wagons for Standerton carrying eight days' supplies for each garrison. He reached Standerton on 12 March but was prevented from continuing on by the flooded Vaal, which it was impossible to cross until 26 March.

Following their inconclusive verbal exchange Cronje invited Winsloe and his officers to enter the marquee formally to discuss the armistice. Once inside French brandy, biscuits and cigars were produced from the hamper that had caused such speculation. Winsloe suggested that if there was already peace on the Drakensbergs it was unnecessary to wait for the delivery of supplies to have a truce at Potchefstroom also and prevent further bloodshed. Winsloe coolly added that he did not intend to ask for any food, as he had enough to last another eight days. Cronje was adamant in his refusal of this proposal saying, 'The terms of the armistice do not allow me to accept this, and my further instructions positively forbid me to do this.' At the same time he refused another request for the Forssman family to leave the fort.

The Boer and British accounts of what occurred immediately after this interchange differ considerably. The Triumvirate officially reporting these events for the consumption of the Transvaal public stated that Winsloe and his staff withdrew outside the marquee to consult, and then returned requesting a twenty-four-hour truce to enable Winsloe to hold a full discussion with all his officers as to whether they would agree to surrender. Cronje and his party then left the tent. When they returned Cronje offered a twenty-four-hour cease-fire after which both sides could meet again on the same spot at 12 o'clock next day. The two commanders verbally agreed that there would be no more fighting before the next meeting and both sides would remain inside their own positions.

The recollections of the British participants are rather more detailed. They maintained that Cronje, having refused to consider the British proposals for an armistice and the release of the Forssman family, handed to Winsloe a prepared document ready for signature, which laid down the surrender terms. The British officers would be allowed to go free, keeping their weapons and private property. This concession was in recognition of the way they had fought and treated Boer wounded. All the rest, 'horse, foot and artillery' and the civilians, were to be prisoners of war. Everything in the fort was to be surrendered to the Transvaal Republic.

Winsloe, recognising that the Boers thought they had the upper hand, made a dramatic gesture. Standing up, he announced he was returning to the fort and promptly marched out of the marquee followed by his officers. They had only gone a few yards when Buskes came running after them shouting that Cronje wished them to return. Winsloe refused but said that if Cronje came himself and gave sufficient reason he might rejoin the meeting. Cronje came out and Winsloe duly went back.

Winsloe considered he had regained the initiative and issued an ultimatum, declaring he would hold out to the last 'extremity'; then after sending notice to evacuate all non-combatants he would fire 300 shells into the town followed by 200,000 rounds of small-arms ammunition; only then would he surrender. This was sheer bluff as he only had some sixty shells left and not a great amount of rifle ammunition. His bluster succeeded and it was agreed to cease fighting and meet again at 12 o'clock next day, Sunday 20 March 1881.

That same afternoon Winsloe held a 'council of war' with all his officers present. Dunne listed the remaining supplies:

Mealies (whole)	1,600 pounds
Kaffir corn (millet)	5,000 pounds
Bran	300 pounds
Preserved meat	24 pounds
Rice	16 pounds
Erbwurst	40 rations
Candles	375 pounds
Brandy	69 bottles
Port wine	45 bottles

Surgeon Wallis commented that the grain was hardly edible and in peacetime would have been condemned as unfit for animal fodder, for which it had originally been purchased. Rundle bluntly declared the mealies were rotten. Summing up, Winsloe concluded that they might just hold out for four days but that it was highly improbable that the provisions from Mount Prospect would arrive in time to save the garrison. He believed that even if bad roads and swollen rivers did not prevent the wagons getting through, it was likely that the Boers would deliberately delay their progress. Dysentery, scurvy and enteric were all rife. There was no means of providing proper care for the sick and wounded. The officers knew they were in deep trouble and at the mercy of the Boers should the enemy discover the true state of affairs in the fort. Only astute and determined negotiation by Winsloe would save the garrison from unconditional surrender. The general consensus was that they should offer to evacuate the fort but insist on taking all their arms and ammunition with them. Winsloe felt constrained on the one hand by the order from Bellairs that had arrived in January directing that 'at last, should no assistance arrive in time, render guns and arms useless' and on the other by the threat he had received from Cronje if he complied with this order.

The following day, Sunday, 20 March 1881, ninety-six days since the siege began, the Boers and British assembled at midday for their second meeting. Cronje wished Mr Bodenstein, chairman of the Volksraad, to be present. Winsloe agreed and sent to the fort for Lieutenant Lindsell to make the numbers equal on both sides. Winsloe began the proceedings by submitting a list of points to Cronje and the negotiations, which were to last five hours, commenced.

The Boers tried hard but failed to force the British to hand over as prisoners all the civilians in the fort: the Forssman family, Raaff's volunteers, the Commissariat drivers and Hudson the spy, who Winsloe thought would be shot. Winsloe in turn requested that all prisoners taken when the Landrost's office surrendered and who were still held should be released on the same terms as finally agreed for the garrison of the fort. Cronje demurred at this, saying he must refer the matter to the war council. However, later that day he wrote to Winsloe confirming that the council would concur.

Despite all his efforts Winsloe eventually had to agree to hand over the two 9-pounder guns that Cronje was so anxious to acquire. The Boers also gained possession of all the Martini Henry rifles. However, in the end Winsloe thwarted Cronje by getting his agreement for all the British ammunition to be placed in the custody of President Brand until after the war. This rendered the guns useless for the immediate future. Conscious that he had disobeyed orders, Winsloe took the first opportunity to explain his actions to General Wood, asking that he be excused on the grounds that this was the only way he could prevent the whole garrison and the civilians becoming prisoners of war as well as the weapons and ammunition falling into enemy hands. He hoped that the Duke of Cambridge would approve.

Once the negotiations were concluded, Secretary Buskes and Lieutenant Rundle were nominated to draw up a contract in triplicate to be signed by both sides the next day. The substance of the conditions to be formalised in the document were:

The garrison would march out with their arms, which were to be laid down some distance from the fort.
They would make good, as far as possible, all the ammunition taken from the magazine.
They would be allowed to take all personal property, the officers being allowed to carry away their swords.
They would hand over any 9-pounder ammunition to the government of the Orange Free State, which would give it back to the British government when hostilities ceased.
No man was to serve again against the Boers in the present war.

On balance Winsloe had secured favourable terms for the British in the circumstances and Cronje had generously acknowledged the bravery of the defenders and their kindness to Boer prisoners by allowing the officers to keep their swords and march out of the fort with the honours of war, the men carrying their weapons. Those who had remained in the fort and had not been party to the negotiations were at first surprised that the 9-pounders had been surrendered undamaged but soon understood there had been no alternative.

The main business over, Dunne lost no time in approaching the Boers to obtain bread, eggs and vegetables for the sick and wounded. The rest of the hungry men watched the arrival of these luxuries; for them, 'the mere sight of decent food once more was pleasant'.

CHAPTER 18

The End of the War

21 to 23 March 1881: Days 97 to 99

At 9 o'clock on the morning of 21 March 1881, ninety-six days after the first shot of the war had been fired in a lane on the edge of Potchefstroom, the British officers signed a capitulation agreement. The signing took place on the same spot as the two previous meetings and once completed, in the words of Winsloe, 'All became couleur de rose.' Describing the atmosphere in the fort, Dalrymple-Hay wrote: 'We can scarcely understand the perfect peace which has so suddenly fallen on us after three months' rain of lead.'

Celebrating Peace

The events that crowded the next two days ran the whole gamut from the mundane and the poignant to the surreal. That morning the very last tin of beef had been eaten and immediately after the signing Commissary Dunne hurried off to obtain provisions. He received the ready co-operation of the Boer commissariat who were anxious to prevent speculators taking advantage of the new situation. Bread, beef, vegetables, coffee and tobacco appeared and the hungry men were soon 'revelling in plenty' as they were given full rations without mealies. Equally quickly Surgeon Wallis managed to acquire from the town the medical supplies and comforts so desperately needed for the casualties.

Under the surrender terms no one was permitted to leave the fort or have any communication with the town without the consent of both commanders. In view of the past vindictive attitude of the Boers it was considered too hazardous to allow the Forssman family or any of the other civilians to stray from British protection, no matter how great their need for essentials such as clothing. For the soldiers with a predilection for liquor the numerous bars and canteens of Potchefstroom remained a dream.

When the formalities were over, Winsloe and some of his party were taken into the town, on the way looking at the wrecked shell of the gaol, the bullet-scarred Landrost's office and other buildings occupied during the fighting. Everywhere they were well received, even by those whose property had been damaged by British shells. They heard how the Steynes had stayed in their house, which was frequently in the British target area, despite all their crockery and best drawing-room furniture being smashed. Only when eighty-year-old Mrs Steyne was wounded did they 'retire from their dwelling'. Women and children confessed to having been frightened by shells and bullets that had missed their target and fallen in the town, but all accepted that this had been accidental and that the British had done their best to spare the inhabitants. Winsloe noticed among the Boers in the streets a number of natives who were carrying rifles, which confirmed reports by sentries in the fort during the fighting that they had seen armed black men in the trenches.

Introductions went on all day, the British party meeting Andries Cronje, the general's brother and commandant of the Schoonspruit commando, Commandant J. W. Wolmorans, commandant of the Mooi River contingent, and Jan Kock, described as the 'fighting general'. Pelser, the gunner in charge of Ou Griet, pressed forward to make himself known, being as pleased as punch when Winsloe congratulated him on his shooting. Daniel van Graan was presented as 'one of our bravest men'; he had one arm in a sling, one eye covered with a bandage and Winsloe heard he also had a third wound. During their perambulations the British received numerous invitations to breakfast, lunch and dinner, stopping to consume 'a quantity of Dry Monopole Champaigne that was surprising'. The visit culminated with an invitation from Cronje for Winsloe and his officers to dine that evening with the Boer commander at the Royal Hotel.

There was a great reunion at the fort when the two sergeants and three corporals captured at the Landrost's office were released at the request of Winsloe, who wrote to Cronje thanking him for the 'courteous consideration of the Courts martial shown to my request'. Having been well cared for they were in better shape than the garrison, but they had disturbing stories to tell, especially of how Buskes had appropriated the rings belonging to Captain Falls and how one of them had been made to work in the trenches under British fire.

That evening Winsloe, accompanied by Major Thornhill, Surgeon Wallis and Lieutenants Browne and Dalrymple-Hay, went down to the Royal, passing the Forssman house they had once known so well and where Major Clarke was still imprisoned. Theirs was to be a strange experience that they would not soon forget. Ushered into a large room, they found thirty rough, hearty, determined-looking men seated at table awaiting them, characters of a type who in Winsloe's opinion 'were in a class to command respect'. Lining the walls three deep stood a crowd of Boers carrying their rifles; every window was crammed with the faces of others outside trying to look in. The British had gone with every intention of enjoying themselves and they were served with an excellent dinner. Surgeon Wallis had warned them not to over-indulge after their starvation diet, advice he himself ignored once the food appeared.

For a while there was an air of genuine *bonhomie* with many speeches and replies from both sides, all being translated by Buskes. The congenial atmosphere evaporated when Cronje, delivering the last speech of the evening, wound up by proposing a toast to the success of Boer arms. Winsloe 'let him have his sweet way', staying still until Cronje sat down 'amidst tumultuous applause, banging of rifles on the floor and shouting in the street'. The colonel watched the reaction of his officers with some trepidation. Seeing the moustache of one subaltern bristle, he felt thankful the young man's sword and revolver were in the next room. When the applause had died down, Winsloe rose and after replying to the first part of Cronje's speech told the assembly that 'the latter part was that he could not respond to'. His words were met with a stony, menacing silence. To diffuse the situation he promptly proposed the health of Cronje coupled with his officers 'lately our enemies now our friends'. There was some subdued response and banging of rifles on the floor, all of which quickly increased in volume as Cronje reached across the table to give Winsloe his hand and they drank the toast together. By his gesture Cronje had restored good relations round the table. The feeling was quickly transmitted to the mob outside the hotel.

Winsloe and his officers now realised that the expressions of friendship were pretty fragile and that anything might happen. When a friendly waiter touched Winsloe on the shoulder he instinctively put his hand down to receive a note, which he surreptitiously read under the table. It contained a warning that some of the mob planned to shoot him on the way back to the fort. The dinner over, the British made their way to leave down a crowded passage where Winsloe had a similar warning whispered to him. Alerted to the danger, Winsloe, who spoke a little Dutch, kept his ears open and heard Cronje charge his officers with the safe return of the British to the fort. Outside it was a pitch dark and as Winsloe climbed into a waiting buggy two of the senior Boer leaders also got in to sit on either side of him while two others positioned themselves behind. The other British officers conveyed in another vehicle were similarly protected as the little cavalcade proceeded at walking pace, at first through a dense crowd and then on without incident to the fort, where the 'escort' took their leave with cordial handshakes.

The British Prepare to Leave the Fort

The next day was devoted to preparing for the evacuation of the fort and the march back to Natal. A priority was the acquisition of the transport needed for a march of over 250 miles. The contingents had arrived at

Engraving published in the Penny Illustrated of 8 April 1881. The only contemporary illustration of events at Potchefstroom, it inaccurately depicts dejected unarmed men carrying cased regimental colours marching out from mountainous walls surrounded by Boers.

Potchefstroom with a total of seventeen wagons, far in excess of the normal regulation allowance because the 2/21st companies from Pretoria had been transported in order to keep up with N/5 Battery and the Mounted Infantry. They had also brought two ambulances and a number of ammunition and water carts. Under the terms of the capitulation all equipment was to be handed over to the Boers. This included vehicles but with the exception of one ambulance and three water carts all others had been burned or damaged beyond use during the fighting. The Boers agreed Wallis could temporarily keep the ambulance on the condition it was returned when the British reached Natal; they also allowed the garrison to have the water carts. Wallis required another sprung ambulance, two wagons for casualties and another for his stores; these the Commissariat would fund without question.

Rigid regulations restricted what Dunne could hire for the main body, which the authorities would expect to march. With no weapons or tents and very little camp equipment or other baggage he would have difficulty in justifying five or so ox wagons even when the Forssman ladies were taken into consideration. Each officer was entitled to a horse, which Dunne would need to purchase; they had kept their own saddles, most of which had bullet holes from the time they had been used to reinforce the parapets. Lindsell's mare Intombe had survived the siege but was wounded and in poor condition.

Given permission by Cronje, Winsloe rode to the Forssman house to visit Major Clarke who was still being held prisoner. They discussed events, Clarke telling how the envoys from President Brand had seen him on 13 March and of the Boer refusal to allow them any contact with Winsloe or permit the delivery of the letters they carried. In turn Winsloe told of how the spy Hudson had brought him news of the armistice and of the subsequent meetings with Cronje who had refused to explain why he withheld the terms of the agreement between Wood and Joubert. He also spoke of Cronje's refusal to allow the Forssman women to leave the fort after the death of Emelia.

Clarke and Raaff were to remain imprisoned until Commandant-General Joubert arrived at Potchefstroom on 1 April 1881 to address a meeting of the burghers. When this meeting ended Joubert visited Clarke and expressed his surprise at not finding the British garrison in the fort and Clarke not reinstated as special commissioner. After consideration Joubert decided that in the circumstances the town must stay under Boer control until Kruger gave a ruling. In the meantime Clarke was to be released. Clarke did not leave for Pretoria until 5 April by which time, at the request of Joubert, Goetze had resumed his functions as Landrost and Raaff, also freed, had gone to Pretoria.

Winsloe with one of the officers took another ride into the town, this time to purchase underclothes and other necessities the men badly needed for the long march ahead. The proprietor of the store where Winsloe tried to place his order explained that he was forbidden by the Boers to sell any such goods. Despite arguing Winslow could get no explanation and had to leave empty-handed.

Apart from the inevitable domestic chores, caring for the sick and wounded, cooking, and emptying latrines, the soldiers were busy cleaning their uniforms and equipment ready to march out the following morning with as much panache as possible. A great deal of time was spent on fencing and decorating the little graveyard at the rear of the fort. Wild flower plants were carefully lifted from the veldt without disturbing the blooms and carefully replanted on the graves. Wooden crosses were neatly marked with inscriptions and the letters IHS or RIP.

By evening the hired wagons had arrived at the fort and the ammunition to be placed in the custody of the Orange Free State was loaded together with the personal belongings that the officers and men were to be permitted to take with them. After dark in a poignant last tribute Lieutenant Rundle led the men carrying lanterns out to the graves where prayers were said bidding their fallen comrades farewell.

The Final Act

At 11 o'clock on 23 March 1881 the garrison paraded at the rear of the fort ready for inspection prior to marching out with the 'honours of war', a distinction of small consolation to the officers and men of the Royal Artillery, who were to endure the stigma of leaving their guns in enemy hands. The ragged men stood waiting with their weapons, turned out in full equipment with water bottles filled, haversacks and rolled remnants of greatcoats. Some indication of how they were feeling was recorded by Dalrymple-Hay, who wrote: 'I was pleased with Corporal Murphy (C Company) coming up to me as we were marching out and telling me he thought he would not have been able to march off if I had had to give up my sword.'

Grooms were standing holding the saddled horses only bought the previous day, ready to be mounted by officers who had never ridden them before, when General Cronje with Brigadier Kock rode up to the fort bringing a splendid white stallion that they wished to lend to Winsloe for the ceremony. Just before 12 o'clock the officers swung into their saddles and Winsloe led his men in the direction of the gaol to a rousing march played by four buglers directed by Sergeant McIlroy. Behind Winsloe rode Rundle holding high the home-made Union Jack torn by several bullets.

The troops were followed by a crowd of about 300 armed Boers who emerged from the trenches around the magazine and the cemetery.

On reaching the Grootvoor, Winsloe halted his men and formed line in open order, the Royal Artillery on the right, then the Mounted Infantry, the 2/21st Fusiliers, the Army Hospital Corps and the Army Service Corps. Behind them stood the bedraggled Forssman family with the other civilians and the Commissariat drivers, and beside them the ambulances and wagons carrying the sick and wounded. Altogether they were 209 souls out of the 322 who had been defending or had taken refuge in the fort ninety-nine days before. To the front of the gaol 300 armed, mounted Boers were drawn up in line; to their left at right angles stood a similar number of armed Boers on foot. The party that had followed the garrison down from the fort took up a position about 50 yards in the rear of the British line. Large numbers of people had come out of the town to watch the proceedings and occupied the tops of buildings and every surrounding vantage point. Winsloe took up his position in front of his men. Cronje with his officers rode forward, grouped around an enormous republican flag, to face the British commander. From the British line, Surgeon Wallis observed Secretary Buskes beside Cronje: 'The villain of the piece – sitting on his horse viewing the remnants of the half starved Garrison, you cannot fail to observe the cunning of a cat teeming from his eyes.'

When all was ready Colonel Winsloe raised his hand in salute to Cronje and in a faltering voice said: 'General, I lay down my arms to you.'

The Peace Treaty

Ironically that same day, after a week of acrimonious negotiations, a preliminary peace treaty restoring self-government to the Transvaal people under the suzerainty of the reigning sovereign of Great Britain was signed by General Sir Evelyn Wood and the Triumvirate, Kruger, Joubert and Pretorius. It was further agreed that a Royal Commission should sit to resolve the outstanding issues affecting the future of the new Transvaal state including its boundaries. The final meetings, which took place at O'Neill's farm on the slopes below Majuba Hill, had frequently come near to breaking down over such contentious issues as the composition of the Royal Commission, and British demands to keep troops in the Transvaal for up to six months. The Boers were particularly opposed to the British intention to retain a large area of the eastern Transvaal, territory to the east of the 30 degree of longitude, where gold and other minerals had been found. It had taken all the persuasive powers of President Brand, who attended the final meetings, to bring the negotiations to a successful conclusion.

CHAPTER 19

The March Out

Leaving their weapons on the ground the garrison reformed in close order and marched off through the town, the mounted Boers riding as an advance guard with the remainder on foot behind. They were escorted for about a mile and crossed the North bridge over the Mooi River where Cronje had entered the town on 15 December 1880. Here the column halted. Cronje delivered a farewell speech and the principal Boer leaders crowded round Winsloe and his officers grasping their hands and wishing them Godspeed. The burghers then formed up on either side of the road and saluted the British troops as they marched between their ranks. Winsloe was most touched by this gesture and recorded that 'no troops in any part of the world could have taken a more polite farewell or behaved more courteously throughout'.

The two Fusiliers dreadfully wounded during the last days of the fighting, Birmingham on 10 March and Jordan on 17 March, had been taken into hospital by the Boers. They both lived long enough to hear the bugles playing as their comrades marched past out of the town. Winsloe led his column to a farm named Vyf Hof owned by Captain Baillie late of the 7th Hussars, which lay on the north-east fringes of Potchefstroom. Baillie had arranged for the garrison to rest on his land before commencing their march back to Natal. The British found themselves surrounded by kindness. One Boer alone sent in fifty ducks for the 'hospital' in which were fifteen badly wounded and eight very sick men. The good captain took Winsloe and the officers to live in his house and when Winsloe told him about the abortive attempt to buy clothing, Baillie led him into a room where the astonished colonel saw piled up everything he had ordered and more. The goods were parcelled up ready for loading on the wagons; all were gifts, and there was enough for officers and men alike.

There remained a sad duty before the garrison could quit Vyf Hof, which was to disinter the body of Captain Falls from the garden of the Standard Bank and bury him properly in the consecrated ground of the town cemetery. With heavy hearts they also had to bury Privates Jordan and Birmingham, the Boers providing the firing party.

Early on the morning of 25 March 1881 the Potchefstroom garrison thanked their generous host and set off on their march to Natal. A route through the Orange Free State had been chosen, as it was likely to be safer and easier to obtain provisions on that route than on a journey through the Transvaal. Next day they arrived at De Wet's Drift on the River Vaal, having been escorted by Commandant Wolmorans who was accompanied by his wife and three burghers. It had been the duty of Wolmorans and the others to ensure that in accordance with the capitulation agreement no armed Boers approached within two miles of the British.

Joubert Presents the Peace Treaty to the Boers

When the British had gone the Boers removed the 9-pounders from the fort and gathered up the rifles surrendered by the British. The Martini Henry rifles were subsequently issued to individual burghers on the understanding that they could be retained after the war on the payment of £7 to the Transvaal government. Everything likely to be of any use was cleared out of the fort: picks, shovels, buckets, barrels plus a miscellany of abandoned material such as corrugated iron, wooden posts and old sacks. Very soon inquisitive burghers and townspeople were scavenging in the fort and the magazine for souvenirs.

Cronje assembled his commandos to thank them for their services, and then, warning them that they must be ready to join the main army at Majuba, sent most away on eight days' leave. However, in less than a week, on 1 April 1881, Commandant-General Piet Joubert arrived to announce that 'he was the bearer of glad tidings, for under the blessing of the Almighty their efforts had been crowned with success, that they had got their country back'.

His audience, which had assembled outside the Landrost's office at 4 pm in the afternoon, comprised the leading local landowners, those of Cronje's men who were not away on leave and a large contingent numbering 300 or 400 who came from the most militant areas of the Potchefstroom district and were passing through on their way home from Majuba. He summarised the main conditions of the peace agreement to a sceptical crowd who were obviously dissatisfied by what they heard. There were many questions concerning the British claim to retain the eastern Transvaal and on local issues such as who would be Landrost and what flag would be flown. Aiming to be moderate and conciliatory he answered the questions, saying the choice of Landrost would be theirs and he would decide on the flag. Eventually he became somewhat exasperated, closing the meeting with the words: 'We did our best. If you don't like what we have done for you, go and fight it out to the bitter end. I need not tell sensible fellows like you what the result of that will be.'

It was after this meeting that Joubert went to see Major Clarke in prison. The very next day, despite what he had said to the assembled burghers, Joubert privately told Goetze that 'no obstacle would be thrown in his way if he resumed his functions as Landrost'. The day after that conversation, all his papers and books were restored to Goetze who obtained the use of a room in the town as an office, the old Landrost's office being damaged beyond use; moreover it had a republican flag flying above it. When Major Clarke departed from Potchefstroom for Pretoria on 5 April 1881 he sensed that the Boers were dissatisfied with the peace agreement negotiated by their leaders and were particularly agitated by a rumour that every man would be compelled to pay a levy of £5 for damage done during the rebellion. Many were declaring that they would fight on rather than comply with such a preposterous imposition.

The March from the Vaal to Ladysmith

The garrison spent 26 March and part of the next day in being ferried across the Vaal. Once over and safely in the Orange Free State they 'felt like birds let out of a cage, free as the air we lived in': no more encircling parapets, no more deadly bullets, no more nights broken by alarms. Having made bivouacs out of their blankets, everyone spent the next two days relaxing, the men sporting about in the river and washing their clothes. Many letters were written and Winsloe settled down under a tree to write his report to Army headquarters at Pretoria. It is a great tribute to Winsloe that this report, which he dated 23 March 1881 from Potchefstroom, contained as much detail as it did. A manuscript copy made subsequently in the headquarters of General Wood at Mount Prospect around 7 May 1881 runs to thirty-five foolscap sheets.

On 29 March Winsloe's column resumed their march heading for Kronstadt, which was reached on 4 April. Fortunately the weather had turned more clement; although still very hot there was less rain; consequently the roads were in better condition and the rivers fordable. Progress was slow, no more than ten miles a day, because marching time was curtailed in consideration of the sick and wounded. In normal circumstances the troops would move off in the cool around 5 am, stopping for breakfast about 6 or 7 o'clock and then marching until midday when they outspanned to avoid the heat and graze the oxen. The march would be resumed about 3 pm for perhaps another two hours until they laagered for the night. Treating the casualties and preparing them for the day's journey made the usual early start impossible.

Union Jacks were flying all over Kronstadt as the British marched through to bivouac under the trees on a riverbank. Then in accordance with the capitulation terms Winsloe handed over all his ammunition to the Orange Free State authorities. Numerous friendly visitors descended on the British camp with invitations to all sorts of entertainment and meals. The soldiers were told how one Boer had hoisted a Transvaal flag only to have it torn down. Of all extraordinary things the troops played a cricket match against a local side, which 'occasioned great excitement, spectators coming from near and far'.

Winsloe rested his men for a week at Kronstadt. When they departed on 11 April they took their leave of the Forssman family who were to stay in the Free State. All the soldiers were truly sorry to part from the ladies who had shared their dangers and miseries with such courage and fortitude, and who had left a sister and brother in the little cemetery with their comrades. The family drove a long way out of the town alongside the marching column before making the final handshakes and saying goodbye. Dr Sketchley as Emelia's husband is not mentioned as part of the family so it is probable that he stayed to assist Surgeon Wallis with the casualties until the end of the march. He later was seen in Newcastle looking underfed and ragged but bronzed and in good health.

The column plodded on day after day over rolling treeless veldt, the skyline broken by distant ridges and kopjes. Beyond the township of Bethlehem they had to negotiate rougher country as the road crossed the craggy ridge that marked the rim of the high veldt. Soon the peaks of the Drakensbergs could be seen on the horizon. They reached Harrismith on 24 April, having covered another 180 miles in thirteen days. Three days were spent at Harrismith allowing the hospital patients to recuperate after the long, jolting journey and to prepare for the final haul over the mountains. Again they were fêted by the local people, who organised a ball where dancing went on until 4 am. At 8 o'clock the following morning most of the officers attended a wedding in the pretty little English church before two hours later they with the whole column marched on once more.

Twenty miles on and three days later they had climbed up 6,000 feet to cross the Drakensbergs by Van Reenens Pass. They descended into Natal by the winding road that led the final thirty miles to Ladysmith, where they arrived at 11 am on 2 May 1881. With regular food and rest, in favourable weather, unencumbered by weapons and ammunition the survivors of the Potchefstroom garrison including the hospital patients had come through a march of some 250 miles with their health much improved.

They found a tented camp awaiting them on the slopes of the hills above the town, a luxury they had not known for five months. From the report by the military correspondent of the *Natal Mercury*, dateline Ladysmith, 5 May 1881, it does not appear that Winsloe and his men received any ceremonial welcome when they joined the troops already encamped at Ladysmith.

Curiously there is no evidence as to whether news had reached Ladysmith of the decision of the Transvaal government to cancel the capitulation of the Potchefstroom garrison. A telegram originated by General Sir Evelyn Wood at Newcastle on 11 April 1881 had been published in the *Natal Witness* at Pietermaritzburg on 13 April, nearly three weeks before, which read:

> Boer leaders admitted to me at Heidelberg that Commandant Cronje broke their promise by suppressing news of the Armistice to the Potchefstroom garrison; they expressed their sincere regrets and proposed that the capitulation be considered cancelled; and they acquiesced in the re occupation of the place. I accepted the apology and proposals. All surrendered material to be handed over at once at Standerton.

Lieutenant-Colonel Gildea at Pretoria had not forgotten his soldiers. Winsloe and his men of the 2/21st found a letter from their commanding officer waiting to greet them at Ladysmith:

> We cannot find words to express the grief we feel at the losses and hardship sustained by our gallant comrades in the defence of the camp at Potchefstroom, but they are proud to learn that all ranks behaved so admirably, and have helped to raise the gallant Regiment to which they belong still higher in the roll of honour, than it stood before. While grieving over the loss of so many comrades and expressing their great sympathy it will always be a comfort to know that they fell in the defence of the honour of Queen and Country.

The thoughtful and practical Gildea had also obtained transport by which he dispatched to Ladysmith the kit and clothing that the companies had left behind at Pretoria when they had marched to either Rustenburg or Potchefstroom the previous year. He also sent for each man 'a new pair of the most serviceable description of trowsers [sic] free'. The issue of civilian trousers in the absence of replacement uniform was not unusual on campaign in South Africa. The regiment had resorted to this on occasions after the Zulu War: 'some were supplied with tweed trousers of various shades and patterns, some were glad to exchange a pair of loud pattern for a quieter pair'.

The Potchefstroom Troops Disperse

There was general surprise when orders were received on 4 May, only two days after their arrival, for Rundle and his section of N/5 Battery to proceed at once to Newcastle. All thought something 'of no ordinary importance' must have occurred that demanded the Gunners to leave again so soon after their long march. Clearly no one associated these orders with Wood's expectations that their guns would soon be returned to Standerton. Rundle had his men ready in no time. Only twenty-eight of the original forty-three NCOs and men had survived the siege and were still fit for duty. A great bond had built up between the Gunners and the Fusiliers, who showed their feelings by cheering the artillerymen until Rundle had led them out of sight.

The absence of Major Thornhill at this juncture gives rise to conjecture as to his movements. After handing over command at Potchefstroom to Winsloe on 12 December 1880, Thornhill seldom receives a mention in any narrative except for allusions to his frequent illness; evidently he took little part in events. There is no indication as to when he may have left the column as it progressed through the Orange Free State, but he was at Army headquarters in Newcastle on 27 April when he answered in writing critical questions put to him by General Redvers Buller as a result of General Wood having read the report written by Winsloe beside the Vaal on 27 March. Thornhill had been too ill at the time of the surrender to ride and had been provided with a spider (a light horse-drawn carriage); therefore it is a rea-sonable assumption that he went on ahead of the slow-moving column to deliver Winsloe's report to Newcastle for onward transmission to Pretoria. Thornhill had a personal interest in returning to Pretoria since his wife had been there throughout the war.

On 17 May 1881 the sick and wounded from Potchefstroom left Ladysmith for Pietermaritzburg in the charge of Surgeon Wallis. Announcing their departure, a report in the *Natal Witness* dated 16 May 1881 remarked: 'It is hoped that the inhabitants of Maritzburg will do something on their arrival to show their appreciation of the conduct of these victims of war.' There is a hint here that Ladysmith had done nothing in this respect. With them went DACG Walter Dunne whose health was severely impaired as a consequence of the siege and continuous campaign service since the 1877 Frontier War. His detailed report on Commissariat aspects of the siege written immediately after crossing the Vaal on 28 March had been included by Winsloe with his own dispatch.

Winsloe and his companies of the 2/21st languished in their camp next to the 14th Hussars, reinforcements from India, as the weeks rolled by: at first while the Royal Commission that assembled on 12 May deliberated, until 3 August 1881 when the final convention was signed, and then on into December when the last British troops evacuated the Transvaal. The Fusiliers performed normal duties alongside other units, taking their turn on detached duties guarding the roads over the inhospitable Biggarsberg hills back to Pietermaritzburg. The companies missed the ceremony at Pretoria on 25 May 1881 when most of their battalion were presented with their long-awaited 1879 Campaign medal for the Zulu War and Sekukuni Campaign. In mid-June, Winsloe took under command a draft of four officers and eighty men of the 2/21st which, having arrived in

Natal after their battalion was cut off in the Transvaal, spent the war as part of the camp guard at Mount Prospect and later at Schuins Hooghte. Two of their number had been killed when used as stretcher bearers in the Majuba battle.

Not until 15 August 1881 did they see Sir Evelyn Wood, who was making a series of military inspections after completing his work with the Royal Commission. His itinerary embraced several regiments fresh from India and Britain; almost as an afterthought when at Ladysmith he included the Potchefstroom garrison. In a letter to the Duke of Cambridge reporting his inspections of the 41st, 2/60th, 83rd, 97th, the Inneskillings and the 15th Hussars, he wrote: 'I saw the 21st detachment very ragged and recruits strikingly unlike their Potchefstroom comrades whom I separated from the others after the inspection and thanked them for their determined defence.'

Winsloe was to recall the address given by Wood:

Men of the Potchefstroom Garrison. I thought there were more of you here as I forgot the Company at the Biggarsberg.

I thank you for the gallant way you defended Potchefstroom and also for the stubborn way you maintained the position.

General Buller has recently been there and the Boers told him that latterly they could hardly show themselves at a loophole on account of your good shooting but then you had plenty of it.

I again thank you for your gallant defence.

I have reported this to HRH the Field Marshal, Commander in Chief.

A few days earlier, on 8 August, Wood had inspected N/5 Battery at Mount Prospect and reported to the Duke of Cambridge: 'I saw N 5 RA in the afternoon and can say only that they have had great difficulties, having lost a division complete at Isandlhwana and another temporarily at Potchefstroom. I shall be glad when the Battery is back at Woolwich to be rubbed up in many ways.'

Winsloe and his men were not finally reunited with the rest of the 2/21st until December 1881 when Colonel Gildea brought the battalion to Pietermaritzburg on their way to embark for duty in India. The Fusiliers with the Mounted Infantry and N/5 Battery were the last British units to evacuate the newly independent Transvaal state. They crossed into Natal on 16 November 1881, marching to Mount Prospect where they left their old comrades N/5. On 4 December, General Sir Evelyn Wood watched the battalion march through Pietermaritzburg 'looking bronzed but in excellent condition'. A day or so later he inspected them formally and afterwards wrote privately from Government House to the Duke of Cambridge: 'The

When Sir Evelyn Wood inspected the survivors from Potchefstroom at Ladysmith on 15 August 1881 he had forgotten one company was on picket duty on the Biggarsberg range. Engraving from The Graphic.

Battalion has not been together since it arrived on the Zulu Border in May 1879 – since that time it has been in five detachments separated from each other by 60 to 200 miles. It would be idle therefore to expect anything like perfection – What I admire most in the Regiment is its esprit de Corps.'

Epilogue

When the news of the Majuba débâcle and the death of General Colley reached London and was digested by the government, they spontaneously appointed General Sir Frederick Roberts, recently returned from his triumph in Afghanistan, to be commander-in-chief in South Africa. Almost within hours, amid public acclaim, he sailed for the Cape. While Roberts was at sea, Wood was instructed by the government, which was more interested in ending the war than avenging Majuba, to continue peace negotiations. On 2 March 1881 the secretary of state for war telegraphed Wood: 'Although Sir F Roberts is going out with large reinforcements we place full confidence in you and do not desire to better your military discretion.' On 4 March he telegraphed again: 'The Queen approves your being granted local rank of Major General whilst employed in South Africa.'

As soon as the interim peace agreement was signed on 23 March, Gladstone announced to parliament that General Roberts would return home immediately and that reinforcements had been stopped. Roberts arrived at Cape Town on 25 March 1881 to be handed a telegram ordering his return. Disgusted, he sailed for England next day aboard the *Trojan*, accompanied by his staff.

Wood, undoubtedly the best man to deal with the Triumvirate, was confirmed in the appointment of acting governor of Natal and high commissioner of the Transvaal, and within days set off to visit Pretoria. By the time he reached Heidelberg on the night of 8 April 1881 he was aware that Cronje had withheld news of the armistice terms from Winsloe. Wood confronted the Boer leaders with these allegations. They claimed not to be aware of Cronje's behaviour, and declared they 'would not let a stain to rest on the people'. The Triumvirate accepted the version of events as given by Wood, and unequivocally offered to cancel the surrender of Potchefstroom, restore everything taken and allow Wood to send the garrison back if he considered it necessary.

In a telegram to Lord Kimberley, the colonial secretary, dated 11 April, Wood explained that he had arranged for the guns and weapons to be returned to the British at Standerton, but that he did not intend to send troops back to Potchefstroom. The government, suddenly eager to salvage some political credibility after all the military disasters, ordered Wood to reoccupy Potchefstroom unless he had some strong military objection.

Wood promptly replied that the idea was impractical; the number of troops he would be permitted to send was too small to be of any strategic value except as a future supply base. In any event the troops would probably be attacked if they tried to make their way through the most hostile part of the Transvaal, whatever efforts Kruger and Joubert might make to keep the peace.

Pompously Kimberley informed Wood that the government would not overlook what had happened at Potchefstroom and insisted that Wood dispatch the 'garrison' with a strong enough escort to meet 'all contingencies'. Furthermore he was to advise the Transvaal government of his intentions. Kimberley stipulated that after occupying Potchefstroom and raising the flag both the 'garrison' and the escort should return to Natal, but that this information was to be kept secret for the moment. On being told of the British decision, the Triumvirate were most co-operative but insisted there was no real reason for an escort as the people would not 'molest the troops'. Joubert himself offered to accompany the British and proposed that two prominent Boer leaders should stay at Newcastle as 'hostages' until the British returned. Remaining sceptical of the whole idea, Wood notified Kimberley that if the Boer safeguards were accepted he believed two and a half cavalry squadrons would suffice as an escort.

On 1 May 1881 Kimberley telegraphed Wood giving government approval for the plans made with the Transvaal government and ordering him to proceed. Two weeks later Wood reported to Kimberley that he had placed the force for Potchefstroom under orders to march but was waiting for the guns to be returned. Wood did not trust Cronje and a letter written by Buskes signed by Kruger, which reached Newcastle on 15 May promising that the guns were expected 'hourly' at Standerton, did nothing to reassure him.

A crisis began to develop as Wood became increasingly irritated by the Boer failure to deliver the 9-pounders as promised. Wood bombarded Kimberley with telegrams that became more and more explosive as the days passed. Finally Wood threatened to give the Boers six days in which to comply or he would advance. Alarmed, Kimberley demanded to know what 'advance' meant; had he not already given authority to reoccupy Potchefstroom? Wood did not mince words when he replied that he intended to march his whole army into the Transvaal and take whatever action was necessary to recover the guns. Sir Hercules Robinson, chairman of the Royal Commission, intervened to defuse the situation, persuading Wood to give the Boers four more days' grace before giving the Transvaal government the six days' notice of his intention to advance into their territory.

In the meantime Joubert, who had travelled to Potchefstroom to expedite matters, sent a message to Wood, which reached the general belatedly by heliograph, that the guns would at last be leaving for Standerton on 19 May. Wood telegraphed Kimberley to the effect that he would not now move without some strong reason, and began a patient wait as news of the guns continued to filter through. On 26 May 1881 when he was satisfied that the 9-pounders were at last on the way to Standerton, Wood ordered the column for Potchefstroom to move north from Newcastle.

On Thursday, 26 May, Lieutenant-Colonel Browne commanding the 94th, who was to bring together the companies of his regiment, which had been scattered across the Transvaal since the ambush at Bronkhorst Spruit, marched his headquarters with 190 officers and men from Newcastle to Mount Prospect. With him went a detachment of N/5 Battery, no doubt including Rundle and some of his men. Two days later, Browne was fol- lowed by two squadrons of the 6th Dragoon Guards and a half squadron of 15th Hussars. On Sunday, 29 May, Sir Redvers Buller, now a major-general and chief of staff to Wood, left Newcastle for Mount Prospect. The column crossed Laing's Nek on 30 May reaching Standerton on 2 June 1881.

Travelling with them was Lady Florence Dixie, special correspondent for the *Morning Post* in London, and her husband, Sir Bernard Dixie. Aged twenty-six, she was the daughter of the Marquess of Queensberry, attrac- tive, highly intelligent but with a caustic tongue. An accomplished horse- woman, she had written a best-seller about a six-month-long riding expedition she had undertaken, *Across Patagonia*. The editor of the *Morning Post*, who like many others did not take the Transvaal rebellion very ser- iously, thought it amusing to invite this patrician lady to be the first female war correspondent for his paper.

On arrival at Standerton the force was reorganised for the final march to Potchefstroom, the detachment of N/5 being left to await the arrival of their guns. The headquarters and men of the 94th stayed behind together with one troop of the 15th Hussars. The main body of the cavalry from New- castle was joined by five officers with 140 men of the 94th, veterans who had recently been besieged at Standerton. The troops were notionally under command of Lieutenant-Colonel Curtis, 6th Dragoon Guards, but Wood had decided that Buller should accompany the column 'as his experience of South African warfare would have been invaluable had there been any opposition'. Buller also carried sealed orders to be opened only on reaching Potchefstroom. A senior Boer commandant named Lombard representing the Triumvirate had joined Buller on 31 May on the road between Laing's Nek and Standerton.

The column left Standerton on 3 June 1881 reaching Heidelberg on 8 June and Potchefstroom on 14 June. Throughout the march the Boers met by the British were civil and willing to sell them any supplies they required. Notwithstanding, it was not an easy journey; the nights had turned cold and the draught oxen suffered terribly from the chill and bad grass. The column had 683 oxen to draw forty-eight wagons and, despite the length of each day's march being decided by the condition of the animals rather than the needs of the men, 300 beasts were lost to lung sickness and starvation on the journeys out and back. The alteration to the normal marching schedule disrupted the feeding of the soldiers, who were dependent on cow dung for fuel. Cooking with this was so slow that they could only have a hot meal before setting out for the day; then they had to wait until laagering for the night before eating warm food again. Buller sanctioned an extra ration of 4 ounces of tinned beef on marching days, which the men could eat cold during the midday outspan to lessen their hunger.

Buller rode into Potchefstroom at the head of his troops with 'all the paraphernalia of a conqueror'. First came the 6th Dragoons riding with swords drawn. Behind them trudged the 94th, dusty, footsore and weary, their uniform worn out and ill fitting, and their helmets battered in; some were even wearing Boer-type felt hats. Last in the procession came the troop of 15th Hussars who by contrast looked spick and span. There were no welcoming cheers from the few remaining loyalists, who stood passively to watch the soldiers pass. Groups of Boers were more vociferous, making disparaging remarks about the poor appearance of the infantry. The column marched down Church Street, turning right into Potgieter Street and out to their camping place by the Grootvoor, three-quarters of a mile north of what remained of the fort. They had passed empty stores and houses, many damaged by shell and rifle fire, some like Jooste's house only a shell.

The next day, 15 June, Buller duly opened his sealed orders to find that he was to abandon the fort and return immediately with his entire force to Standerton. Plans were put into motion to leave two days later on 17 June. Fatigue parties from the 94th had already begun to clear the rubbish still in the fort and the surrounding area in preparation for a ceremony to hoist the Union Jack above the defences once again. A story circulated that as the parade was about to form up it was discovered that Buller had forgotten to bring a flag. Someone fortunately remembered that the Union Jack taken down when Major Clarke surrendered was still in the safe in the Landrost's office from whence it was hurriedly fetched and hauled up the mast. On the day Buller and his column marched away out of Potchefstroom everyone with loyalist sympathies had the feeling that the whole charade demanded by the Gladstone government had left the British without honour, dignity or prestige.

The two 9-pounder guns that had assumed such importance to both sides were eventually delivered by the Boers to Standerton on 31 May 1881 where their owners N/5 Battery were waiting. The 153 Martini Henry rifles surrendered by Winsloe proved even more difficult to recover. By early June

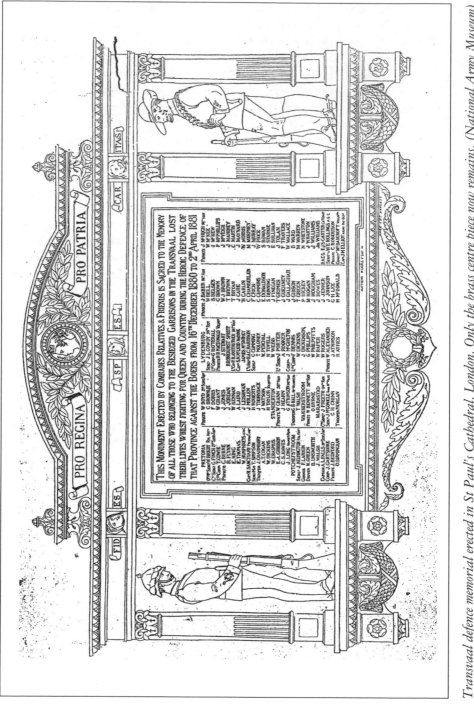

Transvaal defence memorial erected in St Paul's Cathedral, London. Only the brass centre piece now remains. (National Army Museum)

approaching a hundred had been returned but Wood was doubtful if the remainder would come in until the Boers returned from winter grazing on the bush veldt. Not until October was Wood able to advise the War Office that another ten and seemingly the last had been recovered, bringing the total to 133. Twenty had been lost. On a more poignant note, Wood personally sought to obtain the return of the sword and rings belonging to the dead Captain Falls. On 17 May 1881 Kruger signed a letter drafted by Buskes of all people, in which it was said that Joubert was investigating the matter of the sword but that Cronje had already arranged to return the rings to relatives of Captain Falls.

The services of those who had 'defended the honour of the Queen and Country' at Potchefstroom received little recognition. Lieutenant-Colonel Winsloe was promoted brevet colonel and made an aide-de-camp to the Queen. Major Thornhill was promoted brevet lieutenant-colonel. Lieutenants Rundle, Browne, Lindsell and Dalrymple-Hay were mentioned in dispatches, as were Surgeon Wallis and DACG Dunne. Five soldiers were awarded the Distinguished Conduct Medal: Trumpeter Nicholas Martin, Royal Artillery; Driver Robert Gibson, Royal Artillery; Driver Alfred Pead, Royal Artillery; Lance-Corporal Patrick Cunnief, 2/21, Royal Scots Fusiliers; and Private Henry Bush, 2/21, Royal Scots Fusiliers.

Perhaps the attitude of the establishment towards the siege of Potchefstroom was captured by Buller in a private letter to Evelyn Wood written after he returned from reoccupying the fort:

It certainly was a good defence in the sense of a patient enduring defence being a good one. I always try to put myself in another man's place when criticising him and I fancy I should never have defended the place half as long as Winsloe did. Though I might have cut more of a dash at first. He was a real good Badger in a hole.

Select Bibliography

This story of the siege at Potchefstroom has been pieced together from numerous contemporary publications, official documents and correspondence that describe the place, the events and the people involved. Some explanatory notes regarding these sources have been included.

Accounts of the siege by participants

The Official British Report

Winsloe, Lieutenant-Colonel R. W. C. There are three versions of the official report written by Winsloe on 23 March 1881. That published by the government in 'War Office Correspondence relating to Military Affairs in South Africa with reports on the operations of the Garrisons beleaguered by the Boers, 1882' (PRO – WO33/38), edited on the orders of the Duke of Cambridge (PRO – WO 32/7832), differs materially from the original manuscript. The versions are:

PRO – WO 33/38 The printed version purporting to be as submitted by Major-General Sir Evelyn Wood, dated Pietermaritzburg 3 October 1881.

PRO – WO 32/7832 Manuscript version submitted to the War Office by Wood, dated Pietermaritzburg 3 October 1881.

Natal Archives, Pietermaritzburg. Sir Evelyn Wood Papers, Enclosure No 84 dated 7 May 1881. Manuscript copy of Winsloe's account annotated 'Original sent to Adjutant General at Headquarters Mount Prospect'.

Published Narratives

Winsloe, R. W. C., 2/21st, Potchefstroom, *A Military Episode in the Transvaal, 1880–81*, Simpkin & Marshall, London, 1896 (amplification of an article published in *MacMillan's Magazine*, 1883).

Dalrymple-Hay, Second Lieutenant J. R. M., 2/21st, Leaves from Diary December 1880 – March 1881, *Journal of the Royal Scots Fusiliers*, October 1929.

Dunne, Deputy Assistant Commissary-General Walter. A., C&T Staff, African Reminiscences 1877–81, *Army Service Corps Journal*, 1891 (republished in *Eyewitness in Zululand*, Greenhill Books, London, 1989).

Rundle, Lieutenant H. M. L., RA, *The Siege of Potchefstroom*, Royal Artillery Institution, Woolwich, 1884.

Published in Newspapers

Raaff, Commandant Pieter E. Interview given to *Natal Witness*, 30 April 1881.

A Military Correspondent (probably Surgeon K. S. Wallis, Army Medical Department), Daily Diary of the Siege, *Times of Natal*, 22 April 1881.

Official Sources

War Office Correspondence for 1881, MOD Library

Nelson, John, Account of the attack on Potchefstroom, Encl 246.

Parliamentary Papers for 1881 (C2950), MOD Library

Clarke, Major Marshall, RA, Events subsequent to the Armistice, Encl 52.

Hunt, A. W. De La, Postmaster General the Transvaal, Events at Potchefstroom, 16–22 December 1880, Encl 29.

Public Records Office

Binnie, Lance-Corporal Alexander (WO 33/38 Encl 180), Defence of the Landrost's Office and experiences of prisoners of war.

Army Medical Department Report for 1880

Wallis, Surgeon Kenneth S., AMD, Report on the Siege of Potchefstroom, RAMC Museum.

Natal Government Archives – Sir Evelyn Wood Papers A598

Clarke, Major M. Letter to Wood dated 7 April 1881. Describes refusal of Cronje to allow representatives of President Brand to give Winsloe details of the armistice.

Thornhill, Major Charles, RA, Letter to DAAG, Headquarters, Pretoria, April 1881. Accepts sole responsibility for the siting of the fort. Ascribes weakness of citadel to lack of civilian volunteers.

Thornhill, Major Charles, RA, Encl No 3 to E. Wood's No 84, 7 May 1881. Response to official criticism by Major-General Buller regarding his personal handling of 9-pounders during Boer attack, 10 March 1881.

Free State Provincial Archives

Accession Number: GS 1299

Winsloe, Lieutenant-Colonel R. W. C. Letter to President Brand requesting permission to march out through Orange Free State, with nominal roll of military and civilian survivors and details of 9-pounder ammunition to be handed over to Free State authorities.

The Boer Perspective

Weilbach, J. D. and Du Plessis, C. N. J. *Geschiedenis van den Emigranten-Boeren en van den Vrigheids-Oorlog*, Cape Town, 1882.

Davey, A. M. The Siege of Pretoria 1880–81, *Archives Year Book for South African History*, 1953. Summarises official Boer strategic orders including instructions to Cronje regarding the importance of capturing the Potchefstroom 9-pounder guns.

Norris-Newman, Charles L. *With the Boers in the Transvaal 1880–81*, London, 1882. Appendix L is the official Boer government account of events leading to the British surrender to General Cronje at Potchefstroom.

Civilian Accounts

Austen, G. F. *Diary Potchefstroom 1880–81*, edited by Dr J. H. Breytenbach, Cum Books, Roodeport, 1981.

The Forssman Family:

   Forssman, Captain Alric, Biography Chevalier Oskar Forssman, Library of Parliament, Cape Town, 1962.

   Smithers, Elsa, *March Hare*, London, 1938.

   Schikkerling, Roland W. *Commando Courageous: A Boer Diary*, Johannesburg, 1964.

Jolivet, the Right Reverend Bishop of Natal, Journal held in Archdiocesan Archives, The Catholic Church, Natal.

Wallis, J. P. R. *The Southern African Diaries of Thomas Leask 1865–1870*, London, 1954.

Natal Mercury, 1881, Reports on aspects of civilian life in Potchefstroom during 1880–81.

The Reoccupation

Dixie, Lady Florence, Reports in the *Morning Post*, London, 28 July and 8 August 1881.

Buller, Major-General Sir Redvers, War Office Correspondence for 1881, Encl 339. Report on the conduct of the operation.

Further Sources

Africanus, *The Transvaal Boers*, London, 1900.

Atcherley, R. J. *Trip to Boerland*, London, 1899.

Aylward, Alfred, *The Transvaal Today*, London, 1878.

Bellairs, Lady Blanche, *The Transvaal War 1880–1881*, Edinburgh, 1882.

Bengough, Major-General H. M. *Notes and Reflections on the Boer War*, London, 1900.

Blackburn, D. and Waithman-Caddel, W. *Secret Service in South Africa*, London, 1911.

Blair Brown, Surgeon D., AMD, *Surgical Experiences in the Zulu and Transvaal Wars 1879 & 1881*, Edinburgh, 1883.

Brackenbury, Lieutenant-Colonel H. *Chief of Staff's Journal Operations 1879*, War Office, London, 1880.

Bulpin, T. V. *Lost Trails of the Transvaal*, Cape Town, 1965.

Butler, Lieutenant-General Sir W. *The Life of Sir George Pomeroy-Colley*, London, 1899.

Butterfield, Dr P. H. *War & Peace in South Africa 1879–81*, Scripta Africana, 1986.

Carter, Thomas F. *A Narrative of the Boer War*, London, 1883.

Cunynghame, General Sir Arthur, *My Command in South Africa*, London, 1879.

Dictionary of South African Biography, Johannesburg.

Drooglever, R. W. F. *The Road to Isandhlwana*, Greenhill Books, London, 1992.

Du Val, Charles, *With a Show through Southern Africa*, London, 1884.

Duxbury, Colonel George, *David and Goliath*, Johannesburg, 1981.

Heckford, Mrs Sara, *A Lady Trader in the Transvaal*, London, 1887.

Jeppe, Carl, *The Kaleidoscopic Transvaal*, London, 1906.

Knight, Ian, *Brave Men's Blood*, Greenhill Books, London, 1990.

Kotze, Sir John, *Biographical Memoirs & Reminiscences*, Cape Town, 1934.

Kruger, Paul, *The Memoirs of Paul Kruger*, London, 1902.

Lehmann, Joseph H. *The First Boer War*, London, 1972.

Lock, Ron, *Blood on the Painted Mountain*, Greenhill Books, London, 1995.

Mason, Professor R. J. *Archeology of the 1880–81 Fort, Potchefstroom*, University of Witwatersrand, 1975.

Meintjes, Johannes, *The Voortrekkers*, London, 1973.

Nixon, John, *The Complete Story of the Transvaal*, London, 1885.

Rider-Haggard, H. *The Last Boer War*, London, 1899.

Roberts, Brian, *Ladies in the Veldt*, London, 1965.

Stratford House Committee, Reports & Records Russo-Turkish War 1877–78, London, 1879.

Thomason, W. H. *With the Irregulars in the Transvaal & Zululand*, London, 1881.

Walt, van der, Professor A. J. M. *Potchefstroom 1838–1938*, Johannesburg, 1938.

Newspapers and Journals

The *Fusee*, regimental newspaper 2nd Battalion Royal Scots Fusiliers, India, January to December 1883.

South African Military History Society Journal, Vol 15, No 2, December 1980.

The *Graphic*, 1879 and 1881, London.

The *Illustrated London News*, 1881, London.

The *Penny Illustrated*, 1881, London.

Natal Witness, 1875 to 1881.
Natal Mercury, 1880 to 1881.
Times of Natal, 1881.
Transvaal Argus & Potchefstroom Commercial Gazette, 1877 and 1878.
Staats-Courant der Suid-Afrikaanshe Republiek, Potchefstroom, 1881.

Archives
The papers of HRH the Duke of Cambridge, Royal Archives, Windsor Castle. Examined with the gracious permission of Her Majesty the Queen.

Royal Artillery
Survivors of Isandhlwana and Rorke's Drift.
Abbott, Major P. E. *Journal of the Society for Army Historical Research*, Vol LVI, No 226, Summer 1978.
Whybra, Julian, Soldiers of the Queen, *Journal of the Victorian Military Society*, Issue 54, September 1988, and Issue 58/59, January 1990.

APPENDIX A

Campaign Medal

Uniquely this was the only war fought by the Army during the reign of Queen Victoria for which no campaign medal was given. From his correspondence it is evident that proposals from Sir Evelyn Wood fell on deaf ears. General Sir Evelyn Wood wrote to HRH the Duke of Cambridge:

Pietermaritzburg
17th September 1881.

I am extremely obliged to your Royal Highness for permitting me to recommend Colonel Gildea and some of the officers who served in the Transvaal to your favourable notice. I trust you will not see any insuperable difficulty in recommending to Her Majesty some mark of distinction in the shape of a star, or similar form which can be enjoyed by all the soldiers who took part in those gallant and protracted defences. I did myself the honour of writing to your Royal Highness on this subject from Pretoria.

Gun Ammunition Remaining at the End of the Siege

During his negotiations with Cronje on 19 March 1881, Winsloe threatened to fire off 300 shells into the town if he was forced to capitulate. This was sheer bluff. The amount of gun ammunition remaining on that day is recorded in the letter written to President Brand on 23 March giving details of what was to be handed over to the Free State authorities.

Inventory of Ammunition taken away by Colonel Winsloe on evacuating his position at Potchefstroom and to be handed over to the president of the Free State according to clause '2' of the agreement signed by him and General Cronjee on the 21st March 1881

Cartridges filled	61
Shell Common	7
– " – Shrapnel	54
Shot Case	7
Fuzes percussion	35
– " – 15 second	13
– " – 9 – " –	142
– " – 5 – " –	28
Tubes Friction	259
Portfires Common	16
Primers	22

Winsloe Major + Bt Lt Colonel
2/21st Royal Scots Fusiliers
Commanding H. M. Troops
Potchefstroom

Boer Casualties at Potchefstroom

In his account of the war of 1880–81, Charles Norris-Newman published a list of Boer casualties, which he relates were obtained from authoritative sources. The total number was forty-three killed and fifty-eight wounded. Those incurred at Potchefstroom were:

KILLED

Pieter van Vuren	17 December 1880
Jacobus Grundling	1 January 1881
Johannes Joubert	4 January
Hendrik Combrink	27 January
M. J. le Grange	1 February
Frederick Bernardus Muller	10 March

WOUNDED AND RECOVERED

Frans Robertse	16 December 1880
Christoffel Engelbrecht	16 December
Daniel van Graan	18 December
Frederick Berning	1 January 1881
Adrianan Venter	22 January
Frederick Visser	22 January
Hendrick Scheffers	22 January
Karl Buys	22 January
Okkert Botha	22 January
S. Wolfaard	27 January
Bernhard Mahler	4 February
Barth Roelof J. de Beer	5 March
Coenraad Van der Berg	9 March
Marthinus Koen	9 March

APPENDIX D

Roll of Casualties in the Fort at Potchefstroom

16 Dec 1880 – 23 Mar 1881

There are minor differences in dates between this official list and the dates recorded by Surgeon Wallis.

Roll of casualties which occurred in Fort Potchefstroom, from commencement of siege, 16th December, 1880, to evacuation, 23rd March, 1881.

Number.	Rank.	Name.	Nature and Date of Casualty.	
			N/5 ROYAL ARTILLERY.	
			Killed in Action.	
1	Serjeant	Kelvington, J.	Killed	27.12.80
2	Driver	Unsworth	"	20.12.80
3	Gunner	Larkin	"	15.2.81
4	Driver	Green	"	10.3.81
			Died from Wounds.	
5	Driver	Walsh	Wounded on thigh	22.1.81
	"	"	Died	2.2.81
			Died from Disease.	
6	Driver	Crannis	Dysentry	1.1.81
7	"	Bennett	Enteric Fever	27.1.81
			Wounded Once.	
8	Lieutenant	Rundle, H. M. L.	Right side of head, slight	4.3.81
9	Serjeant	Copsey	Left hip, slight	18.1.81
10	Bombardier	Ganley	Chest, severe	23.12.80
11	Driver	Tucker	Scalp, slight	18.12.80
12	Gunner	Price, F.	Wrist "	30.12.80
13	"	Harris, G.	Left shoulder, slight	1.1.81
14	Driver	Pead	Left leg, severe	1.2.81
15	Gunner	Keefe, J.	Shoulder, "	15.2.81
16	"	Evans	Back, slight	11.3.81
17	Driver	Lewis	Right wrist, severe	13.3.81
			Wounded Twice.	
18	Driver	Moss	Chest, severe	16.12.80
	"	"	Head, slight	29.1.81
			2/21st ROYAL SCOTS FUSILIERS.	
			Killed in Action.	
19	Captain	Falls, A. L.	Killed	16.12.80
20	Corporal	Gartshore, John	"	31.1.81

21	Private	Leishman, J.	"	18.12.80
22	"	Dobbs, F.	"	1.1.81
23	"	Roberts, H.	"	14.1.81
24	"	Kennan, W.	"	21.1.81
25	"	Boyd, W.	"	5.2.81
26	"	Laird, A.	"	10.3.81
			Died from Wounds.	
27	Private	Thornback, T.	Right foot, slight	27.12.80
	"	"	Scalp, severe	31.12.80
	"	"	Died	19.1.81
28	"	Jordan, J.	Right side of chest	3.1.81
	"	"	Penetration of neck	17.3.81
	"	"	Died	23.3.81
29	"	Mullen, J.	Left shoulder, severe	28.2.81
	"	"	Fracture of right pelvis, with laceration	11.3.81
	"	"	Died	13.3.81
30	"	Birmingham, D.	Right hand and arm	10.3.81
	"	"	Died	23.3.81
			Died from Disease.	
31	Serjeant	Quegan, T.	Blood-vessel bursting	14.3.81
32	Private	Noble, J.	General dropsy	8.3.81
			Wounded Once.	
33	Bt.-Lt.-Colonel	Winsloe, R. W. C.	Left thigh, slight	5.2.81
34	Lieutenant	Browne, P. W.	Right side of chest, slight	12.3.81
35	2nd Lieutenant	Dalrymple-Hay, J. R. M.	Right ear, slight	11.3.81
36	Serjeant	Troy, John	Head, fracture of skull	13.1.81
37	Corporal	Short, Wm.	Back, slight	12.3.81
38	Lance-Corporal	Davidson, A.	Left forearm and left hip, severe	18.12.80
39	Private	Young, Wm.	Neck and penetration of chest	19.12.80
40	"	Cronan, P.	Left arm	3.1.81
41	"	Foyster, H.	Back, slight	3.1.81
42	"	Woods, W.	Left side and fracture of left scapula	3.1.81
43	"	Jones, W.	Head	3.1.81
44	"	Devine, M.	Neck	17.1.81
45	"	Brown, A.	Left arm	22.1.81
46	"	Colvin, W.	Left arm	22.1.81
47	"	Banks, W.	Left hip	22.1.81
48	"	Smith, A.	Right thigh	23.1.81
49	"	Morrison, S.	Forehead	26.1.81
50	"	Ross, J.	Right side of head with fracture of base of skull	3.2.81
51	"	McCormack, T.	Right cheek	2.2.81
52	"	Conway, J.	Middle finger with amputation	18.2.81
53	"	McCallum, W.	Forehead, severe	22.2.81
54	"	Forscuitt, H.	Scalp, slight	12.3.81
55	"	Woolnough, R.	Head and neck, slight	11.3.81
56	"	Fennessy, J.	Right foreleg, slight	24.2.81

57	,,	McConnell, G.	Right shoulder	28.1.81
58	,,	Lawton, F.	Right arm	17.1.81
			Wounded Twice.	
59	Private	McCluskey, J.	Left wrist, severe	18.12.80
,,	,,	,,	Scalp, slight	6.3.81
60	,,	Cruickshanks, W.	Left elbow, severe	10.3.81
,,	,,	,,	Left forearm, with amputation of arm	11.3.81

2/21st MOUNTED INFANTRY.

Killed in Action.

61	Private	Jones, John	Killed	22.12.80
62	,,	Grant, Wm.	,,	15.2.81

Died from Wounds.

63	Private	Bedford, Jas.	Left chest and arm	21.12.80
,,	,,	,,	Died	27.12.80
64	,,	Watson, J.	Left thigh	2.2.81
,,	,,	,,	Died	8.2.81
65	,,	Brownbill, C.	Right shoulder with penetration of chest and ribs	9.2.81
,,	,,	,,	Died	15.2.81

Wounded Once.

66	Private	King, Jas.	Left hand	7.1.81
67	,,	Cherry, A.	Right knee	5.3.81
68	,,	Coltman, R.	Right side of head, with fracture of cranium, penetrating cheek	5.3.81
69	,,	Flynn, S.	Left shoulder	5.3.81
70	,,	Boyle, W.	Left thigh	10.3.81

ARMY SERVICE CORPS.

Wounded Once.

71	Corporal	Tulle, F. K.	Neck	26.12.80

NATIVES.

Killed in Action.

72	Leader	Class, Abrams	Killed	17.12.80

Died from Wounds.

73	Driver	Tantess	Shoulder	9.3.81
,,	,,	,,	Died	19.3.81

Wounded Once.

74	Driver	Adams, J.	Neck	10.3.81
75	,,	Webb, G.	Left arm	17.12.80
76	,,	Class, F.	,,	19.12.80

Wounded Three Times.

77	Driver	Sam Anthony	Mouth	19.12.80
,,	,,	,,	Foot	11.1.81
,,	,,	,,	Head	15.2.81

ARMY HOSPITAL, CORPS.

Wounded Once.

78	Surgeon	Wallis	Left thigh	4.2.81
79	Private	Barrows, A.	Thigh, severe	6.1.81
80	,,	Wadley, F. C.	Forehead, slight	11.3.81

CIVILIANS – REFUGEES.
Killed in Action.

| 81 | Boy | Taylor, H. | Killed | 24.12.80 |

Died from Disease.

| 82 | Woman | Sketchley, Mrs. | Enteric Fever | 28.2.81 |
| 83 | Boy | Forsmann, A. | ,, | 13.3.81 |

Wounded Once.

| 84 | Girl | Anderson, A. | Left forefinger | 24.12.80 |
| 85 | Volunteer | Benson, J. | Right forearm | 21.2.81 |

R. W. C. WINSLOE, BT.-LIEUT.-COLONEL, R. S. FUSILIERS,

Commanding Field Force.

Return of Sick and Wounded requiring Conveyance.

Regimental Number.	Rank.	Name.	No. of requiring Conveyance.	Wounded.	Other Diseases.	Remarks.
	Private	McCluskey, 2/21st		Wounded		
	L.-Corpl.	Davidson, 2/21st		,,		
	Bombardier	T. Ganley, R. A.		,,		
	Private	Woods, 2/21st		,,		
	,,	King, J. "		,,		
	Serjeant	Troy, J. "		,,		
	Private	Colvin, W. "		,,		
	Driver	Pead, A., R. A.		,,		
	Private	Ross, J., 2/21st		,,		
	Corporal	Stevens, R. A.			Secondary syph.	
	Private	McCallum, 2/21st		Wounded		
	,,	Tobin, D. "			Scurvy	
	,,	McCormack, T., 2/21st			Enteric fever	
	,,	Cherry, A., 2/21st		Wounded		
	,,	Coltman, R. "		,,		
	,,	Boyle, W. "		,,		
	,,	Cruickshanks, W.		,,		
	Serjeant	Hyatt, J., R. A.			Orchitis	
	Private	Daly, P., 2/21st			Dysentry	
	Serjeant	Leedham, J. "			Ulcer of legs	
	Private	Conway, J.			Debility	
	,,	Miller, T.			Sprain of left foot	
	Mule driver	Webb, G.		,,		

Required for Hospital Transport –

Two spring ambulances, two wagons, one store wagon.

R. W. C. WINSLOE, BT.-LIEUT.-COLONEL, R. S. FUSILIERS,

Commanding Field Force.

K. S. WALLIS, SURGEON, A. M. D.,

In charge of Troops.

2nd April, 1881

APPENDIX E

A Portrait of Potchefstroom

In 1880, Potchefstroom was a large and sophisticated community. It was the hub of an extensive electoral district administered by the Landrost, Andreas Goetze, and the venue for regular sessions of the Transvaal High Court. Significantly it lay at the heart of the most militant republican area of the Transvaal.

The town grew from the settlement of Mooiriviersdorp, established in 1838 by Potgieter after the historic Boer victory over the Matabele at Kapain the previous year. Unfortunately the location had been chosen in the dry season, and when the first heavy rains fell in 1840 the area became a swamp. A new site was found, an hour's ride down the river, where in 1841 a spacious town was marked out in a rectangular grid pattern and given the quaint name Potchefstroom, said to be derived from 'the stream of the chief Potgieter'. An extension of the Voortrekker route through Transorangia with access to the distant sea coast through Natal, Potchefstroom became the gateway to the Transvaal.

The town grew steadily in size, boosted after the British annexation of Natal when Pretorius led his supporters back over the Drakensbergs to settle in and about Potchefstroom. Pretorius assumed the place of his rival Potgieter who had moved north again to distance himself from the British. These were turbulent years for the embryo republic as disputes between political factions led to armed confrontation. On one occasion Kruger used the old cannon Ou Griet against opponents at Potchefstroom. In an attempt at reconciliation the new constitution of 1857 decreed that Potchefstroom should be the capital of the republic and a newly built town, Pretoria, the seat of government.

This era saw the arrival of many of the cosmopolitan families who were to figure in the war of 1880–81. In 1846 Oskar Forssman journeyed from Natal with a wagonload of trade goods and founded his business empire. Roland Schikkerling, of Dutch and Huguenot stock, came up from the Cape to trade in ivory, horn and skins. An Englishman, F. W. Reid, opened a store across the square from Schikkerling in 1851. Dr Poortman, a highly respected physician from Holland, followed Pretorius from Natal. The Reverend Dirk van der Hoff arrived from Holland in 1853 to be the first permanent pastor of the Hervormde Kerk, built in 1841, the earliest erected north of the Vaal river. He became an influential figure in the religious affairs of the republic and designed their flag, the Vierkleur. Jan Borrius, born in Amsterdam, bought his press in 1866, becoming government printer and the proprietor of multilingual newspapers.

In 1859 Potchefstroom boasted 100 houses, with fruit trees planted round the boundary of each property, overhanging the streets. The main thoroughfare, Kerk Street, was one mile long. By 1867 the population had grown to 1,200, occupying 250 dwellings. Just before the war in 1880 British intelligence assessed the numbers residing in the Potchefstroom electoral district as 6,000 'Dutch' and nearly 2,000 'non Dutch'. Pretoria district, in comparison, had just under 6,000 'Dutch' and 1,000 'non Dutch'. Roman Dutch law was the common law of the country, enforced by lay Landrosts, although in time qualified advocates arrived from Holland. Several, like Advocate Buskes at Potchefstroom, were appointed clerk to a Landrost.

In addition to the ever-growing number of businesses that exported ivory, ostrich feathers, skins and wool and imported ready-made clothes, groceries, beer, wine and other luxury goods, there was also a strong market for local produce. Much of the commercial growth of Potchefstroom derived from the local fertile farming country where cattle thrived and there were high yields of wheat and barley. Potchefstroom soon attracted entrepreneurs, becoming the centre for financing land development and mineral exploration. The Cape Commercial Bank opened its first branch there in 1874, followed by the Standard Bank in 1877.

The expanding Kimberley diamond fields opened up a market for all types of produce, and soon the volume of commercial activity between Kimberley, Potchefstroom, Pretoria and the Lydenburg gold fields created a demand for passenger and mail services. Transport companies sprang up in the 1870s, using stage-coaches of the American pattern.

The traditional Hervormde Kerk served most of the Boer community, but in time it had rivals, the puritan Doppers and the modernising wing of the Dutch Reformed Church whose pastor, Reverend Jooste, was an ardent supporter of British annexation. The cosmopolitan element of the townspeople brought with them their own congregations, Anglican, Wesleyan and the Berlin Mission.

Throughout the years of migration and isolation the Boers retained a high regard for education, employing itinerant teachers of doubtful quality and background on their scattered farms. The later arrival of teachers from Holland was greatly welcomed in Potchefstroom. A government school was in being by the 1860s and several private schools were opened through the 1870s, including the young ladies' seminary for 40 pupils where Dames Watt and Malan (who were involved in the siege) taught.

As the town expanded so did the amenities and the social life. During the

1870s Potchefstroom was said to have more canteens and bars than any
other town in the Transvaal. There were two main hotels, the Royal and the
Criterion, which apart from accommodation offered wedding breakfasts and
ball suppers with waiter service within a radius of 60 miles of the town. The
Masonic Billiard Hall offered 'wines and spirits of the choicest brands'.
There were public balls with dancing until 4 o'clock in the morning. Race
meetings were popular, with large prizes: the Potchefstroom Plate in 1878,
run over $2\frac{1}{2}$ miles, was worth £100. Shopkeepers catered for every luxury,
from ladies' hats to biscuits and confectionery, and there was even a sub-
scription lending library. Several pharmacists dispensed drugs and patent
medicines. Artisans such as builders, blacksmiths and farriers all functioned
in the town.

The war left this once vibrant society divided and scarred. Business was
more or less paralysed; stores owned by loyalists were forsaken and their
homes remained empty. Many of the buildings in the vicinity of Kerk Street
and the square were riddled with bullets or reduced to a shell. The forlorn
remains of the fort, the magazine and the cemetery stood as a grim reminder
of events. On all sides there was scorn and contempt for Gladstone and his
government. Boer belief in British power had vanished.

Index